CHILDREN'S THEATRE

PRENTICE-HALL SERIES IN THEATRE AND DRAMA

Oscar G. Brockett CONSULTING EDITOR

The Actor at Work,
Robert Benedetti

Century of Innovation:
A History of European and American Theatre and Drama Since 1870,
Oscar G. Brockett and Robert R. Findlay

Children's Theatre: A Philosophy and a Method,
Moses Goldberg

Play Directing: Analysis, Communication, and Style,
Francis Hodge

Theatre in High School:
Planning, Teaching, Directing,
Charlotte Kay Motter

Playwriting: The Structure of Action,
Sam Smiley

Three Hundred Years of American Drama and Theatre:
From Ye Bare & Ye Cubb to Hair,
Garff Wilson

CHILDREN'S THEATRE

A PHILOSOPHY
AND A METHOD

MOSES GOLDBERG
Florida State University

PRENTICE-HALL, INC., ENGLEWOOD CLIFFS, NEW JERSEY

Library of Congress Cataloging in Publication Data

GOLDBERG, MOSES
    Children's theatre; a philosophy and a method.

    (Prentice-Hall series in theatre and drama)
    Bibliography: p.
    1. Children's plays—Presentation, etc.
I. Title.
PN3157.G65   792'.0226   73-12954
ISBN 0-13-132605-8

© **1974 by Prentice-Hall, Inc., Englewood Cliffs, New Jersey**

Printed in the United States of America

10 9 8 7 6 5 4 3 2 1

Prentice-Hall International, Inc., *London*
Prentice-Hall of Australia, Pty. Ltd., *Sydney*
Prentice-Hall of Canada, Ltd., *Toronto*
Prentice-Hall of India Private Limited, *New Delhi*
Prentice-Hall of Japan, Inc., *Tokyo*

TO PAT

CONTENTS

A PROGRAM NOTE

This book is intended primarily for the theatre student seeking knowledge about that specific sub-group of theatre experience intended for children, particularly children aged five through fourteen years. It is hoped that teachers, parents, recreation directors, community leaders, and other individuals will also find this book of value. I have, however, assumed a minimal knowledge of theatre history and practice on the part of the reader. In other words, this book will not tell you how to build scenery, make props, make out a rehearsal schedule, identify Realism, etc. There already exist many fine books which contain such basic information to which the reader may resort if he desires this material.

This book also does not spend a great deal of time discussing children's theatre performed by children—which is herein defined as "recreational drama." This is not to disparage recreational drama, as recreation is by no means a minor value in the modern world, but rather to assign to it a proper role as a *performer*-centered activity, as distinguished from "children's theatre," an *audience*-centered activity.

I have subtitled this text *A Philosophy and a Method*. It contains both, but the reader will soon discover that there is more philosophy than method, and that even the "methods" are little more than applied philosophy. The reason for this apparent imbalance is that, in methodology, the "children's theatre" is basically the same as the "adult theatre." There is, however, a special set of historical traditions, goals, and technical emphases which constitute a sub-group of theatrical experiences—those intended for an audience of children. Besides the age group of its target audience, the significant difference between the children's theatre and the traditional adult theatre is the strong philosophical ideal which underlies it. It is to assist a study of these philosophies and the methodological emphases that are a direct result of these philosophies that this textbook has been written.

One component of the children's theatre deserves an additional word: its literature. It is often necessary to draw upon examples to illustrate concepts and methods. Unfortunately, excellent scripts for children are few and are often difficult to locate. I have tried to draw my illustrations from a limited number of the better plays. Hopefully, the student will take the time to read at least these few samples of drama written for children. Those plays mentioned most often in the text are:

Androcles and the Lion, by Aurand Harris
Reynard the Fox, by Arthur Fauquez
The Tingalary Bird, by Mary Melwood
Hansel and Gretel, participation script, by Moses Goldberg

A list of the principal publishers of children's plays will be found in Appendix A.

I am indebted to many sources of encouragement and information, but particularly to Geraldine Siks, for her inspiration; Richard Fallon, for his support; Oscar Brockett, for his advice on the manuscript; the McMillan Foundation at the University of Minnesota, which provided funds for the travel that resulted in chapter three; and to the leaders of the American Children's Theatre Association and the international organization of children's theatre, ASSITEJ, for their assistance in gathering photographic materials.

Moses Goldberg

part one

A PHILOSOPHY

The typical children's theatre worker is a dedicated person. No doubt there are many in the field who consider it "convenient" or "easy" to work in *children's* theatre, but the majority of those who dedicate their lives to children's artistic education do so out of idealism.

More than in any other kind of theatre, in the children's theatre one acts, or directs, or produces, or writes because one wants to bring something to children. Perhaps because it is a way of influencing the development of mankind; and is, therefore, a kind of immortality. Perhaps it is an attempt to salvage values, ethics, or morality from the kaliedioscope of modern technological confusion. Perhaps it is a sincere desire to help children to become their unique selves.

Whatever the reason, the result is clear: children's theatre is strongly driven by the philosophies of those who work in it. The first half of this book will, therefore, deal with a philosophy of children's theatre—including its history, cross-cultural patterns and differences, an impression of its audience, and, finally, a suggested developmental sequence. The first necessity, of course, is a definition of the phenomenon under investigation.

one

CHILDREN'S THEATRE:
WHAT AND WHY

The children's theatre is a theatre where no distinction is made on the basis of economic class, race, sex, religion, or national origin; it is attended by a complete cross section of the population. This theatre brings joy to its audience and also helps them to become better human beings. And it does all this with only a fraction of the critical notice, financial outlay, or community support commanded by the more famous American theatres. The children's theatre is a theatre with little prestige, few artists, and not much dramatic literature. Yet it has the potential of reaching 100 percent of the population and becoming the foundation of a new American theatre tradition. What is this theatre all about? Why does it struggle—against all odds—to find its audience? What are its limits? What are its possibilities?

DEFINING THE TERMS

Part of the confusion surrounding the area of dramatic activity by and for children stems from terminology. On a theoretical level, artistic

3

education involves four kinds of exposure to art. There is *appreciation, performance, analysis,* and *sociological awareness.* Artistic *appreciation* involves an observer's reactions to the art. The goal is to increase the sophistication of such reactions, i.e., the knowledge behind the responses. *Performance* involves the learning of techniques, by which all artistic media make themselves manifest. *Analysis* is an intellectual dissection of the specific experience—it necessarily follows appreciation—in order to find its philosophical relevance. The study of art as a *sociological phenomenon* is the application of psychology and history—in fact, of all the social sciences—to the role of the arts in the life of man. Artistic education fails to be complete unless it tackles all four problems. Theatre, as one of the arts, should be subject to the same four kinds of study, depending, of course, on the age and sophistication of the pupils. Generally, these concepts are only applied to adult education. Within the theatre, however, there exists another set of terms having usage relative to the area of children's artistic education.

"children's drama"

This term is the most inclusive one. Generally speaking, it means all forms of theatre by and for children. It rarely includes the idea of classes about theatre taught on a junior or senior high school level, but does include nearly every other form of theatrical artistic education for children. Children's drama includes those phenomena described below as "creative dramatics," "children's theatre," "recreational theatre," and also the rare formal classes for elementary school children in acting or stagecraft.

"creative dramatics"

Creative dramatics refers to an informal activity in which children are guided by a leader to express themselves through the medium of drama. Its goal is not performance, but rather the free expression of the child's creative imagination through the discipline of an art form. Other goals include the development of the whole child through a group process, and the fostering of an appreciation of the theatre. Creative dramatics can be related to psychological therapy in that many of its techniques are similar. Creative dramatics can also be used as a part of a total educational unit in which the child concretizes his learning about, say, social science or literature by enacting the characters or situation he is studying. Further uses of creative dramatics are found in socialization therapy or speech therapy. Also, creative dramatics can be used as a technique in teaching drama to adults, in which situation it resembles improvisation.

The essential technique of creative dramatics is the leader's use of divergent, or open-ended, questions to allow the participants to solve the problems of dramatization in their own creative way. The skillful leader can thus cause the group to find an internal validity behind all of the so-called "rules" of the drama—such as consistency of characters, verisimilitude, interaction, staging for the benefit of an audience, etc. All of this is true even though performance for an audience is rarely a part of creative dramatics. "Playmaking," "story dramatization," and "educational dramatics" are roughly equivalent terms for creative dramatics, and all may be found in the literature of the field.

"children's theatre"

The term which defines the basic subject matter of this book is "children's theatre." This term can be defined as a formal theatrical experience in which a play is presented for an audience of children. The goal of children's theatre is to provide the best possible theatrical experience for the audience. To this end, children's theatre employs all of the techniques and principles of the theatre, using some of them in special ways which will be examined later. "Youth theatre" is the equivalent term for children aged fourteen through eighteen.

There is frequent confusion about who the performers are in children's theatre. In common usage, the term "children's theatre" does not distinguish between children performing for other children and adults performing for children. To avoid some of this confusion this book invokes a new term, "recreational drama," which will be used to refer to a formal theatrical presentation where the development and experience of the performers is as or more important than the aesthetic enjoyment of the audience. Under this terminology, school pageants, camp skits, or recreation department programs in which children act for other children will be referred to as "recreational drama." Hopefully, the term "recreational" connotes no mere diversion, but rather an activity which re-creates the self. "Children's theatre" then, will nearly always be reserved for the performances in which adults act, although a child may be used in a child's role in such plays. If the audience's enjoyment is the main consideration, and the occasional child was chosen because he is sufficiently talented to project the role, rather than because he needs the opportunity to develop poise or self-confidence, then the name "children's theatre" will apply.

"puppet theatre"

Puppet theatre should be mentioned, also, since it is frequently part of a total program of introducing theatrical values to children.

Again, it may consist of children performing creatively for their own development and expression—as in "creative dramatics"; or it may be done by children for other children, for the development of both performer and audience—as in "recreational drama"; or, finally, it may be done by adults, the primary goal being the appreciation of the audience—corresponding to "children's theatre."

There are obviously many forms of puppet theatre, from marionettes to shadow puppets. This is a rich theatrical form almost totally disregarded in this nation, but, in fact, a significant form of theatre in some lands. One has only to visit an adult puppet theatre in Japan, Russia, or India to realize that it can be a serious artistic medium. It cannot be discussed within the scope of this text, but it is recommended for corrollary investigation to the reader who is interested in the total range of theatrical opportunities for children.

an organizational guide

Throughout this book various organizations will be referred to; and, as we are defining terms, this is a good time to identify these groups.

The American Theatre Association (ATA) is the organization of all branches of non-commercial theatre. It includes college and university theatre personnel, as well as community theatres, secondary school theatres, military theatres, and children's theatres. The Children's Theatre Association (CTA) is the children's theatre branch of the ATA. It operates through the parent organization and also sponsors its own conferences and publications. Founded in 1944 by Winifred Ward, it is, today, the most important American grouping of children's theatre practitioners. It's purposes are listed in the Operating Code as follows:

1. To encourage experience in live theatre for all children everywhere.
2. To promote in all communities children's theatre activities, including creative dramatics, by educational, community, and private groups.
3. To encourage high standards in all types of children's theatre activity throughout America.
4. To provide a meeting ground for those interested in children's theatre by sponsoring an annual meeting, and encouraging regional meetings and the work of CTA committees throughout the year.
5. To coordinate and generally direct the activities of its regions.

The Producer's Association of Children's Theatres (PACT) is an association of professional children's theatre producers in the New York area who have banded together to secure benefits for commercial children's theatre, especially through unified negotiations with trade unions.

It is a relatively new organization and its influence remains to be determined.

The Associated Junior Leagues of America, Inc. (AJLA) is an organization of women's community service groups. Each community League operates more or less independently, but the national organization provides guidelines and expert assistance when requested. The national League occasionally retains a part-time drama consultant, since most of the member groups have some sort of children's theatre project. AJLA philosophy is to provide cultural and sociological resources for the community. They have often led the way in establishing children's theatre programs either by performing plays themselves, or by financially sponsoring professional, university, or community theatre productions for children.

Association Internationale du Théâtre pour l'Enfance et la Jeunesse (ASSITEJ) is the international association of children's and youth theatres. Organized in 1964 by over eighteen national centers, it serves to unite all those interested in drama for children everywhere in the world. CTA serves as the United States Center of ASSITEJ. The goals of this organization are set down in the charter as follows:

1. To promote contacts and interchange of experience between all countries, encouraging theatre artists to become mutually acquainted so as to estimate their own work, and in this spirit influence their public.
2. To promote study tours for individuals or groups, as well as engagements for producing companies travelling abroad.
3. To introduce and support, at its discretion, proposals made to competent national and international authorities, for furtherance of its work.
4. To promote the formation, in countries where there is none, of national associations uniting all organizations and persons interested in theatre for children and young people.

Whether this organization can survive the diplomatic trials facing all global unions remains to be seen, but as of this writing, the chances are it will become a major influence in the upgrading of children's theatre throughout the world.

CHILDREN'S THEATRE
IN A TOTAL PROGRAM

This chapter began with a cursory view of artistic education—the total exposure of the individual to the phenomenon of art; and then proceeded to distinguish various existing approaches to the theatrical artistic education of children. It is now appropriate to discuss the relationships between these several approaches. Children's theatre should be seen as only one facet of a total program. It should provide the aesthetic culmination in a series of exposures to the art of drama. Ideally, it should be related—on every appropriate level—to creative dramatics, recreational drama, curricular study of the drama, and a study of the other arts.

children's theatre and creative dramatics

Children's theatre presents children with a product; creative dramatics involves them in a process. Some use the process of creative dramatics to develop a product, which is then presented to an audience. This technique is used by many in the adult theatre, who make heavy use of improvisational approaches to staging and writing plays. Two examples are Joan Littlewood and Megan Terry. Most practitioners, however, prefer to separate product completely from creative drama. The end result of a "product" is, in fact, regarded as a minor sin by some. Similarly, some vocal leaders shun the idea of examining process in a children's theatre event. For them, stage magic should take over the child's imagination and all thought of acting, scenery, staging, and plot should be lost in open-mouthed reverie. Both positions are, in part, justifiable, but are extremes.

In a creative dramatics sequence for children, performance is not the major goal. The focus is on development of the child's creative personality. In fact, when creative dramatics are shown to parents and visitors, it is usually through a "demonstration" session—where there is no performance, but only a "typical" period of creative process. This is certainly valid, since, if the emphasis is on the process, it is more relevant to show the process than the product.

The need for culmination remains, however. The child in creative dramatics must find out that the process which he is exploring does lead to a finished product. The obvious solution is to expose the creative drama group to a first-class children's theatre experience. By seeing a production by experts, the children absorb a sense of purpose behind the drama techniques with which they "create" in creative dramatics class. The effect of children's theatre on the creative dramatics student is to provide him with an objective—the culmination of dramatic processes.

The effect of creative dramatics on children's theatre is, moreover, to increase appreciation of the product. Having just tried to create a character, the child becomes aware of, and appreciative of, characterization. Having wrestled with the problems of dramatic compression and revealing dialogue makes him a better appreciator of plot structure and stage language. To say that this awareness interferes with his enjoyment of the play is to say that one enjoys music better if one has never played an instrument. It is true that knowledge of process makes a child more critical but that is a goal of artistic education, not an anathema.

To summarize this relationship, the child should learn process through creative dramatics, culminating in exposure to a dramatize product. Creative drama teaches appreciation of children's theatre and the latter provides a motivation for the former.

children's theatre and recreational drama

In recreational drama, the emphasis is on both process and product. The child learns how to project vocally, to dress stage, and to interact with the other characters. He knows that there is an audience to please. He knows that success and failure are possible end results—unlike creative dramatics in which there is no ultimate evaluation. The child in the audience often recognizes the achievements of his peers, and desires to emulate them. The child on stage often gains confidence in his abilities—especially in his ability to impress his parents and friends. On the other hand, failure, ridicule, boredom, and loss of self-confidence, can exist for both performer and audience. Extremely careful guidance is necessary to avoid putting a child in a situation where he may experience a traumatic failure. What is more seldom realized is that equal guidance is necessary to avoid exposing an audience to dull "showing-off." To be effective, recreational drama requires an enthusiastic, sensitive leader who can reliably judge the capabilities and limits of his performers and inspire them to the creation of an exuberant production. Effective recreational drama is even harder to achieve than is effective children's theatre. For this reason, I tend to de-emphasize its place in a total program. The most logical place for recreational drama is as the conclusion of a creative drama experience, where the children have had unlimited time to creatively develop a performance, and the leader is sure of the children's success before he announces the presentation.

Once again, children's theatre fits in by being an inspiration—an example of standards which should be striven for. Children who see a good production will not necessarily be interested in becoming performers in a recreational drama. They may, instead, get very interested in the dramatic process as explored in creative dramatics. Regardless of the path their interest takes, children's theatre motivates further development. Of course, there is always the exceptionally talented child who becomes inspired—sometimes by seeing a single production—and dedicates himself to becoming a serious performer. This child usually reaches out for whatever informal drama experience he can find, and hopefully finds both recreational plays and creative drama opportunities.

children's theatre and curricular drama

Curricular drama for children is rare in the United States. Not many elementary schools or school districts have theatre specialists or classes. Ideally, every student should have some exposure to theatre from kindergarten through college. Creative dramatics is a logical beginning; supplemented by classroom study of acting, design, and playwriting from about the fourth grade, and history of the theatre from about the seventh. Hopefully, a trend towards theatre education is beginning. Investigators are currently at work, for example, at CEMREL (Central Midwestern Regional Educational Laboratory, Inc.), to develop a curriculum that will analyze drama into steps which can be absorbed by children at various levels. Such a curriculum is usually referred to as "spiral" because it begins with one phenomenon at a simple level, and then returns to it later with more complexity. If successful, this project will be the most significant accomplishment in the field of artistic education since the acceptance of art and music into the elementary curriculum. When theatre becomes a widely accepted schooltime subject, attendance at children's theatre will obviously be bolstered. The performances of children's plays will become a logical point of focus for these classes, leading directly to preparation for, and analysis of, the theatre experience. In some parts of the world, field trips to the local theatre are required by school curricula, along with follow-up sessions back at the school. Formal plays should be only one phase of the curricular program, however, as all students should learn some appreciation of the theatre and its sociological relevance, even if they seldom go to a play.

In any case, curricular drama will greatly benefit children's theatre, if only to teach children that the theatre is an institution which has had and still has relevance to some portion of the populace. Children's theatre, again, serves as a culmination of curricular study, an example of a finished product, and an impetus to continue one's study of the drama.

children's theatre and the other arts

The study of theatre in any form provides an opportunity to integrate all artistic education. Theatre can include other artistic media— especially music, art, dance, and architecture. An exposure to a well-produced children's play can be a means of motivating a study of these arts. The approach may be toward isolating the visual or auditory elements of the production, or it may be toward seeing how they all fit together. The child who can be brought to a realization that music can say the same thing that color or form or bodily movement can, is well on his way to an aesthetic sensitivity that will enable him to extract and learn from each art media. Since this is the goal of artistic education, it would seem that music and art, among other media, will benefit from the child's guided exposure to theatre. The reverse is also true, since an art or music background helps the child to an understanding of the theatre. Often this understanding is one-sided, as the child neglects movement and focuses on design; but at least this gives him an entrance into the world of the play. Once in, his own short attention span will cause him to become aware of the multitude of other stimuli, and gradually his narrow understanding becomes a broad one. Knowledge of other arts provides, therefore, an initial impetus toward theatre. Exposure to theatre provides a synthesis of all artistic education. The total program should, therefore, involve other arts, especially art, music, and drama, in the preparation for and analysis of the theatre.

a sample program

To design an integrated program of artistic education will require the work of many minds and long experimentation. What follows is merely an untested hypothetical construction aimed at indicating the space of time and subject mattter necessary for the program. If a school week equals approximately 25 hours of effective teaching time, the following outline would apply. A good project for an education student would be a carefully supported revision of this informal proposal:

kindergarten-third grade

dance	3 hours weekly
art	3 hours weekly
music	3 hours weekly
theatre	3 hours weekly of creative dramatics; see 2–4 professional productions during year.

fourth-sixth grade

art	3 hours weekly
music	3 hours weekly
theatre	3 hours weekly creative dramatics 1 hour weekly culminating in recreational production at end of year; acting, design, playwriting 2 hours

weekly in units, 3 months each; see 4–6 plays during year.

seventh-ninth grade

art   3 hours weekly
music   3 hours weekly
theatre   3 hours weekly
                creative dramatics 1 hour weekly, culminating in 2 or more recreational productions when ready; acting, design, playwriting 2 hours weekly in units, 1 year each; see 4–6 plays during year.

tenth-twelfth grade

art   1–5 hours weekly (student's choice)
music   1–5 hours weekly (student's choice)
theatre   1–5 hours weekly (student's choice)
                All students must take 1 hour of creative dramatics, culminating in recreational productions when ready; acting, design, playwriting, theatre history, and stagecraft, as electives; see 4 or more plays during year.

college

course work on elective basis; see 4 or more plays during year.

While the above outline is probably very remote and represents an ideal situation it is worth proposing, if only because it may well be necessary to ask for nine hours (out of 25) devoted to the arts, in order to eventually get four or five. The plays mentioned above could be performed by a locally-based or a regional touring professional repertory company.

THE NEED FOR
CHILDREN'S THEATRE

It is easy to write, "We should have a children's theatre and an American artistic tradition." It is too easy! The lover of the arts tends to feel that the arts require no justification. However, to expand successfully, the arts must be recognized and subsidized by leaders of society—

especially educators, businessmen, and politicians. The arts must be justified in a language that these leaders will understand. This, perhaps, is
the significance of such recent books as the *Rockefeller Panel Report:
The Performing Arts,* which suggests better business practices for arts
institutions. Children's theatre is probably a good thing, but it does not
become accepted as such merely by saying so. The more complex the
demands are on public men, the more facets of our society that clamor
for their attention, the more concise and articulate must we be in answering the question, "Why should we have a children's theatre?"

an artistic tradition

The most glib answer is, "to build an artistic tradition." It is a
good answer, but not a very pragmatic one. It is logical to assume that
exposure to good theatre as a child will make the future adult more
likely to be a theatre-goer. There is, however, no concrete evidence to
prove that this is so. No research or audience survey has yet succeeded
in demonstrating that child theatre-goers become adult theatre-goers.

One obstacle to proving this relationship statistically is the phrase
"good theatre." If "good" children's theatre makes adults go to the
theatre, should not "bad" children's theater make them avoid it? In order
to test this hypothesis, according to the principles of controlled social
scientific experimentation, it would be necessary to expose two matched
groups of children to a certain number of theater experiences—one group
to "good" theatre and one to "bad," as rated by some valid judgment,
probably that of a panel of trained experts. Then one would simply
have to wait twenty, thirty, or forty years (or at all three periods) and
send out questionnaires to determine how many times a year the individuals concerned went to the theatre. Other statistics, such as how many
contributed money to educational theatres, or how many were actually
working in theatre in some capacity, would also be collected. A third
group, exactly like the other two except that it saw no theatre during
the childhood period, would complete the experiment. The results would
show statistically that the three groups were not different, or else that
one or more groups were significantly higher in attendance, support,
and participation. The prediction, of course, would be that the "good"
theatre group would be the highest. It would be interesting to discover
whether the "bad" theatre or the "no" theatre group was lowest! This
study has not been done, probably because no children's theatre group
with a research facility has existed for long enough to contemplate it.
Such theatres do exist in Eastern Europe, but no controlled study was
ever possible because nearly all children from one area were exposed to
the same amount and quality of theatre.

There is, however, non-quantifiable evidence to support this hypothesis, both in Eastern Europe and in isolated U.S. cities. Disregarding quality control, those centers which have had some kind of children's theatre for the longest period of time seem to also have perceptibly broader adult audiences. The Soviet children's theatre is fifty years old, and the adult theatre there seems to attract a far greater percentage of the adult population than does the American or English theatre. Of course, it is hard to evaluate the influence of governmental pressure in support of the arts—which is much less than formerly, but still probably a real influence. Several American cities have had strong university-sponsored children's theatres for more than a few years. Evanston, Illinois; Minneapolis, Minnesota; and Seattle, Washington, are among those providing the most continuous exposure. I venture to predict that all three cities would have adult theatre attendance figures considerably above the national average for residents in cities of equal size. Of course, population mobility weakens the statistical evidence which could be found by this kind of investigation. Half of the adults in Evanston were probably not living there as children, and so may have missed the exposure.

Even if one could demonstrate the validity of this prediction, of course, it does not prove that an artistic tradition is a desirable thing. Some will argue that love of the arts only makes a society effete. Other arguments must be found in favor of children's theatre.

values to children

Kenneth L. Graham, in an article published in 1961, states the values to children of good theatre as five-fold: entertainment, psychological growth, educational exposure, aesthetic appreciation, and the development of a future audience. My own terminology relates to his five goals, but I tend to think of "entertainment" and "audience development" as aspects of aesthetics, and to enlarge the term "educational" into its widest meaning by changing it to "pedagogical." Aesthetics, pedagogy, and psychology are, therefore, the three basic areas into which I group the values to children of good theatre.

The primary aesthetic value is emotionally stimulating entertainment through participation in an act of creation. This phenomenon has, at some time in man's history, been classified as a religious experience. The creative act was largely a symbolic one, such as an enactment of seasonal rebirth. Today, when the experience is recognized as an artistic one, the symbolic nature of the work probably becomes less important than its relevance to the current social fabric. In either case, the aesthetic experience is not confined to children, although their naivete and lack of preconceptions about theatrical form make them more receptive to it. It is worth noting that the essence of this aesthetic value is participation. In French, "to attend" a play is *assister;* i.e. to "assist" in the performance. If the child is not present at the performance, that is, if he sees it on TV or in a film, his chance of participation is reduced considerably. (Young children still will try to participate, of course, as the live form of theatre is the only natural one—to them. That is why they will scream and cheer when the cavalry rides onto the screen to save the hero.) If the children feel a lack of receptivity on the part of the actors, this also lessens the opportunity for participation, and, therefore, lessens the children's aesthetic enjoyment. Presence, interaction with the actors, and belief in the ongoing action are the keys to participation. It must be stressed that this value, and the two below, are not confined to children's theatre. Adults seek this value in the theatre, although with a more inhibited expression. Children can find these values in well-produced adult plays, although sometimes their participation is lessened by their feeling that they don't comprehend everything. (It is all right not to comprehend, but *feeling* that one does not comprehend interferes with participation.)

Pedagogically, the children's theatre can be a powerful force of far-reaching consequence. All learning is increased by motivation, and the motivational situation of an enjoyable diversion has obvious advantages over the typical formal classroom. This does not mean that plays should be formal lectures, lest they lose their motivational advantage. The play, indeed all art, teaches indirectly—by exposing truths and ideas to the choice of the spectator. Any learning that goes on is then the learner's responsibility, not the teacher's. Pedagogical theorists will agree that such self-chosen learning is faster and more thorough than the externally inflicted sort. Yasha Frank's often quoted remark bears repeating: "Children love to learn, but hate to be taught." As far as *what* children can learn from plays is concerned, the answer depends on the play and its staging. I can recall a scene from a children's movie, set in Japan, in which two playmates run in from the schoolyard, late for class, hurriedly remove their shoes and place them in a rack, and dash to their classroom. Happily, nothing was said by any narrator to the effect that, "Japanese children remove their shoes indoors." But such information was there to be taken in by any observer. One could see that lateness to school was a serious business, that shoes were removed as a matter of course, that Japanese schools were different from ours architecturally but much the same in function, and that dawdling on the way to school and then having to run to make up time is a universal human trait. The child could learn about morality, foreign customs, geography, and human psychology without a word of "instruction" being given. Safety rules, mathematics, political science, the makeup of social institutions, the use of language and vocabulary, etiquette, history, athletics, and any other subject matter can be the content of a play, and thereby ingested by the child. He also learns the conventions of the theatre, or other arts, by simply watching *how* the play is revealed to him.

Psychological values are also important benefits—in most cases more so than in the adult theatre. By seeing problems solved, one learns: a) that problems can be solved, and b) that the specific problems one may have currently, have been encountered and solved by others, at least by fictional others. In the adult theatre, the same principle operates, but since we are all different, and have different problems, it is rare that we see a character in whom we can recognize ourselves and our exact problem. Occasionally it happens, and we leave the theatre either shaken or pieced together—in either case psychologically matured. In the child audience there is a far greater communality—as far as psychological growth is concerned. Every child needs to develop a positive self-concept, and to learn to recognize that others are different from himself. Such a development probably reaches a crisis around age seven or eight, although with vast individual differences. A play can deal with this specific problem and be shown to this particular age range. As the child enters puberty he develops strong peer needs. The feeling of being different becomes a psychological handicap. This phenomenon occurs in nearly all children, at nearly the same age. A play in which the hero solves a similar problem can provide a vicarious psychological lift to nearly all the children in the audience, if the age level of the audience is correctly matched with the approximate age level of the developmental crisis. Of course, the above examples are generalized. Nevertheless, by careful understanding of the audience's needs, and some control of which age group sees which play, the normal psychological values of good theatre can be heightened enormously in the children's theatre.

In general, the theatre can offer the child enjoyment, a chance to participate creatively, an opportunity to learn, and a stimulus to psychological growth and mental health. It can offer all of the above, and still not lead to an artistic tradition. It can, perhaps, do both.

values to society

The final rationale for children's theatre is perhaps the most potent one, in terms of convincing politicians and businessmen. It, too, may exist as a value with or without the values of developing the arts and developing the child. It is the use of theatre as a tool by the society of adults.

The prime function of pedagogy is to serve society by molding children into citizens. There are two possible approaches to this service, however. One can serve the society of today—those who pay for the education—by bringing up citizens who will fit into existing conditions; or one can serve the society of tomorrow—those who receive the education—by preparing them to be creative, responsible citizens of the world. One can inculcate the mores of the present, or one can develop ethical judgment for future needs. Children's theatre can be a pedagogical tool for the accomplishment of either goal. The latter objective assumes a stress on creative problem-solving. The theatre must show individuals who solve problems without regard for morality or tradition, but with suitable ethical values which *they have chosen* to hold. These plays often offend strict moralists because the hero may flout authority if his principles require it. Arthur Fauquez' *Reynard the Fox* is an excellent example of a play oriented toward the society of the future.

The bulk of today's repertory for children, however, seems to favor the other approach—the one that strengthens today's morality. Plays in which the hero must learn and adapt to an *external* value are plays of this sort. Modern society, for example, places a high value on modesty. The young hero in a typical moral play learns not to boast about his achievements, however grand they may be. This is not to challenge the validity of modesty—only to point out that it is probably an externally applied value. To continue the example, moderation is probably *internally* valuable. If a play attacks *excessive* boasting, or *excessive* modesty, it might be' considered in the category of oriented toward the future society.

More obvious examples of plays which strengthen today's value structure are those which openly defend it, usually by means of the biographical play about a paragon of modern virtues. Historical children's plays are almost always of this type. George Washington is shown as the founder, not only of our nation, but of our morality. Through identification—a most powerful psychological event—the child learns: a) about the history of this nation, and b) to emulate Washington's morality as demonstrated on stage. Every nation has heroes in its history or folklore who epitomize the moral code of today. It makes no difference that this code is different from the one actually followed by this ancient figure. The point is that the theatre can teach existing mores through identification with an immediately recognized hero.

The reader will have realized by now that the children's theatre can be a political tool, as well as a moral one. Shifting only a few mores can cause as dramatic a political shift as the one between democracy and totalitarianism. A political regime can maintain itself indefinitely if it can succeed in inculcating the present morality into succeeding generations. It is a changing moral code that brings about a revolution (whether

violent or not), and if one can freeze the morality, one can freeze the political structure as well. American political upheaval may be in the offing
simply because our national morality is changing. Similarly, the Church's
grip on morality acted to freeze the Middle Ages into a rigid political
structure.

Society's need for a children's theatre could depend upon the values of the leaders, usually political leaders, of that society. Lenin wanted
to change the Russian peasant morality into the Soviet worker's morality.
Stalin wanted to freeze that worker's morality as long as possible. Both
used children's theatre as one tool to achieve their purpose. On a smaller
scale, occasionally in this country, high-minded and well-intentioned moralists have used the children's theatre to try to freeze the American suburban morality. What the children's theatre *should* be used for is not the
purpose of this chapter. But what the theatre *can* be used for is exactly
the point: any specific mores sought can be inculcated; any specific mores
not desired can be discouraged; any pattern of ethical behaviors can be
influenced; or, any developing revolution can be checked or bolstered
through the proper use of the children's theatre—provided only that sufficient time is available (at least one generation). Soviet dictators have
been most aware of this tool in modern times, although theatre professionals from Aristotle through Grotowski have written about it. Of course,
the theatre can be a sociological tool only if people attend it; hence its
increased value to a totalitarian state which can enforce attendance.

Unless America can encourage large-scale theatre-going, perhaps
through an elementary school showing of carefully done plays, the socio-
political values of theatre will remain subdued. These uses of theatre
should, however, represent an important part of any campaign to convince business and political leaders of the need for children's theatre. In
this country we have seemingly assumed for a long time that our democratic values were hereditary. Now we must find ways to bring such values back into the lives of our children. Theatre might be one such means.
Or perhaps, should our society collapse, the theatre could be used to train
children to cope with the resultant anarchy, or totalitarian state. Faced
with these alternatives, few of society's leaders should be inclined to dismiss the theatre as unimportant.

A PRIMAL
THEATRE EXPERIENCE

The easiest way to grasp the institution of children's theatre is to
attend it, surrounding oneself with children and sharing the aesthetic
experience on their level. For the reader with no opportunity to see a

play for children, however, it may be helpful to describe a typical experience. Ideally, children should start formal theatrical activity at about five to six years of age, when they start school. More typically, they begin at about nine or ten with a trip to the university theatre in a school bus, or at an assembly in the gym with a group of housewives presenting a classic fairy tale. The following is a fairly accurate description of a better than average experience in an American university town:

For several weeks, preparations have been going on in the fifth grade class. Every year, the fifth grade goes to see a play at the university, and the time is nearly upon this year's fifth grade. First, the teacher passed out "flyers" announcing the play, and requesting the parents to send a quarter to school to cover the admission price. The week before the play, which is to be Aurand Harris' *Androcles and the Lion,* the teacher told the class the basic plot of the play, based upon a study guide which he received from the play's producer. The guide also suggested several possible class activities, both before and after the show. Half of the teachers will only read the plot summary to their pupils, but some teachers will also discuss the original Roman legend, have the class draw pictures of a lion costume, put on their own play based on the story (using creative dramatics, perhaps), discuss the Commedia dell'arte as the style of this production, and even write essays on related topics—such as the Commedia troupes, or Roman slave practices.

At last, the day has arrived. The children no sooner get settled in school than they are taken out to the buses. It is necessary to be at the theatres by 9:45 a.m. for the play starts promptly at 10:00. One late bus throws the schedule off, and then everybody ends up late to lunch, so punctuality is the rule. There is no cause for concern, however, as nobody is dawdling. This is an eagerly anticipated event, and most buses arrive early—in fact, so early that the house staff at the theatre doesn't want to let them in, knowing that too long a wait in the theatre will dampen the children's enthusiasm. The children line up on the sidewalk for a while, and finally are admitted to the "temple of Dionysus." The auditorium holds about 500, so there are five or six different schools at this performance. The best seats are rotated from year to year, so that each school must take its turn in the back rows, where involvement is, necessarily, less.

At first, there is a sense of awe in the audience. They find themselves in a strange hall, poorly lighted, and with rows of seats facing a large curtain, similar to the movie theatre. There is a mystical difference, however—today's "movie" is to be *alive*! Gradually, this awe fades, as the children are seated to wait. Conversation, trips to the rest room, occasionally songs and games, take over the hall. The cast backstage is convinced that 5000 children have been crammed into 500 seats—just by the noise. A few teachers are already shushing their students, determined that their class shall be well-behaved, no matter what. A few have strolled out for a cigarette, assuming that the whole trip is only a planned relief for them. The best ones are sitting with their classes sharing their animated anticipation.

Suddenly, it happens. The ushers have seated the last group, and the hour has arrived. The house lights dim to half their previous intensity. It is invariably the signal for a universal cheer. No adult audience ever cheers the lowering of the house lights, but for these children, it is the beginning of an adventure, and they spontaneously explode into applause and shouts of joy. As their cheers die away, the music starts. This is the signal for quiet. Immediately, the house lights go out, the curtain opens, and the lights come up on the stage. The play has begun.

Among the first considerations for the children is to figure out who is the hero. Until the audience has aligned its sympathies, it will show little curiosity as to where the action takes place, or even as to what the story is about. The visual milieu is important, more so than in the adult theatre, but, at this stage, mainly because it helps us to find out whose side we are on. This play begins with actors introducing the plot. Immediately, we meet Androcles. We are told he is a poor slave. He looks kind and sincere. He is young and attractive, although in an undernourished way. Without a word of dialogue we accept him as the hero. The young girl, Isabella, is introduced next. She also is young and pretty. She looks sad. She obviously has a problem. She, too, gets our support. Then we meet the Captain and Pantalone. They are older. They look mean and stingy. Their attitude is one of smug superiority. They are smiling, with a gloating air. They must be the villains. About Lelio, the girl's lover, we have no thoughts as yet—he seems too stupid to be a hero, but too nice to be a villain. We will see whose side he is on, and then decide. The Prologue is our friend because he talks sincerely to us, and introduces the others. We accept him as a storyteller, friendly, but not important to the play, since he doesn't *act*, but only talks. Later, when he appears as the Lion, we will be caught up in the story. We will, therefore, respond to him as Androcles does—first, with fear; then pity; then friendship; and finally, dependence. Now we are ready to discover the story of the play. Fortunately, the playwright is ready to reveal it. A couple of lines deal with the conventions of this production so that we can see how the troupe sets up its own scenery and props in order to tell the story. A more spectacular play might hide such devices from us, thereby setting up different conventions. Whatever the conventions are, we absorb them quickly. Whatever is done must be the way to do it. We have never seen a play before, so we assume that all is correct.

Then, the story starts. Androcles is treated badly. He tells us of his capture and enslavement. We sympathize. We see him pushed around by Pantalone. We sympathize even more. We learn of Isabella's money, illegally kept by Pantalone, and see how eager Androcles is to help her. We want to help her, too. The Captain enters to guard Isabella. We wish him ill. When Androcles tricks him, we roar with laughter. The pompous deserve to be made ridiculous. It is even funnier to see the two villains argue with each other. That gives Isabella time to escape, and punishes their stupidity. Isabella escapes. Good. She forgets her money. Bad. Androcles runs to give it to her. Good. That makes Androcles a runaway slave. Bad. The playwright carefully plays upon our short attention span. A slow scene is followed by a fast one. A comic scene by a serious one. A building rhythm of varied and yet contributing events has taken over the stage, and captured our attention. We sit open-mouthed, forgetting even to squirm in our chairs, unless an insincere actor reminds us that this is only fake. Suddenly, a lion runs on. We are uncertain how to react. There is a relaxation of plot, necessary to avoid over-straining our ability to sit still. The lion sings. We find him comical, but nice. He goes into his cave. "What's going on," we think, "what has happened to our story line?" Androcles runs on, chased by Pantalone. Immediately we are back in the grip of the plot. Androcles hides in the cave. We try to warn him, but he doesn't hear. As soon as Pantalone and the Captain leave, Androcles runs back out in terror. The lion will eat him, we fear. He fears that, too. Then the lion gets a thorn in his paw and all is safe. "Run away," we scream to Androcles. But he doesn't run. He defies our instincts, and goes to help the lion! This makes a big impression on us. Someone we respected has conquered his fear to help someone in trouble. We will have to think about that—but afterwards, for the plot has started up again. Pantalone and the Captain return. Androcles tricks them again, and we laugh. Then they catch him! It is the show's lowest moment. They drag him off to be sacrificed to wild beasts. All is lost! But wait, the lion returns. He says he will help Androcles. He wants to save his new friend. Surely he is strong enough to help; Androcles cannot free himself. We scream and shout, "That way! That way! Hurry, free him!" The lion shouts that he will, but we don't hear him over our own yells. The actor playing Lion has a song to sing, asking which way they went, but he finds it advisable to cut the song, since the audience won't stop screaming until he follows in pursuit. Still, it's nice to have the song there, in case he happens upon an inhibited audience and needs to fill in that gap. Today, he couldn't be heard anyway, so he does a few "false" starts, and then streaks off after Androcles.

Suddenly, the play stops. Lelio announces, "Intermission," and the lights come on. This is an unpopular decision. We want to know what's going to happen. We do get a chance to stretch, however, and renew our concentration abilities. Many productions eliminate this intermission since the play is so short, others keep it in, but only as a stretch period of two or three minutes. Quickly, we jump up and down with our teacher. Then the lights dim—and again we cheer. The second act begins.

We are somewhat slow to get resettled, so the second half begins with a quiet scene, to make us listen. We see the lovers acting foolishly. Finally, they realize Androcles' plight and hurry off. Lion follows them on a merry chase, back to Rome. During the chase, the set is changed to the arena. At last, the climactic scene is upon us. Androcles is led in and thrown to the wild beast. We worry. The Lion is shoved on as the "wild beast." We cheer. Then we can relax and laugh, for we know all will end well, even though our hero doesn't. We enjoy the "fight" and dance upon the mutual recognition. Then Lion grabs the villains. Quickly, they are punished, the hero rewarded and the play ends. Just as it should end. We cheer and clap. The actors come back onstage and bow. At first we think this is a third act, but we take a cue from our teachers and the ushers and learn that this appearance is only so that we may cheer for our favorite characters. We clap loudest for Androcles and Lion, of course; but we appreciate Pantalone and the Captain's comic villainy, and clap for them too. If there had been a really evil character, like a witch, we might be more inclined to boo, unless we are sure that this is the actress now, not the witch. Taking off a wig would convince us, or seeing the witch die convincingly in the play would help us learn that the curtain call is a convention, not a continuation of the play. Besides, by the fifth grade we are old enough to separate fiction from truth, even in stories that we read.

The play ends on a warm glow. In orderly rows, we return to our buses and school. After lunch there will be a chance to discuss the play, and perhaps draw pictures of our favorite scenes or write letters to the actors. For the next few days we may have related projects in creative writing, social studies, or creative dramatics. Finally, the trip to the play will fade to a few select memories—perhaps the moment when Androcles pulled the thorn, or the wonderful way the Lion scared the Captain at the end. The most important memory is that we went to a play, felt it was exciting, and felt a warm glow afterwards. Upon that aesthetic experience will be built our future as a theatre-goer.

All children do not have this opportunity, of course. The town might be too small to have a theatre. There might not be a producing group. The group may not do plays for children. The schools may not cooperate, so that only parental interest can get a few children to the play. Or, worst of all, the play might have been bad. We could have been bored and restless, welcoming the intermission as a relief and the bus ride back to school as the highlight of the day. The actor playing Androcles could have been insincere, destroying our concern. Or the directing so bad that we couldn't follow the plot through onstage actions. Or the script could have been a weak one, using cardboard characters in trite situations. In other words, it could have been a disaster. Fortunately, it wasn't.

THE NEED FOR
HIGH STANDARDS

"High standards" in the children's theatre means basically the same thing as does "high standards" in the adult theatre: artistically unified productions that achieve the highest possible quality in each area of theatrical endeavor. Visual communication is especially powerful for the child audience, so directing, acting, and design probably are slightly more critical, and voice control and playwriting slightly less critical than they would be in the adult theatre. A necessary ingredient for a successful children's theatre program is a respect for the audience and for the artistic work to be done. Above all, the children's theatre artist, like any artist, must find fulfillment and satisfaction, and the opportunity to grow in his art. Otherwise there can be no communicative quality in his work. These standards are only trivially different from those which would apply to any area of the performing arts. The importance of adhering to them, however, is greater in the children's theatre than in the adult theatre.

Stanislavski has been quoted as saying, "It is necessary to act for children as well as for adults, only better." The principles of acting and the need for good acting are identical in adult and children's theatre, but the penalty for failing to achieve high production standards is greater when working for children. Three possible reasons for this increased importance can be shown. First, the child audience is not polite. They will not accept a poor production. An adult who does not like the play will think of something else—his business, his last meal, etc. He will try not to disturb the other members of the audience, and will even clap politely at the end of the act. Not so with a children's audience. If they do not like the play, they will squirm, talk, throw spitballs, make paper airplanes of their programs, fight with their neighbors, run up and down the aisles, and, eventually, stage a riot. *High standards are necessary because the play cannot continue without them.*

Secondly, the child audience is developing an attitude, not just toward the present play, but toward all art. The adult who dislikes a play will tend to avoid that author, or this particular acting group, or if he is very perceptive, that director. If he is only an occasional theatre-goer, he may avoid the particular genre of this play for a while; or even the entire theatre for a certain period. The frequent theatre-goer will be disappointed, but probably not put off. He has learned that some theatre is bad, and some is good. The child, however, is having what may be his first experience in the theatre. He is also more impressionable, and quick to form judgments about what he does and does not like. Observe his eating habits, for example. Having eaten a certain food—say, eggplant—fixed a certain way—say, baked—and not having liked it, he will refuse to eat any eggplant in any form—often for the rest of his life. He will insist, if asked, that he "doesn't like eggplant." Someday, when he is grown, he will be a guest in his boss' home for dinner, and fried eggplant will be served. He will force himself to eat, and will discover that he really likes some eggplant—but not baked. The same is true of theatre. Should the child's first theatre experience be unenjoyable, he will probably never try again. If asked, he will reply, knowingly, that he "doesn't like theatre." On the other hand, a single, deeply moving theatre experience at this impressionable age will perhaps be sufficient to make him want to keep coming back, even through subsequent poorer shows, as he seeks to repeat his first enjoyable exposure. *High standards are necessary because the child's future attitude toward theatre may be set by his first exposures.*

Thirdly, the child audience is capable of a more total appreciation. A play may be good enough to avoid causing chaos in the auditorium, and good enough to encourage the child to try theatre again, and still not reach the highest possible standard. As we have seen above, the child has the naive potential to experience a true catharsis in the theatre. He is far more susceptible, emotionally and intellectually, to a total empathic response. It is difficult, even with very high standards, to achieve a full rapport between an adult audience and the actors for more than a few brief moments. When it happens, even for an instant, it is a most satisfying aesthetic event. It is much more possible to achieve such an event with a naive audience. The artistic quality which will grip an audience of adults for a few seconds, will probably bring children to the edge of the chairs and cause their open-mouthed transfixion. They react more, probably because they have not learned the social inhibitions which prevent self-expression. The rewards to the artist, however, are heightened by this fact. Since children are capable of more, and since that capacity adds to the satisfaction of the artist, it is doubly important to ensure the quality of the play. *High standards are desirable in theatre for children because they produce a greater aesthetic effect than they would in sophisticated adults.*

two

THE AMERICAN

SCENE

The American children's theatre movement was not originally a theatre movement at all. If it has become one, it is due mainly to the theatrical sensitivity of several of the leaders in the original group of its advocates, and the subsequent attraction to the field of a few gifted artists. After only seventy-odd years of existence, it is still too soon to say what will become of children's theatre in this nation, but there does seem to be a definite direction to its development. This direction seems to be a basic one, leading from an emphasis on theatre as a social welfare device towards theatre as an aesthetic device. The major goal for children's theatre workers has not changed—to develop children into mature, creative citizens; but the means of approaching this goal seem materially altered and are still undergoing modification. Perhaps it is helpful to discuss the American scene in terms of tense: past, present, and future.

THE PAST

The student interested in the history of the American children's theatre would be well-advised to examine Nellie McCaslin's excellent book on the subject: *Theatre for Children in the United States: A History.* McCaslin's text is thorough and readable. It would be pointless to duplicate her efforts here. However, some abbreviated description of the history of the movement is necessary to enable the student of theatre to understand the significance of what now exists, and of what is projected as a trend for the future.

the settlement houses

The first children's theatre in the United States was the Children's Educational Theatre in New York, founded in 1903 by Alice Minnie Herts. It was conceived as a recreational project for the entire neighborhood—mostly Russian Jewish immigrants. The theatre experience provided an introduction to the English language and to American social behavior for many of the participants. Since most of these immigrants were literate, but unfamiliar with America, the project was a direct appeal to their interest in cultural enrichment as well as an attempt to integrate them into a new community through a neighborhood project. The first production was *The Tempest,* and for many parents in the neighborhood, this script became their first English book.

The pattern set by the Children's Educational Theatre—using a theatre project to boost community involvement, cultural integration, language acquisition, and other social welfare purposes—became a common approach at settlement houses around the nation. During the first twenty years of the century, Hull House in Chicago, Peabody House in Boston, Henry Street Settlement in New York, Karamu House in Cleveland, and other community welfare centers followed Miss Herts' experiments with their own. This pattern, really a recreational drama approach, dominated the children's theatre movement during the first decades of its existence. Strong programs at the Neighborhood Playhouse (Henry Street) and Karamu House lasted for years. The latter program, begun in 1918, still is thriving as a powerful means of inculcating Black awarenesss into the residents of its Cleveland neighborhood.

Most of these programs eventually succumbed to a lack of specific theatre interest, to a shift of social needs away from the pressing need to integrate a diversity of immigrants into American life, or to financial obstacles. The Children's Educational Theatre itself folded in 1909 when laws were passed forbidding Sunday matinees—its best-attended performances. But before its demise, it received enormous public attention, attracting Samuel Clemens, among others, as an outspoken supporter of its objectives. The settlement houses thus provided the first children's theatre in this nation. Their purpose was social welfare, and theatre was merely a handy group activity with cultural overtones. The quality of theatre which these groups offered varied considerably, depending on the talents of the person in control; but since these projects were conceived and administered primarily by social workers, theatre quality was probably of minor interest. It is unfortunate that this latter attitude was also one of the strong influences on the early children's theatre movement in the United States.

leagues and communities

If the settlement houses began the children's theatre movement in this country, it was the community theatre movement which spread its influence. During the first thirty years of the twentieth century there was enormous interest in local theatricals; nearly every town worth a drug store had a little theatre group. In 1910 the Drama League was founded. One of its goals was the establishment of non-commercial community theatres across the nation. In addition to publishing plays and an index of children's plays, the Drama League provided production advice and a chance to share ideas about community theatre, including theatre for children performed by adult and child casts. The Drama League disbanded in 1931.

Other community-oriented organizations furthered the movement. The Association of Junior Leagues of America (AJLA) is primarily a women's service organization, but children's theatre has been one of its national objectives since 1921. Often the ladies themselves donned makeup and trouped to the schools. Occasionally, they sponsored educational or professional productions. Although much of the theatre presented by the AJLA has been unskilled, it cannot be denied that the energy, commitment, and financial assistance of this group was highly significant, and was, perhaps, the most important single factor in spreading the idea of children's theatre across the nation.

Recreation programs in various municipalities quickly picked up the idea of children's theatre—or its recreational equivalent. One of the Drama League's methods was to persuade local recreation programs to include theatre activities. Many fine theatres were begun under such sponsorship, especially on the West Coast. In the late 1920s and early 1930s, programs flourished in Oakland, San Francisco, Tacoma, New York, and various other cities. The landmark program was the Palo Alto Children's Theatre which opened in 1932. This theatre is part of a community recreation complex which includes a children's museum, outdoor playgrounds and equipment, and an adult community theatre. It is still in operation and will be discussed further later in this chapter. Other significant theatres began under recreation sponsorship in Nashville, Tennessee, in 1931 and in Cain Park, Ohio, in 1938.

Most of these recreational programs represent links with adult theatres, as is the case with the Palo Alto, Cain Park, and Nashville theatres. In addition, dozens of other "adult" community theatres have sponsored occasional children's plays. Many still do so today. An excellent example is the Midland, Texas, Pickwick Players—the children's branch of the Midland Community Theatre.

Another early kind of community program was the sponsoring committee, set up specifically to bring professional touring plays into a community. These groups did not produce plays, as a rule, but acted as entrepreneurs by offering a season of selected activities for children. The pioneer work in this area was done by Dorothy McFadden, who began with a group of parents in Maplewood, New Jersey, in 1933. In 1936 she started a nationwide network of sponsoring committees, called Junior Programs, Inc. Several plays were produced by Mrs. McFadden professionally and toured throughout the Junior Programs network. Plays produced by other professional groups were also circulated among the various local committees. When Junior Programs folded during the war years, at least one branch kept going: the Seattle Junior Programs, Inc. Founded in 1939, it still flourishes, and will be discussed later as an example of a sponsoring organization.

the universities

Many universities or other educational organizations began their work in children's theatre during the same period as the community theatre expansion, but the real spurt in educational interest came just in time to pick up the slack in community resources caused by the depression and the Second World War. The first college coursework and production of plays for children was inaugurated at Emerson College in Boston under the supervision of Imogene Hogle. Her work began in 1920. Five years later, the most significant university program in terms of subsequent influence was begun at Northwestern University by Winifred Ward, a founder of the creative dramatics concept. Northwestern opened the Children's Theatre of Evanston, which still operates, although no longer with university funding. Other early programs were launched at the King-Coit School of Acting and Design (1923), and at the Goodman Theatre, an actor-training academy operated by the Chicago Art Institute (1925). The Goodman Children's Theatre was later directed by Charlotte Chorpenning, from 1931 to 1955. During most of these years she was the most prominent American writer of plays for children.

The real growth in educationally-sponsored children's theatre began in the late 1930s and continued vigorously for over twenty years, spearheading the American children's theatre movement during that period.

The Universities of Minnesota, Denver, Washington, Iowa, Delaware, California at Los Angeles, and many others began programs during these years. An association of leaders in the field was begun in 1944, known as the Children's Theatre Committee of the American Educational Theatre Association. This Committee actively promoted and proselytized children's theatre, primarily through the educational contacts of the parent organization. By the 1960s, surveys revealed that 350 colleges and universities had children's drama programs, and an additional 250 had at least one course or presented at least one production annually. Activity is centered today at Northwestern, Minnesota, Washington, Kansas, UCLA, Denver, New York University, Florida State University and elsewhere. The program at Florida State will be described later as an example of a university's approach to the field.

the government

Before the mid-sixties, federal involvement with theatre was confined to two episodes—both of limited scope, but great potential. The Federal Theatre was established in April 1935, with Hallie Flanagan as director. Although not specifically a theatre for children, it did sponsor a considerable number of productions for them between 1936 and 1939, especially in Cleveland, New York, Chicago, and other large cities. Since the goal of the Federal Theatre was not simply entertainment, new scripts were developed with educational content, audience research was carried out, and children's involvement in the playmaking process was also explored. Financial shortages and suspicion of Communist influence are the two reasons generally given for the dissolution of this project by Congress in 1939. The other attempt was the creation of the American National Theatre and Academy (ANTA), which was chartered by Congress in July 1935, but which has never received federal financial backing. This organization has served as a clearinghouse for information about children's theatre, and as a link with the international movement, largely through UNESCO and the International Theatre Institute. Even these services have been reduced, however, as CTA and ASSITEJ have expanded their influence and taken over these functions. It remains doubtful that ANTA will operate on a significant level until national funds are added to the national charter.

In more recent times, however, a large contribution to children's theatre has been made through governmental financial interest, both on the national and state levels. In 1965, the National Foundation for the Arts and Humanities Act and the Elementary and Secondary Education Act were both passed. The former act created Endowments for Arts and Humanities—funds to encourage theatre activities, including those for children. In Title I and Title III of the Education Act, expenditure of government funds for children's theatre was also authorized. Other relief acts, such as the Economic Opportunity Act, which created Headstart, included provisions for cultural enrichment funding. This nation now has a National Council on the Arts, and money is appropriated annually to foster theatre programs. Most of this money is funneled through state Arts Councils; some is given directly to applying professional theatres.

As the money comes to the states, they have all had to establish Arts Councils in order to distribute it. This has resulted in a state-level organization which has, in some cases, led to significant additional appropriations by the states. New York's Arts Council actually preceded the national one, and in the past has spent almost as much to subsidize the arts as has the entire United States Congress. California, New York, and North Carolina have established schools of performing arts with state funds, and, hopefully, other states will follow. However, some states spend nothing on the arts, and only maintain a volunteer state Arts Council to qualify for their share of the federal money.

Municipal governments have, in many cases, contributed most generously to the arts—usually through recreation programs such as those described above. Private foundations are also beginning to take some interest in children's theatre. The Rockefeller Foundation has given the Minneapolis Society of Fine Arts Children's Theatre a large grant, and the J. D. Rockefeller III Foundation supports, almost exclusively, aesthetic education projects in school systems. It is to be hoped that the new interest of private and governmental sources of funding will soon rival that of some of the European nations. Significant funding on a more than municipal basis dates only from the late 1960s. It is too soon to foretell of its long-range impact, or even its continuation.

the professionals

From its inception in 1903, there has been a growing interest in theatre for children by professional companies. The growth has been uneven—slowed by war and depression, spurred by the new subsidies, and always tied to individual artistic leaders. But the direction has been upward, and the trend is clearly toward further growth. Basically, there are two kinds of professional theatres: commercial and non-commercial. Both try to bring in as much money as they can from customers, patrons, or subsidies. The non-commercial theatre can expect to survive a deficit, but the commercial theatre cannot. Broadway, of course, is highly commercial. Children's plays have been done there—at adult ticket prices and for family audiences—but rarely. The first *Peter Pan* production in New York was opened in November, 1905. Other titles done on Broad-

way, or in the imitative stock companies, have included *The Blue Bird,
Little Women, Rebecca of Sunybrook Farm, Snow White and the Seven
Dwarfs,* and Eva Le Galliene's *Alice in Wonderland* in 1932. *Peter Pan*
was revived often, and the musical version starring Mary Martin played
first in 1955. Outside of these relatively isolated ventures, Broadway has
not found it profitable to play this kind of show. Even the musical *Peter
Pan,* a classic, only ran for four months in its initial engagement—not a
profitable length.

A series of off-Broadway companies have sprung up for children,
however, almost always touring, and usually barely surviving financially.
The first significant company was one of the best—that of Clare Tree
Major, the first important children's theatre leader with a strong theatrical background. In 1921 she began working for child audiences, performing fairy tales. Two years later, she added classical productions,
especially for high school students. By 1931, her company was visiting
twenty-five cities; by 1938, it was touring coast-to-coast with six separate
troupes of actors. By the entry of the United States into World War II,
she had her own actor-training program and a regular series of teacher-
training workshops in the summertime. Her company lasted until just
before her death in 1954, and its impact on communities across the nation
is still evident. Other touring companies followed Miss Major's, notably
those of Edwin Strawbridge and Monte Meacham. School entertainment
programs were also packaged and toured by many groups, particularly
after the war.

Today's New York and touring company offerings include solo
performers, dance troupes, poetry readings, mime groups, and plays. Unfortunately, many of these commercial theatres try to appeal to parents
instead of to the children with musical spoofs, theoretically in order to
sell more tickets or bookings.

Some have specialized in the school assembly package—for example,
Children's Theatre International.

Others focus on doing the traditional tales with as much color and
spectacle as possible, such as The Traveling Playhouse. This company
is the oldest in continous operation, dating from 1948, and grew out of
support from the Y.M.H.A. on 92nd Street in New York, which is still
its home base.

Another creative company is The Paper Bag Players, under the
direction of Judith Martin, who work with bags, boxes, string, and other
everyday objects to create free-form dramas before the children's eyes.

Recently, some of the more permanent companies in the New York
area have banded together as the Producer's Association of Children's
Theatre (PACT) in order to negotiate contract's with Actor's Equity.

Hopefully, this will increase the seriousness with which children's theatre work is regarded. Among the best known of these companies are the Traveling Playhouse, the Performing Arts Repertory Theatre (which specializes in musicals depicting the lives of great men), the Prince Street Players, Periwinkle Productions, Children's Theatre International, the National Theatre Company, and Maximillion Productions. Other commercial groups, outside of New York, include the Everyman Players of Shreveport, the National Children's Theatre Association of Dallas, and Casa Mañana in Fort Worth.

Non-commercial theatres for children are usually attached to museums—as in Minneapolis, Chicago, Detroit, or Sarasota; or to adult regional companies—Atlanta, New Haven, Washington, Waterford, or Huntington. They depend on private or governmental patronage to make up deficits. Most of these companies have very strong involvement in educational programs for school children and teachers. The Minneapolis Society of Fine Arts Children's Theatre will be described later as an example of this kind of company. Nearly all of these non-commercial operations have begun since 1965, following the regional repertory movement out from New York to the American public.

organizations and publications

It would be an oversight to conclude this brief historical survey without a reminder of the significance of certain key organizations, and a summary of helpful publications. In 1944, the Children's Theatre Committee of the American Educational Theatre Association began its work. It soon became the Children's Theatre Conference, and, in 1971, the Children's Theatre Association—still affiliated with ATA (which dropped the "Educational" from its name in the same year). As more and more leaders in the field have joined CTA, it has quickly become the most important children's theatre organization in the nation. ASSITEJ began in 1964, and its impact on Americans has grown steadily, especially since 1972, when the United States and Canada co-hosted the International General Assembly in Montreal and Albany, New York.

The other significant groups have been the publishers. Although print may lag behind production concepts and philosophical positions, it is only through eventual publication of scripts or theories that real communication can spread. The Children's Theatre Press began in 1935, and has since become the Anchorage Press. It is the major United States publisher of children's plays, and has also issued several key textbooks in the area. Other significant publications have included the Drama League periodical (published from 1911 to 1931); the December 1952 issue of *World Theatre*, which was devoted to children's theatre; various play anthologies by Montrose Moses and Stuart Walker; *Players Magazine;* the *Educational Theatre Journal;* the Coach House Press, another specialist in children's scripts, which dates from the mid-1950s; texts by Geraldine Siks and Hazel Dunnington (1961), Winifred Ward (1939), and Jed Davis and Mary Jane Watkins (1961); and the *Children's Theatre Review,* founded as the *Children's Theatre Conference Newsletter* in 1950. Many other scholarly works are listed in the bibliography.

THE PRESENT

There exists in the United States, today, an enormous diversity of operations which call themselves children's theatre. Some are closer to what this book calls recreational drama, in that they stress using child performers as a means to the child's development. Others use mixed casts, or adults. Some use amateurs only, some professionals, and some combined casts. Some produce plays, others only sponsor them. Some do only a few performances a year for children, others over 400. It is impossible to describe every operation in detail, or the various philosophies behind them all. In order to give some idea of today's range of activities, I have selected six companies for further description. Each of these companies represents a different mode of operation: a community producing theatre, a community sponsoring organization, a high school children's theatre, a university children's theatre, a commercial professional theatre, and a non-commercial professional theatre.

palo alto children's theatre

The children's theatre in Palo Alto, a suburban town of about 56,000 people with a large proportion of university services (Stanford is located there) and the site of electronics industry, was begun in 1932 by Hazel Robertson, who directed the group for over twenty years. In 1936, the City Council of Palo Alto decreed the theatre's operation an official responsibility of the Recreation Department, and it has received city funding ever since. The children's theatre building was provided by a private citizen, Mrs. Lucie Stern. In fact, Mrs. Stern created an entire complex of recreational buildings, including a community theatre, a junior museum, and a community center. The new theatre opened on January 29, 1937, with a production of Jessie Braham White's *Snow White and the Seven Dwarfs.* A five-year remodeling project, completed in 1974, was designed to update the theatre's equipment and appearance. The theatre works closely with the adult community theatre and the city's visual arts and music programs in order to share staff and produce multi-media experiences. Among its regular offerings are included ballet and puppet workshops.

The goals of the city's Art Department, through which the theatre is currently funded, are listed as:

1. Entertainment, enlightenment, and enrichment through a wide variety of quality exhibits and productions for all the citizens of the entire community;
2. Opportunities for individual citizens of all ages to participate in creative activities in a climate that stimulates growth and development in talents and skills;
3. Encouraging organizations and individuals to cooperate and support art activities in the community; and
4. Development, maintenance, and extension of leadership, equipment, and facilities necessary to the practice, enjoyment, and development of the arts in the community.

The first goal covers children's theatre; the second, recreational drama. In a sense, the Palo Alto Children's Theatre is primarily doing the latter because only children and teenagers are used in the casts. Because they do emphasize quality of production and select their casts competitively from literally hundreds of applicants, they qualify as a children's theatre. In fact, they represent a large segment of "children's theatre" operation in this country which tries to be both production-oriented and recreational.

In announcing its productions, the theatre invites the community's children to audition, usually specifying an appropriate age group, depending on the size and complexity of the roles. Three hundred or more children often arrive for tryouts—as many as a third of them might be used in large shows, like *The Blue Bird*. A typical season consists of five productions, for example: *The Firebird* (the Stravinsky ballet), *Cat on the Oregon Trail, Beauty and the Beast, Tom Sawyer,* and *The Hobbit.* The theatre also sponsors occasional films and touring productions by professional groups. Children's tickets sell for thirty cents, adult's for one dollar. Income for a year is around $22,000; expenses are figured around $54,000. The theatre is therefore 59 percent subsidized by the city government. In addition to performances, the theatre staff offers year-round classes in acting, costume sewing, creative dramatics, dance, make-up, puppetry, stage craft, and musical theatre. They also produce an annual pageant for the city's May Day Children's Festival. Outside of the professional director, designer, choreographer, and a staff of instructors and technicians, all positions are filled by teenagers or children, who have been trained in the theatre's classes.

There is little doubt that Palo Alto is an exceptional theatre community, with four decades of municipal support to boast of, and one of the rare physical plants built especially for children's plays and drama classes. A fascinating book describing this theatre's beginnings is *Children and Theatre* by Caroline Fisher and Hazel Robertson. Few of the children's theatres in this country have as colorful and as long a history as the Palo Alto Children's Theatre.

seattle junior programs, inc.

As an example of a sponsoring organization, this group of parents and civic leaders would be hard to better. Founded in 1939 as a part of the national Junior Programs circuit, its goal, as stated in its *Children's Theatre Manual* published in 1944, is as follows:

> The purpose of this corporation . . . shall be to present the junior citizens of the community educational and entertaining programs in the field of drama, music, science, and interesting arts, with the purpose of raising the standards of such programs to the highest level and developing audiences of young people who will come voluntarily to enjoy the finest cultural programs, in their leisure time.

Before the war, Seattle Junior Programs mainly sponsored attractions sent out from New York by Junior Programs, but when travel restrictions halted the touring of the parent group, they turned to the northwest community for their producing organizations. In 1942 they began booking the University of Washington School of Drama for one or more productions a year—a cooperation between university and community organization which lasted for many years. A local professional theatre and a ballet school also contributed shows.

In more recent times, the Seattle group has started producing some of their own shows, which they then tour around the state of Washington. They still rely on outside groups for much of their season, however. The spirit of cooperation continues—they have worked out facility sharing problems with the Seattle Repertory Theatre, and coordinated educational tours with the Washington State Educational Enrichment Program. Typically, they sell season tickets to over 15,000 children, who each see three or four productions, such as *The Tortoise and the Hare, Thomas Edison and the Wonderful "Why,"* or a classical ballet. Ticket sales bring in about $40,000 annually, and expenses average around the same. As a non-profit corporation, excess funds are spent on "research and development," especially the sponsorship of their nationally famous playwriting contest. Often the winning play is produced by the theatre using local amateur actors, as one of their own rare productions. Groups sponsored in recent years have included the Holiday Theatre from Vancouver,

British Columbia, the Everyman Players, and several New York companies. The group's manual is a highly informative guide for other communities desiring to start a sponsorship program.

hopkins eisenhower high school

Unfortunately, good high school drama programs are rare in this country. They exist only through the lucky coincidence of a brilliant teacher director and a sympathetic administration. Such a combination occurred in Hopkins, Minnesota, a suburb of Minneapolis, in the late 1950s when Tony Steblay took over as theatre director of the high school. He has built a sound drama program of classes and productions—all done by students. The program features regular activities intended for junior high and elementary school children. The Hopkins group makes a specialty of using children's theatre scripts, doing original plays and classics such as *Tom Sawyer* or *The Emperor's New Clothes.* They perform for 2,000 bused-in grade school children annually and often tour to many other schools with selected shows. For the junior high students, they offer classics such as *Julius Caesar, Billy Budd,* or *Mother Courage.* Their most successful work is improvised, including an exciting rehearsal collaboration between director, playwright, choreographer, composer, mime, sound technician, and designers. The group also plays to adults, using scripted and original material.

Hopkins High School contains two theatres: a 500-seat modified thrust stage, and an arena stage, seating one hundred, and built entirely—from platforms to light board—by the students. The inspiration of Mr. Steblay is, of course, the most important factor in this theatre's success, but local support and funding of tours by the state Arts Council has certainly helped its reputation. The operation is subsidized through the regular school budget, but admission is charged and brings in roughly 50 per cent of the theatre's total expenditures.

Students need not take theatre classes to participate in plays. Nearly all rehearsals are outside of school time. The spirit and morale of the high school students are significant by-products of this operation, and the plays themselves are excellent. The fact that these young performers enjoy playing to younger children has been well-utilized by Steblay, and offers a suggested method for building administrative support in other secondary school settings. Principals who balk at school productions of avant-garde plays for adults, done by their students, are apt to be more positive about the productions of plays for the neighboring elementary schools. The Hopkins model is one that can be studied for means of winning local and even national recognition—and children's theatre production is a cornerstone of this model.

The Karamu Theatre of Cleveland, Ohio, in a scene from *Mean to be Free* by Joanna Kraus. Courtesy Reubin Silver.

The oldest permanent home for an American children's theatre is this building in Palo Alto, California. Courtesy Palo Alto Children's Theatre.

Seattle Junior Programs presenting *Pippi Longstocking*. Photo by Lester Gallaher. Courtesy Seattle Junior Programs, Inc.

The Capture of Sarah Quincy performed by students at Hopkins Eisenhower High School, Hopkins, Minnesota. Courtesy Tony Steblay.

One of the United States' oldest children's theatres is Theatre 65 of Evanston, Illinois. Courtesy Jane Dinsmoor Triplett.

Ed Graczyk's Pickwick Players of Midland, Texas, perform his *To Be,* an adaptation of *Hamlet* for the modern world. Courtesy Midland Community Theatre.

The Atlanta Children's Theatre, a full professional company, performing in *Treasure Island*. Photo by Charles Rafshoon. Courtesy Chuck Doughty.

A visual poem by the Little Theatre of the Deaf of Waterford, Connecticut. Photo by Peter DeNicola. Courtesy Eugene O'Neill Memorial Theatre Center, Inc.

Children's Theatre International of Bronxville, New York, presents *Petey and the Pogo Stick.* Courtesy Vera Stilling, producer.

New York University's Program in Educational Theatre performing Euripides' *The Cyclops* for youngsters. Courtesy Lowell Swortzell.

The imagination of the Paper Bag Players of New York City. Courtesy
Paper Bag Players.

The Trial of Tom Sawyer at Eastern Michigan University, Ypsi-
lanti, Michigan. Photo courtesy of Eastern Michigan University.

Aurand Harris' *Rags to Riches* performed by the Pixie Theatre for Young People at the University of North Carolina, Greensboro. Courtesy Tom Behm.

The exciting Children's Theatre Company of the Minneapolis Society of Fine Arts in John Donahue's *Hang On To Your Head.* Courtesy Children's Theatre Company.

florida state university

Florida State University is a relatively new entry among the universities and colleges with strong child drama programs. It is significant for the range of its activities in the field, and also for the integration of these activities into the total program of the theatre department. F.S.U. is located in Tallahassee, a city of 100,000, which, although it is the capital of Florida, is not near any major population centers. The university theatre department also operates a professional theatre—the Asolo State Theatre—in Sarasota, an even smaller city which does experience some tourist traffic. The University System of Florida has three published goals: teaching, service, and research. All three of these goals are carried out in the children's drama program at F.S.U. Graduate and undergraduate courses are offered in children's theatre, recreational drama, creative dramatics, puppetry, and all the traditional theatre areas. In children's theatre twenty class hours are available, plus individual study beyond these regular courses. Degrees offered include the BA, MA, MS, MFA, and PhD—all of which can be earned with an emphasis in children's theatre. Frequent courses and workshops for local children and teachers throughout the state are given at the university. The department faculty includes two specialists in children's drama.

Among the many services the group performs is included the production of plays for school children. They also provide a consulting service throughout the Southeast. The department sponsors, through the Asolo, a state-wide tour. Advanced students are paid to take a quarter off from regular classes in order to bring productions to elementary school children from Pensacola to Miami. Besides their salary and expenses, these semi-professionals get a full quarter's credit for the touring experience. In 1971, over 200 performances of two plays were toured to nearly 60,000 children. These activities receive some state funding through Asolo, which is the state theatre of Florida. In a single year, F.S.U. will produce, under faculty direction, eight or more plays for children: two for grades 1–3, one specifically for grades 4–6, one for grades 7–9, one "family show" as a part of the Tallahassee main stage season, and three plays done on the Asolo stage for ages nine–adult as a part of the Asolo repertory. These latter plays are acted by advanced students in the final year of their program as paid interns in the Asolo's professional training program, or by MA/PhD students intending careers in professional theatre for children. These students are often supplemented by the best of the program's graduates who have entered the professional world. Plays range from audience participation versions of classic fairy tales, to original scripts, and old stand-bys. A typical season might include *The Legend of Sleepy*

Hollow (Gaines), *The King Stag* (original adaptation by Eb Thomas), *Jack and the Beanstalk* and *Aladdin* (improvised), *Two Pails of Water* (Greidanus), *Johnny Tremain* (original musical version by Humphrey and Goldberg). In addition, numerous student-directed scenes and plays are performed as a part of the theatre student's training.

Research is also conducted at F.S.U., which boasts a strong interest in an experimental approach to theatre research. Creative dramatics classes and children's theatre productions are often research laboratories for both students and faculty at F.S.U.

Many other universities have some or all of the same kinds of activities. Weaknesses in university programs often come from a lack of acceptance of children's theatre as a full-fledged departmental activity, and the normal weaknesses of university actors. These problems are minimized at F.S.U. through heavy faculty commitment and a serious attempt to put children's theatre acting on, at least, a semi-professional basis.

children's theatre international

Among the many commercial children's theatres, there are a few that have established a unique style—a signature on all their work. Children's Theatre International, founded in 1961 by Vera Stilling, is such a company. This group is completely self-supporting, although an occasional grant to a sponsoring organization indirectly serves to pay the theatre for its work. Primarily, this is a touring company with a strong commitment to theatre as a part of the child's school experience.

Their trademark is variety and originality. Their first production, still in the repertory, was *Petey and the Pogo Stick,* a modern musical fantasy including a trip around the world and an outer space adventure by the boy inventor of the "atomic pogo stick." Since then, they have produced plays about Japan, India, Ireland, and Holland, as well as a series of social awareness plays dealing with history, ecology, drug abuse, and the Cherokee Indians. They do no traditional fairy tales, feeling that the market is already deluged with this type of entertainment. They also do occasional productions for young adults, such as an adaptation of Boucicault's *The Streets of New York.* Some of this company's uniqueness is traced to their willingness to do plays as difficult and daring as *Melinda,* an honest story about a young girl's near tragic adventures in a fantasy world of drugs; and *Arrows to Atoms,* a light American history play, mostly in mime, which includes creative dramatics participation by the children. Another unusual aspect is their repertory approach which sends out one company of eight actors equipped to do four different plays for four different age groups.

In 1969, this company began sending its actors into the classroom to present creative dramatics and other experiences. Performers work with an entire class on mime, movement, and improvisation. One such project was funded by a grant from Project CREATE and involved the actors for a week in each school. The children learned about Japanese customs and culture. They studied the Kabuki theatre and put on traditional Kabuki makeup. They improvised scenes from the Noh drama, and studied Haiku poetry. The culmination of the week was a full-scale production of *A Box of Tears,* a Japanese style play, by the actor/teachers.

This company's success is due to their educational orientation and creative designs and scripts. They use Equity actors on the PACT-negotiated children's theatre contract. There are problems, however, in keeping actors on the staff long enough to establish good ensemble playing, and in finding enough tour bookings to guarantee financial stability. Showcase appearances, personal salesmanship, and considerable advertising are all necessary, and company management is a full-time job. All the PACT companies have similar problems. This one serves as a good example of a commercial theatre because of their high standards and commitment to developing a broad audience for the American theatre.

the minneapolis children's theatre company

The Children's Theatre Company of the Minneapolis Society of Fine Arts is a non-commercial professional company, which includes several amateur performers. It was begun in 1961 as the Moppet Players by three young adults, one of whom, John Clark Donahue, is still the director of the company. At first the group played in a local restaurant, then in an old police station. The company moved to the Minneapolis Art Institute in 1965, and the growth of the ensemble dates from that year. Donahue and a staff of four produced a season of plays in the Institute's theatre for 26,000 spectators. Only seven years later, the staff numbered fifty, the season included fourteen plays, and the audience was nearly 100,000. This theatre has received several significant grants, including $250,000 from the Rockefeller Foundation, and sizable endowments from the National Endowment for the Arts and the Minnesota State Arts Council. These grants have been given to foster professionalism in the children's theatre, the preparation of the theatre's scripts for publication, touring productions, and the theatre's school program. A new theatre/classroom building, completed in 1974, was designed by Japanese architect Kenzo Tange as this company's new home.

The philosophy of this theatre relates to the spirit of both adult and child. In this particular theatre, the adult audience is as important as the child audience. Often 30 percent of the audience is composed of adults.

This group is never condescending toward the child. To quote John Donahue,

> In my life in the theatre, I am surrounded and involved with children who do not know or even care what the word "art" means. They come to the theatre with a pure approach, no preconceived ideas of how to respond or react but eager to laugh and cry and clap and shout. They come to any "art" happening with tremendous candor. They admire and wish for great leaps, huge choirs of angels, secret meetings of witches, and a sturdy kite with the ability to fly three blocks in the air. Nureyev and the Beatles both lead "art" lives. An old lady weaving lace on a home-made loom is kin to Rembrandt. Both may lose out to their pet dog or the trapeze artist on a given day, but only to remain in reserve to be called upon for aid and inspiration at some later time. Such is the plenty of the child mind. They do not know and do not need to know what everything they see means, but to recognize the beautiful, pure and true and cherish it.

The actors in this theatre are predominently the adults on the staff and the teenagers in the school, with occasional community volunteers or guest artists. Live music is almost always used. The plays done on the Institute stage are nearly all original, and range from traditional tales and ballets for the youngest audiences, such as *Peter and the Wolf* or *Hansel and Gretel,* to *Robin Hood* or *Madeleine and the Gypsies* for older children, and *School for Scandal* or *The Lower Depths* for teen-agers and adults. There is annually a poetic piece intended for all ages, such as Donahue's own *Hang on to Your Head* or *Good Morning, Mr. Tilly.* These experimental odyssey plays have been hallmarks of this theatre's individuality. Both of those mentioned have been seen at na-tional or international children's theatre meetings. All these plays are presented on weekends for adults and children, as well as during the week for bused-in school audiences. In addition to the plays at home, there is a touring Commedia dell' arte troupe with its own portable stage.

Obviously, the theatre is heavily supported by the Minneapolis Society of Fine Arts, the governing and supporting organization for the Children's Theatre Company, the Minneapolis Institute of Arts, and the Minneapolis College of Art and Design. Facilities, including the new building, and promotional assistance are two valuable contributions which the Society provides. Financially, the theatre projected an income for 1975 of $300,000 from ticket sales, against a budget of $550,000. The total subsidy from all sources thus amounts to 45 percent.

In addition to being a theatre, this company is also a school. All artists act as teachers in a program worked out and financed with the Minneapolis public schools, with several grants to assist its realization.

Over one hundred students from the local high schools are accepted by audition into the performing arts classes, which include pantomime, ballet, modern dance, gymnastics, fencing, karate, singing, music composition, voice, acting, playwriting, and gardening. These students take basic courses at their home school each morning, and then are transported by school bus to the theatre for their afternoon arts classes. In effect, this combined program is a high school of the performing arts for these talented youths. They also serve as apprentices in technical areas, and as full-fledged members (unpaid) of the acting ensemble. Many will never become professional artists; many will. All are having an enrichment program rarely equalled in this country.

The Children's Theatre Company of the Minneapolis Society of Fine Arts is a model of commitment and excellence in the field of theatre. That it happens to specialize in theatre for young people is extremely fortunate for those dedicated to that audience. For the range of its activities, its ensemble morale, its strong philosophical stand, its educational achievements, and its performing skill, this company is truly a model for study.

THE FUTURE

The six companies described above are examples of existing operations with a common goal of theatre for children in the United States. They will grow, change, or disappear. Others of equal stature exist now, or are appearing on the scene. In the coming years it seems probable that American children's theatre will grow—at least in terms of quality—as much or more than it has since its beginnings in 1903. Predicting the future is hard work, but four trends are visible, and they seem likely to continue for several years. No one knows what the centennial of children's theatre will find when it arrives in 2003, but some inferences may be drawn from these four directions—three of which concern the operation of children's theatres. The fourth concerns a new kind of dramatic material.

the community's role

More and more Junior League groups are leaving their costumes and wigs at home and becoming sponsoring organizations instead of producers of plays. More and more community groups are organizing themselves and their neighboring towns into circuits in order to bring in outside groups that can tour plays to a series of local sponsors. These circuits enable regions of the country to bring in one professional production for the cost of six or seven locally-produced and usually inferior amateur productions. There is a loss of diversity, but a gain of excellence; a loss of recreational value to the volunteer performers, but a gain of artistic value to the child audience. The outside groups brought in to replace the local production are almost always professionals, or at least semi-professionals with strong university support. The cost of bringing in these plays is usually higher unless shared by several communities in a circuit, but the frustration of production with inadequate facilities and know how is avoided as a result.

The community organization can then devote its energies to other problems besides production: organizing the schools to atttend the plays, finding local private or corporate sponsors to underwrite the costs, persuading the school board to give financial or moral support, establishing good public relations, and insuring that all segments of the local child population have equal opportunities to participate in the theatre experience. The artistic problems can be relegated to the professional artist, who, hopefully, is best-suited to solving them.

Communities which have not gone so far as to abandon production entirely have often gone part of the way by hiring professional directors and/or a nucleus of professional actors to take the major weight of artistic responsibility off the shoulders of the amateurs. This trend is growing. The community groups are turning to professionals for their product, and concentrating their own activities on community arousal and participation.

the university's role

The change in the university's role in the field of children's theatre is not as widespread as is that of community organizations, but it is roughly in the same direction—toward more professionalism. Several universities have begun professional or semi-professional children's theatre companies, either as a part of a total program of providing cultural events for their home community, or as a means of providing advanced experience for their students and graduates. Such companies may be composed of Equity actor/teachers, of graduate students on acting fellowships, or of advanced students paid to tour a specific play or, perhaps, produce a summer season. Several colleges and universities with professional activities of some kind have banded together to form the University Resident Theatre Association (URTA), a branch of ATA. While most of these academically sponsored theatres are intended for adults, more and more children's plays, or separate children's theatre companies, are coming into being under their auspices. Some universities with no URTA liaison and no adult professional company have been financing semi-professional children's productions, especially on a touring basis.

As the cultural organization with the broadest financial base and access to relatively inexpensive student labor, the university is ideally situated to lead a move toward regional professional children's theatre. The theatres created by universities generally also serve a function comparable to a teaching hospital, where students can graduate from class projects and amateur productions into internship roles under practicing professional artists. Future performers and managers of children's theatres are undoubtedly to come from such apprenticeship programs. Obstacles, such as developing new ties with the professional unions and convincing college administrators of the validity of the cutural service function of the university are quickly being worked out. The university is in a unique position to provide the artistic product, the development of future artists, and a critical liaison between the community, the academic world, and the professionals.

Children's theatre production/training is only one aspect of the new role which the university will be playing, but it is a sign of the field's new acceptance that many of the university professional programs do include theatrical activities for children, and nearly all offer special programs for youth of high school age. As an added benefit, the inclusion of children's theatre in these academic professional companies is helping to dispel the old image of children's theatre as a social welfare activity for amateur performers.

the regional theatres

The slowest trend to develop, but, in the long run, the most significant, is the beginning of full-scale children's theatre work by the regional repertory theatres of the nation. Since their beginnings in the 1960s, these theatres have been dedicated to establishing an American theatre tradition. It is only natural that they should make considerable use of theatre for young audiences to accomplish this purpose. But many have done nothing in this area. The social welfare image of children's theatre, and the scarcity of respected artists who can write, direct, and act for children have been responsible for the initial resistance of most of these theatres. As outstanding professional work is created by university sponsored groups, or by the growing number of competent specialist children's theatres, the regional theatres are beginning to become aware of the artistic potentialities of children's theatre.

Ideally, the best place to do children's theatre would be in a resident professional company. Such a group could provide both excellence and continuity of theatre exposure into adulthood. The children's plays should not be done by a separate company within the resident theatre, but by a single company which plays the full range of dramatic literature from Aeschylus to Aurand Harris, from *Hamlet* to *Cinderella*. The resident acting pool should be large enough to allow all the actors to play for all ages, without being overextended. The term "children's theatre" would then lose its connotation of separation and become a stage in the developing theatrical awareness of the individual. Such a regional company would be the most fully-realized performing unit in America, and it would consider, of necessity, the level of its audience and the artistic development of its ensemble at every step. With capable, far-sighted leadership and solid community support, such a theatre could become part of our everyday lives in a way that no recreational theatre, no university theatre, and no temporary professional company could ever equal.

participation plays

The fourth significant trend visible in the United States likely to be of continuing importance concerns the increasing development of scripts which rely on audience participation. Typically, such plays are done in-the-round, for a limited number of children, varying from sixty to two hundred and fifty. They are almost always done for specific age groups, and most often for younger children, under nine years old. The plays may be based on traditional fairy tales, legends, or original plots, but they always require the audience to actively assist at some point in the play. Perhaps the audience has to help say the magic words (which can be done from their seats); or grow into berry bushes with their bodies so that Hansel and Gretel can pick berries and go home (which can be done by rising in their places); or perhaps they must help the actors to build a runway so that an airplane can land in an isolated village with supplies (which requires them to organize into several groups, each led by one of the actors, and actually dramatize various physical actions on the stage).

These participation plays are done in various ways by different groups around the country, and their popularity is spreading. Generally, they all grow out of early work in this area by Brian Way in England, although there have been other influences. The advantages of this method are its economy, its adaptability to the particular ideas of each new audience, and its hypothesized ability to stimulate the young audience to develop its own creativity instead of accepting the creative product of the actors. The major disadvantage is the extra skill required of the actors, who must be sincere and energetic to elicit a response, and then flexible enough to deal with whatever response the children make, even if it carries them away from the rehearsed sequence. These plays are often improvised by the performing group, but scripts are also being circulated, and two publishers in this hemisphere now specialize in participation scripts: New Plays for Children, and Young Audience Scripts (see Appendix A).

This technique is particularly good for children under nine as it provides a bridge for them from their own spontaneous play into the formal drama, where actors play all the roles for the spectators. In a sense, this means the participation play can never be a complete aesthetic experience because the audience cannot be removed completely from the action. The use of these participation plays might best be decreased as the child matures. They may be exciting and valid experiences, but they are not identical to the experience of watching a fully-staged play, and should not replace these plays in the child's life. In the introductory stages of any new idea, advocates are apt to go overboard in its use, and the new participation plays are no exception. They are not panaceas, but they are useful new forms. They can also serve to introduce the child to the more formal plays. In my own participation plays, I include a prologue in which the actors prepare to do the play. This demonstrates, hopefully in an interesting way, how plays are done. I have never done such plays for children over nine although other groups have found effective ways to involve older children without condescension.

Participation plays are often used because they can draw on the audience for ideas and themes from which to develop improvised plots. Such a use is especially common among those groups working with ghetto children, who have unique cultural backgrounds, and who often find traditional fairy tales or suburban American plots completely irrelevant to their own lives. Such a use of participation is helpful at every age level, including the adult level, as long as the actors are sensitive and skilled at improvisation. Many times participation plays of this sort, or more traditional kinds, draw on the "revue" format, employed so effectively by Sesame Street and other good children's television programs.

The continued use of these kinds of plays is assured. They lend themselves to various individual company's needs and shoe-string financing. What their relationship to the more formal kinds of plays will be is not yet known. It is hoped that they will not replace them, but only serve as an extra means of firmly establishing the theatre as a relevant part of the life of the American child.

three

THE EUROPEAN
SCENE

In some instances the best way to learn how to do something is to watch someone else do it. If their circumstances are slightly different from ours we can extract and use the applicable aspects of their performance. As the American children's theatre movement grows and develops in many different communities, in different kinds of organizational structures, and facing different obstacles, it is useful to share information. It is also useful to examine full-grown children's theatres in other lands, where the idea of a theatre for the young may have flourished or struggled under different local conditions. There was little communication about this movement between the nations until the middle of the twentieth century, and yet children's theatre seems to have gotten started simultaneously in most of the areas of the world. The children's theatre is a world-wide movement of this century, and not only a national one, which means that throughout much of the world there has arisen a belief in the usefulness of the arts in shaping the child's development. There is good reason to assume that the progressive education movement of Pestalozzi and John Dewey was an impetus to this awareness. The social and political reforms of the early twentieth century must also be considered as factors. In any case, we have much to gain from examining international patterns of development, and the large variety of circumstances which have surrounded the rise of children's theatres.

INTERNATIONAL PATTERNS

It is hard to generalize about the children's theatre's development except in broad philosophical ways. Each nation, in fact each community, has different traditions and resources. Several widespread factors, however, serve to help categorize the European children's theatre. To an extent, these over-riding influences separate our American children's theatre from theirs, but they also have significance as shaping forces in the movement throughout the world.

patronage

In the Renaissance, the artist was the responsibility of the European nobility—the ruling class. Without the personal protection and financial security provided by some powerful courtiers, Michelangelo, daVinci, and their colleagues would have perished. The theatre, too, came under the patronage of the political elite. Molière was often nurtured by the King himself, and Shakespeare's company had need of shelter from above from time to time. In fact, the court jester or minstrel is the prototype of the performing artist, supported entirely at the expense of a nobleman. These performers, like the Fools in Shakespeare's plays, probably supplemented their income by clowning around the town, but their basic bed and board was provided by their patron. The tradition is well-established in Europe that one of the responsibilities of the elite or of the powerful is to support the artist. This explains the competition between breweries in Scandinavia to see which can give the most to the arts, and the underwriting of symphonies, theatres, or galleries by business firms throughout Europe. It also explains why many Europeans assume that the government should heavily endow the arts—it is a traditional role of those in political power.

In America, which was theoretically created to combat the concept of elitism and nobility, the tradition of patronage has not flourished until very recently. It is significant that only when the American economic elite—the Kennedy's and the Rockefeller's—also became its political leaders was there a surge of governmental patronage for the arts. The common man in this country has still not accepted what every German takes for granted—the arts must be supported by the state as a fundamental responsibility accompanying its power.

As a result of these centuries of private and political patronage, there is now an artistic heritage in most of Europe. The thousands and thousands of Americans who flock to Europe every summer do not go primarily to study history, or to sample foreign food. They go to steep themselves in an artistic tradition which they rarely find at home. They go to see architecture, painting, and sculpture, which was created under a system of patronage and has now become the legacy of an entire nation. Americans go to the theatre in England to see serious dramas and Shakespearian tragedies, who would not dream of giving up a night of television for a play in their American home town. Europe is so strong culturally that we have tended to make it a substitute for our own cultural environment. What Europe has that we lack is a heritage caused by a tradition of patronage. Even in places where the government support for the arts has an ulterior motive—such as education or propaganda—there is still an expectation that the artist must be provided with a chance to create as a part of the leadership function of the rulers.

A heritage of artistic participation does not guarantee high artistic standards, of course. A heritage of political participation in this nation has not guaranteed excellent statesmanship. Nor does it mean that every citizen will make use of artistic means of recreation. But it does mean that most citizens expect the arts to exist by public endowment, even if they don't use them, just as most Americans have agreed that the schools are a public responsibility, even if they personally have no children. And, usually, it also means that the standards will be higher than they would be in places where there is no heritage; or at least more uniformly consistent. If there is one excellent theatre in a European town, it usually means the others are not far behind. If the adult theatre is excellent, it usually means that the children's theatre is, too. Since more people expect the arts to exist as a matter of course, they are more willing to render candid and critical judgments about specific works of art, and to be more comparative in their evaluations. Competition for attendance in Europe seems to depend more on quality than on stars or choice of scripts, which is not always true in the United States. A European critic can more easily attack a production without the fear that his readers will assume that he is attacking the theatre itself. For better or for worse—and it definitely works both ways—the arts are taken for granted much more in Europe than they are in the United States.

east and west

Although still subject to individual differences among themselves, there is unquestionably a totally different pattern of children's theatre in those countries under the influence of socialism. Both sides of the Iron Curtain have similar goals and problems, but there are at least three distinctive differences between them: amount of subsidy, priority of goals, and kinds of plays.

In Eastern Europe, an average of approximately 80 percent of the total budget of the children's theatres comes from outside support, usually direct grants from the national government. Often this grant takes the form of a payment per ticket sold according to the difference between a full adult admission and the low price set for a child admission. Thus the theatre can set the price as low as it likes with no penalty, for the state picks up the resulting loss entirely. Other grants are fixed sums, or special allocations for staging certain kinds of plays. In the Western European theatres, outside support averages less than 50 per cent and is rarely from national sources. Usually these theatres must put together subsidies from local foundations, private businesses and individuals, or municipal governments. National funding is minimal for children's theatre, even in places like West Germany where there is significant adult theatre subsidy. The increased financial resources in the East almost invariably mean a better grade of artist can be attracted by the theatres. In fact, that is one of the government's major reasons for granting the subsidy. By paying higher salaries than do many of the adult theatres, the Soviet children's theatres are able to ensure high standards, complete enjoyment by the audience, and effective achievement of the government's goals for the theatres. This point cannot be overstressed: by providing more money for better artists, the Socialists guarantee the effectiveness of their theatres for children as instruments of pedagogy or propaganda.

This leads to the second difference. In Eastern Europe, the theatre is frankly regarded as a pedagogical tool. Both Eastern and Western European children's theatres stress the importance of individual development as a goal of exposure to the arts, but in the Socialist nations another highly emphasized goal is the development of citizens for the Socialist state. This emphasis stems from the origins of children's theatre in the Soviet Union, where Lenin sought to capitalize on the new movement and gave it the full weight of his support. It is likely that Lenin is responsible for the state of all of the arts in the USSR today, as he insisted that they had a key role to play in the shaping of a new ideology among the Russian peasants. It was quickly discovered that poor quality and boredom in the theatre would undo the pedagogical hopes held for the arts, so high standards and entertainment were made priorities. The result, with some natural fluctuation, has been a generally good children's theatre, which is officially recognized as a part of the total educational exposure of the child. Even in the bleakest periods of Soviet adult drama, especially right after World War II, the children's theatre still turned out excellent and effective behavioral models with regularity. Because of the extra political goal for children's theatre in the East, there has been more public support, and more pride in the theatres themselves. The local children's theatre building is a landmark in most Socialist cities, because the residents are justly proud of institutions upon which their way of life depends.

The third big difference between East and West is the matter of genres of plays. The Western European theatres seem relatively satisfied with traditional fairy tales and adventure stories. Fantasy predominates, as it does in the United States. These kinds of plays are also common in the East, but with the addition of a genre largely absent in the West— the realistic problem, or "today," play. The days of Socialist Realism are over in the theatre, and *Peter Pan* is as popular in Russia as it is in England, but the heritage of the Socialist Realist movement is still evidenced by the frequent plays about the modern child. Plays for all ages are set in schools, family groups, Pioneer Clubs (Scouts), etc. The audience sees characters who are close to themselves in every way, and sees them cope with problems—both personal and political—of great contemporaneity. The closest to this genre that the Western repertoire comes is the rare modern mystery with a child hero, although the popularity and influence of the "today" play has started to spread.

assitej

The other large pattern of influence in Europe is the relatively new organization of international children's theatres, ASSITEJ (Association Internationale du Théâtre pour l'Enfance et la Jeunesse). Because the European nations are geographically closer to one another than they are to the United States, any sort of international organization will have a greater impact among them than it will have in America. A large variety of languages and cultural patterns exists within a day's car travel of almost every European capital. Under the auspices of ASSITEJ, touring companies from neighboring lands are swapping visits at a highly accelerated rate. Italian companies appear regularly in Switzerland, French companies in Belgium, and Bulgarian companies in West Germany. Each nation has an annual festival to which foreign companies are invited with the ease with which Americans can invite companies from the next state. These exchanges have led to augmented translations of good plays, benefiting the repertory of every land. International contests of children's art work based on drama have also been held with inspirational success. More and more, there will be international tours, local festivals, translations of scripts, information exchanges, and internationally sponsored research projects to spur the growth of the children's theatre movement throughout Europe. America has a disadvantage of distance in terms of capitalizing on this cross-cultural infusion.

Under the constitution of ASSITEJ, each member nation is required to establish a national center—the CTA (Children's Theatre Association) is the American center. This forced organization on the local level is another benefit of the international union. Through pooling information and joint solutions to mutual problems, the development of the children's theatre movement is accelerated by the existence of ASSITEJ. This influence is spreading to nations with no existing children's theatres, as the organization pursues its goal of bringing the movement to new territories.

NATIONAL HIGHLIGHTS

The influences discussed above serve as a background for a myriad of local solutions to the problem of how to build an effective theatre for the young. The remainder of this chapter deals with specific nations. What are the conditions under which children's theatre has arisen in various countries? What has shaped its present status? How does it typically function in these different environments? It is not possible to describe in one chapter every theatre or every national picture. Some examples will have to serve to illustrate the range of activities that exists.

england

Although companies of boys performed for adults in Shakespeare's days, the tradition of performances *for* young audiences in England dates back only to the early eighteenth century, and then only if the Christmas pantomime is to be included in the category of children's theatre. These performances are traditionally lavish, with a lot of adult humor, and have developed certain conventions all their own—such as the use of a woman to enact the hero, and a male to play the old crone. They are almost always musical revues of little literary interest, with a great deal of topical satire and vaudeville clowning. Of course, they were originally (and still are) aimed at adults and family audiences, not primarily at groups of children. Besides these seasonal offerings and the occasional adult play which happened to attract children, there was little done for youngsters until the First World War. The Christmas Pantomime tradition is still evident, however, and makes it much easier for British adult companies to accept the notion of performing for children—as the Royal Shakespeare, the National Theatre, the Mermaid Theatre, and many other well-known companies have done in recent years.

The real beginning of drama aimed specifically at children came around 1914 when Jean Sterling Mackinlay tried a season of children's plays as a substitute for the pantomime in the Christmas season. In 1918, Ben Greet's company performed Shakespeare for the London schools. The first company set up on a regular basis for children was probably Bertha Waddell's Scottish Children's Theatre in 1927, followed by several other experiments, most of which have not survived. Peter Slade's work in the 1930s has remained influential, even though Slade himself turned to creative drama and shunned the theatre experience for children. His theories led to a major part of today's British children's theatre—the participation plays. It was not until after the Second World War, however, that the real growth of children's theatre in England began. John Allen's Glyndebourne Children's Theatre, and the Young Vic Players, under the guidance of George Devine and Michel St. Denis, both began shortly after the war, and both eventually received subsidies through the Arts Council of Great Britain. In 1948, two other significant companies were launched —by Caryl Jenner and John English. The former grew into the Unicorn Theatre Club in London; the latter into the Midland Arts Centre in Birmingham. In 1952, unfortunately, government funds were cut off from children's theatres. The local educational authorities filled in financially as much as they could—which led to extensive touring programs by most of the major companies, who needed to find funds from as many local authorities as they could reach. The Young Vic was a casualty of this period, but happily was revived in 1970 as an auxiliary of the National Theatre.

In 1953, also subsisting on local education authority funds, Brian Way began his Theatre Centre, Ltd. Way's experimental form is undoubtedly the prototype of all participation drama in the English-speaking countries of the world. Together with Margaret Faulkes, Way—who did some of his early experimenting with Peter Slade—evolved a style of arena production with absolute simplicity of decor and heavy involvement of the young audience in the drama. At his productions, the children are always limited in number to a group that can participate creatively in the action of the play. His work drew immediate attention from interested school officials, and eventually the group received financial support from a private source—the Nuffield Foundation. In 1970, the Theatre Centre was operating seven professional companies simultaneously, covering the entire nation. Although his ideas about participation drama have not been widely published, they have been spread by reporters and critics, and Way's work is the inspiration for much of Canadian, Australian, and American experimentation with audience participation and open staging.

When governmental financial support for children's theatre was reinstated, in 1967, it touched off a great spurt of growth in professional companies which specialize in children's performances. Many of these companies consist of teams of actor/teachers attached loosely to leading repertory companies. These so-called Theatre in Education (TIE) teams do most of their work right in the schools, attempting to bring both creative dramatics and children's theatre within the educational framework. Their activities include performances, but also a lot of work with the children in improvisation or in the crafts of the theatre. Among the most successful TIE teams are those in Coventry, Sheffield, and Watford. Training programs aimed at developing actor/teachers for the TIE teams have begun at the Rose Bruford College and the Central School of Speech and Drama. Community action programs using improvisational techniques are also being developed, most notably by Ed Berman in London.

The present status of theatre for children in England is best described as booming. With the resumption of federal funding, the widespread acceptance of the TIE teams, the college level specialization in aesthetic education, the re-creation of the Young Vic, and the great interest in international relations has come—as far as quantity is concerned —a great surge of growth. The quality is improving, too, as competition and artistry develop. Among the patterns of operation, in addition to the educationally sponsored touring groups like Brian Way's and the TIE teams, one finds a magnificent arts and recreation complex, the Midland Arts Centre, which is a vast collection of buildings containing four theatres. The Centre offers puppet and live theatre for ages two through twenty-five and also provides recreational drama activities. The Unicorn Theatre is a club whose members generally buy out all productions in advance. This theatre is located in the West End of London, and is especially significant in its discovery of new playwrights, at least two of which—Mary Melwood and Jackson Lacey—have superior contributions to make to the international repertoire. In addition to professional activity, there is also a large amount of amateur production for children throughout the nation, usually by drama clubs, which are, in effect, community theatres.

England is one of the few countries in Europe with an extensive interest in the drama as a *process* in developing the child. It is little wonder that there is a great interest in creative dramatics, recreational drama, and forms of theatre which heavily stress process, like the Way, Berman, and TIE methods. This emphasis on development may act to inhibit an emphasis on entertainment, but, fortunately, the movement is dominated by professionals with solid theatre backgrounds. Although faced with limited funds, insufficient scripts, and a difficulty in attracting top actors to children's companies, due to the frequent liaisons with adult companies—all the way up to the National Theatre—there is hope for the current surge to continue in the British children's theatre. Such a surge obviously benefits the other English-speaking countries, including the United States, in terms of models for study and scripts for immediate availability.

france

Although there is a strong national conference of children's theatres, there is almost no nation-wide recognition or support of theatre for children in France. Thus, every theatre has to secure its own financial stability and develop its own patterns of operation. Since education in most Latin countries is traditional by comparison with the rest of Europe, this usually means convincing the local education council of the validity of the arts for the child. Many are very resistant to this concept. French theatres generally receive proportionately less outside subsidies for children's plays than almost any other nation. Their scripts are freer, however, of some of the dangers of overemphasized morality, and one often finds challenges to the young minds from witty, fast-paced plays.

The French children's theatre dates primarily from the late eighteenth century, when Madame Stephanie de Genlis was writing and producing moralistic plays with and for children of the French aristocracy. Her plays were first published in 1779, the earliest volume of plays specifically for an audience of children. It is believed that she was very much influenced by the educational theories of her acquaintance, Jean-Jacques Rousseau. In particular she was influenced by his concern for children as individuals with spiritual needs as opposed to half-formed adults with few developed needs, which was the contemporary way of regarding children.

There was little continuity in the French children's theatre, however, and the next period of activity did not come until the late 1920s. One of the leaders of the modern world movement was Léon Chancerel, whose own theatre activities for children spanned the period from 1929 to 1963. Besides his own companies, which included the Comédiens Routiers and the Theatre of Town and Field, Chancerel taught and organized most of today's children's theatre leaders in France. He founded the journal, *Theatre: Childhood and Youth,* which today is the official publication of ASSITEJ. He also was a member of the group that issued the original invitation for a meeting of national leaders, a step which led to the formation of today's international organization.

Following Chancerel's example many different children's theatres have been formed. The Fifreli de Lutin, in Toulouse, was founded in 1947 and does both puppet and live plays for children and adults. Catherine Dasté's reknowned Théâtre de la Pomme Verte encourages the development of plays by children, and involves professional actors directly with youth in the creative process of theatre. The plays at la Pomme Verte are taken from stories told by youngsters, and developed into scripts using classroom discussions and writing projects. The children involved are guided into free expression and artistic discipline in order to create the plays. The adults who enact them are protected from stuffy morality or adult verbosity by their continual association with the children. Dasté's theatre is located in Sartrouville, a suburb of Paris.

In Nancy, Henri Degoutin has created, since 1964, a tiny professional company, which tours throughout eastern France with great energy and enthusiasm. His company is at the mercy of local educators. After five years of operation, his home town of Nancy would still not allow him to perform at the municipal theatre inside the city limits. Touring is the only means of existence for this troupe, with all its limitations and difficulties. By appealing to innovative educators in administrative positions with an in-depth program, Degoutin manages to carve an existence for his troupe.

There are also many marionette theatres and amateur companies playing for children. Without strong national interest, however, the French children's theatres are reduced to a difficult existence—paying low salaries and losing their best actors to adult companies. When the local educators are sympathetic, they survive. When they are not, they disappear. In many ways they have the same problems facing small American theatres for children.

italy

The problem in Italy is similar to the one in France: a retarded interest in progressive education, and a consequent mistrust of artistic "frills." The few theatres that do exist are subject to the whim of local educators, or the goodwill of some private sponsor. Very few professional theatres have found the solution.

The Teatro per Ragazzi in Milan has the most secure conditions of all Italian children's theatre companies. Founded in 1953 and partially underwritten by Angelicum, the church-owned recording studio, it was the first professional theatre in Italy to perform all year for children. It tours northern Italy and Italian-speaking Switzerland, where school officials welcome school-time performances, but at home in Milan it is restricted to playing on school holidays or weekends. It attracts some good actors and some interesting, if highly moralistic, playwrights. It, too, is on precarious financial grounds due mainly to the lack of acceptance of the validity of aesthetic education. Other theatres have come into existence in recent years, notably the Teatro dei Ragazzi in Rome, but the same restrictions prevent any kind of significant impact, even in the largest cities of Italy. The Venice Biennale has hosted international festivals of children's plays, but most of the companies have to come from outside Italy.

west germany and scandinavia

The countries of northern Europe have fairly strong traditions of governmental support of the arts, but comparatively little transfer of this principle to art for children. Where children's theatres do exist, it is usually by the recent efforts of a single person.

The Theater der Jugend in Munich was founded in 1953 as a private theatre, was given some city funds, and then taken over completely by the city in 1969. The theatre is now tied to the Münchner Kammerspiele, from which it draws mature actors; and the Falkenberg Drama School, from which it draws advanced students for the younger roles. Such cooperation is typical under government mandate, but is comparatively recent for children's plays. The theatre in Nurenberg is slightly older (1948), and has its own excellent company. Both German theatres are trying to break the mold of moralistic expectations in favor of exciting contemporary plays, and both have full cooperation from their local schools. There is also a private children's theatre and a cabaret theatre for children that develops original material, both located in West Berlin.

In Stockholm, the school board operates a network of neighborhood theatres and a small company which tours around the circuit. There are also school council theatres in Denmark and Norway, with strong local support. Many private amateur productions are performed throughout Scandinavia for children. One organization exists in Oslo—the Skoltheatret, established in 1931. They commission adult professional theatres to do plays for children, and then arrange school-time audiences for the productions.

So far there has been little literary activity in this part of Europe which has attracted attention internationally. The exception is the work of Erich Kastner, especially *Emil and the Detectives,* a modern mystery play.

austria

In all of Western Europe, the highest production standards of children's theatre are found in Vienna, where there is little distinction made between theatre for children and theatre for adults. The same actors that work in the adult Viennese theatres are hired for the Theater der Jugend. Founded by the city in 1932, this theatre publishes its own magazine, *Neue Wege,* and does between fifteen and twenty plays a year for all ages, using three different buildings. Under the strong artistic direction of Peter Weihs, and the administrative supervision of the local educational office, this theatre regularly employs the finest actors in Austria. There is no special concern for the educational or social values of theatre—they are simply included in the aesthetic values. As a result, the productions of this theatre range from excellent to mediocre, but for artistic reasons, not because of condescension or overemphasis on morality. One gets the distinctive impression that theatre for children exists in Vienna because theatre exists, and for no special reason beyond that.

Outside of Vienna there is an occasional production for children by the various state theatres and operas, but there is no major children's theatre company.

the soviet union

Children's theatre is an old custom in Russia. The second production done by Stanislavski at the new Moscow Art Theatre was a play of interest to children—*The Blue Bird.* In July 1921, a young woman named Natalia Satz, who already had considerable experience in children's theatre, founded a permanent theatre for children in Moscow. With the aid of the new Soviet government, this theatre quickly became the headquarters of a vast network of specialized children's theatres. In 1937 the state donated a building to this company, designated as the Central Children's Theatre—right next to the Bolshoi and Maly Theatres, on what is known as Theatre Square (Sverdlov Square). In 1970 this theatre had over 340 permanent employees—the largest theatre for children in the world—plus a studio to train actors for the children's theatre, and a theatre "club" for amateur and recreational drama. Only a few months after Madame Satz, the "mother" of Soviet children's theatre, founded her theatre in Moscow, Alexander Briantsev, the "father," founded his own in Leningrad. The premiere production was *The Hunchbacked Pony* by Peter Yershov. The date was February 23, 1922. That same pro-

The Riga Theatre of Young Spectators (Latvian S.S.R.) performing Kastner's *Emil and the Detectives*. Courtesy Soviet Center ASSITEJ.

A modern musical at the Theater der Freundschaft, East Berlin. Photo by Egon Radloff. Courtesy German Democratic Republic Center ASSITEJ.

Many leading Soviet play-
wrights write for the children's
theatres. Here the Moscow
Central Children's Theatre performs Victor Rosov's *Good
Luck*. Courtesy Soviet Center
ASSITEJ.

The Voronez Theatre of Young Spectators (U.S.S.R.) in *The Tales of Pushkin*,
a typical offering for the youngest children (7–9). Courtesy Soviet Center ASSITEJ.

Plays about America do well in Eastern Europe. Here is *Catcher in the Rye,* performed most successfully by the National Youth Theatre of Bulgaria, Sofia. Courtesy National Youth Theatre.

The Diary of Anne Frank at the Jiřího Wolkrá Theatre, Prague, Czechoslovakia. Photo by Miroslav Tuma. Courtesy Jiřího Wolkrá Theatre.

A Slavic legend, *The Firebird and the Red Fox,* at the Jiřího Wolkrá Theatre, Prague. Photo by Miroslav Tuma. Courtesy Jiřího Wolkrá Theatre.

The Theatre in Education Company (Theatre Vanguard) of the Sheffield Crucible Theatre performing in an English school. Courtesy Crucible Theatre.

"Los Grillos," a Peruvian company, performs *Puss in Boots* in Lima. Courtesy Sara Joffre de Ramon.

On Trial performed by Youtheatre, Montreal, Canada. Courtesy Youtheatre.

Teatro do Gerifalto, Lisbon, Portugal, presenting *Arlequin et Ferrailleur*. Photo by J. Marques. Courtesy Teatro do Gerifalto.

The Theatre for Children and Youth, Tel Aviv, Israel, in *Winnie the Pooh*. Courtesy Orna Porat.

An all-Arab company performs *The Olive Jar* at the Theatre for Children and Youth, Tel Aviv. Courtesy Orna Porat.

An example of international cooperation stimulated by ASSITEJ. The Ion Creanga Theatre of Bucharest, Romania, on tour in Italy with an Italian play—*Pinnochio* by don Lavagna Rafaello. Courtesy don Lavagna Rafaello.

duction, slightly restaged when the Company's new building was occupied in 1963, is still in the repertory after more than fifty years! It is still a colorful, exciting theatre experience and a truly communal one, as nearly every one in Leningrad has seen it at least once. Briantsev was the man who provided the theoretical link between twentieth century pedagogy and the theatre for the Soviets; and he is also credited with the standard design of all children's theatres built since the new Leningrad Theatre for Young Spectators opened in late 1962. This prototype is a wide amphitheatre seating nearly 1000 children comfortably within 60 feet of a well-equipped thrust stage and curved front curtain. Unfortunately, Briantsev died just before the building was completed. The Leningrad Theatre also operates a studio for the training of specialist actors, including the famous *travesty* actresses, who take the roles of children and young men in the productions. The theatre also stresses the continual in-service training of its entire professional staff.

In addition to these two leading companies, there were almost fifty regional children's theatre companies throughout the Soviet Union in 1970, excluding puppet theatres and adult theatres which play occasionally for children. All these theatres are subsidized—up to 90 percent of their operating budgets—when they play to children. In cities where there is no specialized children's theatre, the law requires that a certain number of performances for children be given by the adult companies. Approximately half of the fifty-five million dollars spent in 1969 for direct subsidy from the state went to the hundreds of theatres covered by this law. The remainder was split among the children's theatre companies. This total is for direct grants for children's plays and does not include other benefits such as rent-free theatre buildings or discount housing for the actors, which also are provided by the government.

As had been mentioned, the Soviet children's theatre is heavily influenced by pedagogical and social goals. Each theatre has a high-ranking administrator, called the "theatre pedagogue," in charge of educational programs and liaisons. Artistic quality is preserved, of course, as the government is well aware that dull teaching is worse than no teaching. In order to insure the effectiveness of the message it desires to impart, the theatre must first guarantee aesthetic excellence. Normally, the audience at the children's theatres is divided into three age groups: seven to ten years, eleven to fourteen, and fifteen to eighteen. Outside of the Russian Republic, the theatres are normally bilingual, performing both in Russian and the local language.

The Soviets place a great deal of emphasis on children and education as a means to achieve their national goals, and aesthetic education receives a natural and significant portion of that emphasis. The Soviets are extremely active in spreading this priority to the nations under their general influence. All of the Socialist nations have children's theatres—whether of their own devising or under Soviet guidance. When one sees how effectively Soviet theatres succeed in inculcating the Socialist morality, without compromising artistic standards, one cannot fail to see ways in which the Western countries could bolster the sagging national image from which they sometimes seem to be suffering. A creative, uncensored, but idealistic use of the arts media might be an answer to the modern loss of values felt in some nations. As was discussed in chapter one, the theatre can be used to help preserve the status quo, or to help train future citizens to solve new problems creatively. We have much to learn from the Soviets, while retaining our own ideology.

bulgaria

In Bulgaria, a little-known country of great poverty which was, nevertheless, the crucible of the Slavic languages and culture, the patterns of development of the Soviet children's theatre were repeated during the closing days of World War II. Emerging from turmoil into political independence under the Bulgarian Communist Party, and with the strong support of the Soviets, the government early in 1944 established a National Youth Theatre. This theatre, located in Sofia, is the main children's theatre in Bulgaria today. It is supplemented by several specialist theatres in the larger towns, and other theatres, which generally play to adults but make use of Youth Theatre advice for the scripts and stagings of occasional plays for the young. The National Youth Theatre performs for two age groups: children and youth. They perform mostly fairy tales, modern problem plays, patriotic histories, and the classics. There is a strong liaison with the National Theatre in Sofia (the adult company), and many actors go back and forth from one theatre to the other on subsequent nights. One of the outstanding features of the Youth Theatre company is its extremely high morale, caused by the opportunity which the actors have to grow as artists. It is mandatory that these actors alternate between roles in children's and adult theatre, and this experience is felt by them to be highly satisfactory.

There is also amateur children's theatre activity in Bulgaria, as there is in the Soviet Union. Every cultural center has theatrical schools for children, and many regular schools have recreational drama activities.

east germany

In 1946, the occupying Soviet army ordered the East German government to establish children's theatres. A theatre was started that same year in Leipzig, and, four years later the Central Children's Theatre was founded in East Berlin, under the management of Madame Ilse Rodenberg. The building was donated by the Soviet army, and called the Theater der Freundschaft, the Friendship Theatre. Several other theatres have been founded since, all having a highly skilled staff and playing to three age groups: five to nine years, ten to thirteen, and fourteen to eighteen. The Berlin group has a brilliant ensemble and an active artistic cross-fertilization with the Berliner Ensemble, recognized as one of the world's finest companies. Their plays are extremely well-acted, very open and theatrical, and thoroughly committed to developing Socialistic ideals. What is really noteworthy in this nation is the way in which theatres for children have established an image for themselves as desirable places for artists to work, and as exciting theatres for adult as well as child viewers to attend, and all in the relatively short time since their creation by political fiat. By 1969, less than twenty years after its creation, the Friendship Theatre had become one of the foremost theatres in East Berlin—as far as both actors and the general public were concerned. The Germanic traditions of theatre attendance are probably stronger than the Slavic, for the East German theatres have rarely relied on forced attendance during school hours to fill their auditoriums. They have succeeded on the basis of building a good ensemble and producing a large variety of plays, with a special emphasis on modern and classical adventure tales for ages ten through thirteen. In comparison, in the USSR, attendance was required for many years before it was felt that the tradition was firmly established. In 1968, laws were passed converting most Soviet children's plays to the after-school hours.

czechoslovakia, yugoslavia, and romania

These three nations, while in the Socialist bloc of nations, seem to be less politically committed to the Communist ideals, and this is perhaps reflected in their children's theatres which, although excellent, are less ideological. In Czechoslovakia, the Jiřího Wolkrá Theatre was founded in Prague in 1935 by Míla Mellanová, and is one of the principal children's theatres in Eastern Europe today. There are also strong theatres in Ostrava and Bratislava, and many others—both professional and amateur—which play regularly for children, usually during school hours. Adult theatres also play an average of seventy performances a year for children, and there are newly-formed "little theatres" intended for adolescents. The Czechs have been more resistant to the Soviet forms of theatre, and remain fairly close to the traditional fairy tales and musical satires, which are their national heritage.

The patterns in Yugoslavia and Romania are fairly similar. Both nations are led by a few strong children's theatres, with a lot of supplementary activity at smaller specialist theatres or adult theatres. Unlike that of the Soviet, Bulgarian, and East German Theatres, the repertory is more folk and traditional than modern or psychological. These theatres also get heavy state support, but are less established than the Soviet ones, probably because salaries are not usually given an extra boost for children's theatres in these three countries. It is probable that the lessened emphasis on the political role of theatre is partly responsible for the lower image, or it may simply be that these nations have much younger traditions—in Romania, the biggest children's theatre, the Ion Creanga, dates only from 1964, although it has already established an enviable artistic reputation.

other nations

There are a variety of patterns in the other nations around the world having children's theatre activities. In Poland there is a dominance of puppet theatre, with only scattered post-war performances of live theatre for children. These are almost always by adult companies presenting extra offerings designed for children. In Holland, there are three major companies that perform for children: the Scapino ballet, the Carrousel Mime Troupe, and the Arena Theatre Company. Scapino dates from 1945, the other two from the 1950s. One interesting feature is the high degree of cooperation between the three groups, illustrated by the combined showings they perform on occasion. Of course, all three use different approaches—dance, mime, and theatre. In Spain, a very vigorous development of children's theatre activity is being spurred by the existence of ASSITEJ, and also by the application of theoretical studies of child development to the theatre. Spanish theatre leaders have organized a course in order to have themselves trained by pedagogues and psychologists in the needs of children. They have reciprocated the students of pedagogy with courses designed to awaken interest in the possibilities of children's theatre. Several large scale contests are sponsored annually in Spain to stimulate amateur and professional productions for children. The other nations of Europe have, typically, small companies which operate part-time for children. Nearly all of them were originally composed of amateurs; some—like the well-known Company of Four Thursdays in Geneva—remain amateur.

Outside of Europe, there are active children's theatres in South America, Africa, the Middle East, India, Japan, China, Australia, and, of course, Canada. Canadian and Australian children's theatre parallels that in England and the United States. There is a considerable amount of participation drama, and heavy support from local education councils. National financial subsidy exists in both nations to some degree. Creative dramatics and recreational drama are also found there; they also occur in India to a much smaller extent. Among outstanding Canadian companies, there are several that play in French, and some, like the Young People's Theatre in Toronto, which include experimental programs, touring programs, and student training programs.

In Iran, an unusual children's theatre program was established by the Queen of Iran. It regularly performs in a network of public libraries, also built by the Queen. Further east, one finds that puppet theatre and folk theatre were the direct ancestors of much of the theatre done for children. There are few companies which play exclusively for children in the Orient, although there were some in Japan before the war, and they are beginning to return in that nation.

Children's theatre in the People's Republic of China was begun in 1947 by an American, Gerald Tannenbaum, who was serving as Executive Director of the China Welfare Institute—an organization primarily devoted to the medical and nutritional needs of an underdeveloped nation. Beginning in Shanghai, Tannenbaum's group used child actors— many of them taken from the streets—to build a communal ensemble which did plays incorporating both the modern drama and the traditional Peking Opera style. With the Communist Liberation in 1949, came vast support for the children's theatre. The actors became adult professionals, the material became frankly political, and the financial resources were multiplied enormously. By 1972 there were six specialist children's theatres in China, plus children's departments in many of the regional adult theatres. The Soviet model, followed for a time, was abandoned completely during the Cultural Revolution of 1966, and the plays done for children in China today are all modern, realistic, and political. One interesting feature of the Chinese children's theatre is the virtual elimination of the playwright. Scripts are evolved by the entire ensemble, usually "on location" in a factory or village where some incident has occurred which illustrates an important political concept, and is thus a worthy subject for a play. Most Chinese schools also have recreational drama programs, frequently coordinated through the large "Children's Palaces" located in most neighborhoods.

It is difficult to make any overview accurate, especially for nations with little children's theatre tradition. These are usually the places where financial problems cause an almost daily change in the existing companies. Typically, there is first some kind of amateur activity, strongly educational in orientation. With financing comes professionalism, and with professional artists comes, hopefully, aesthetic quality. Only if the financial support lasts long enough for an artistic reputation to be established is there any kind of security in the operation of these theatres, and there is often danger that the patron who financed the educationally-oriented amateurs will lose interest in the artistically motivated professionals. Even after stability is reached, there is continual need for outside subsidy. Up-to-date information for the student planning a visit or a study can usually be obtained through the various ASSITEJ centers (see Appendix B).

It is worth becoming familiar with foreign patterns of children's theatre both because we can learn from their successes, and because we can avoid their errors. It is also true that the children's theatre movement constitutes a rare international force for the development of creative and peace-loving citizens of the future.

four

THE CHILD
AUDIENCE

Consider the child. A semi-mysterious, ever-changing, intolerant, complex set of behaviors with an unknowable capacity for experience. The child attracts the hopes and projected fears of every adult member of his species. The child is to be feared and loved, for he represents both the challenge and the hope of salvation for the world of today. Some people can relate to the child; some cannot; but no one can truly claim to understand him fully. The child is, by definition, a potential—a potential anything. Expose him to Greek, and he will speak Greek; expose him to hate, and he will learn hate; expose him to the wonderful, and he will wonder. This chapter attempts to outline some minimal information as to who the child is, what his needs are, and how the children's theatre acts to meet those needs. One chapter is not enough to explain properly the child—nor is a set of volumes. But the children's theatre practitioner need not be a professional child psychologist, as long as he is aware of child psychology, principles of pedagogy, and the basic behavioral patterns and interests of his prospective audience.

THE AGE GROUPS

By dividing the child audience into four age groups—under seven, seven through nine years, ten through thirteen, and fourteen through eighteen—we can speak more meaningfully about the interests and capabilities of each group.

Of course, no individual fits exactly into any set of categories. Children are no exception. Some talk at ten months, others not until twice as old. Some like horror stories at age twelve, others never do. But, generally, we make the attempt to categorize large groups of children as having certain shared physical and emotional abilities, and certain interests and psychological needs in common. One of the goals of the children's theatre is to correlate the theatre experience with these common needs.

five and six years old

This is probably the youngest age for which theatre is attempted. Often even these children are considered to be too young to sit through a performance, unless it is in a small audience, or at a play which invites creative participation. These children have very short attention spans and need fairly constant adult supervision. When they are at play they often prefer to have an adult near-by. They are characterized as capable of responding totally. They cry with their whole energy, and laugh the same way. They respond physically as well as emotionally to stimuli—it is almost impossible for them to be sitting still and enjoying something. Some level of physicality always accompanies their concentrated appreciation. This child, therefore, needs pacing. He requires moments of relaxation and security so that he may be calm and content. The adult responsible for him must guard against overextension of the child's resources.

The child at this age is curious. He likes anything new, particularly new movements or shapes—strong visual impressions. He likes other children, but may seem to ignore them when he plays. The Swiss psychologist Jean Piaget refers to a stage of language development called "collective monologue" when a child will talk to himself, but only if there is another individual in the room to trigger his speech behavior. This is a step toward learning that one speaks *to* others. Children of five and six sometimes play the same way—using other children as catalysts, not really as playmates. Five is a relatively stable and secure age. Six is more under pressure. Psychologically, this marks the final stages of developing self-awareness. Not until seven or eight can the child put himself into another's place, but at six he begins to be aware of the consequences of his actions on others. This may make him tempestuous or easily frustrated when he senses an undesired response from a peer or parent. The child of this age is learning the rules of the environment. He becomes wary of things that can hurt, like cars or strange animals. He is especially afraid of the loss of security. A death in the family can be particularly traumatic at this age level, as it is easily generalized to the death of the mother, or his own death. He needs a lot of love, especially physical cuddling, when under stress.

This child is idealistic. He must have his optimism reinforced. He needs to feel that his ideas and his sense of humor are appreciated. He can be creative with his toys, creating new designs with blocks or add-on sets, but he needs to be assured that this fanciful play is accepted and approved. His group games are simple, like tag, or straight-forward ball catching activities. His biggest interest is in his immediate environment. He loves animals and real life stories about mothers and fathers and children. He is interested in the big machines he sees, like trucks, airplanes, and steamshovels. He is interested in little creatures that "move funny," like caterpillars and frogs. He also loves parties and holidays, especially birthdays and Christmas. He likes picnics, celebrations, company for dinner, or anything else that is both immediate and novel.

When these children choose library material, they generally prefer stories and pictures about fantasy creatures, humor, animals and nature, holidays, birthdays, and fairy tales. On television they watch mostly cartoons, puppets, and animals. They also like stories about daily life, such as going to work or family relations, but probably not as much as the children of this age group from forty years ago. Television and increased travel opportunities have undoubtedly caused children's interests at various ages to change. Most reasonably well-exposed youngsters of five and six are ready to move from simply playing house to playing special events within a familiar setting—a step upward in maturity. They also like to play that they are animals or fantasy heroes. This age group is in the beginning stages of socialization—most have just begun school—and they profit from trying out roles, if the roles are familiar enough to be recognizable to them.

This child's dramatic interest and comprehension is suitable to some sort of controlled theatrically-oriented activity. He is finding out about society's institutions, and is especially interested in those that offer new stimuli and a chance to experience humor and special happenings in the familiar world around him. If the theatre experience takes cognizance of his activity level and attention span, he is capable of a positive first experience in the theatre.

seven through nine years old

This glorious period of childhood is best characterized as the time of rules and roles. The child of seven, eight, and nine is finally getting control of himself physically. The seven year old can manipulate small objects and begin to enjoy hobbies and collections and active games. By eight he is beginning group sports and organized indoor games. By nine he is testing the limits of his physical prowess—climbing trees, walking rails—threatening to overdo everything. This is a process of building physical confidence. At last the child knows who he is, and that he controls certain parts of his environment, but not others. These children still respond with total bursts of energy, but have much more poise and balance than they used to. They can still be overextended and require adult attention, but are more willing to abide by pre-determined limits and boundaries.

This is a strong socialization period, and group activities are preferred by many children of this age. They are very concerned with rules and fairness. As they learn about adult rules and expectations, they apply them to their own activities. Groups are structured on a firm standard of right and wrong, and indecisive or inconsistent adults will seriously frustrate the children. They are sensitive and emotional. They express themselves freely, and enjoy vicarious emotional experiences. But they need to know what is real, and how to apply their behavioral code to each new situation. Their attention span is still very short, but they can sit and discuss for brief periods. They are willing to codify anything they can understand, and will work out the details of expected behavior for every circumstance. They show some verbal skill, and occasional patience. They like "good" and "bad" to be clearly defined. Then they can begin to generalize these values to new situations.

By nine, the child is willing to plan his own time and has his own strong interests. Girls and boys usually divide into separate activities at that age. The years from seven through nine are marked by strong involvement with stereotypes which teach rules of behavior. This, of course, is the age level of the classic fairy tales, which embody the values of the culture. These children begin to be able to identify strongly with a heroic character, and so they especially love the deeds of heroes which also offer guidance to society's moral code. In their reading, they still choose animal tales, but fables, myths, fairy tales, foreign lands, and mysteries are also widely sought. Some interest in biographies is evident in nine year olds. They are interested in discriminating and making choices; they will reject complexities in favor of simple statements. Their literature helps them to learn the rules and to experience the range of emotions available through role identification.

ten through thirteen years old

The ten year old is a relatively stable, individualized, and capable child. Great sex differences are apparent at this age, and also individual differences. But the seeds of adolescent trauma are obvious in the strong peer-seeking behavior and the growing anticipation of adulthood by this age group. The rest of this four year period will be fraught with an increasing need for acceptance and individual responsibility. Each child belongs to a group, and must establish himself as making a contribution to that group. There is a growing awareness of the specific traits which define the leader or the successful group member, and the child is learning that individual abilities count for more in the real world than does a knowledge of right and wrong. If the seven to nine year olds insist on fairness, the ten to thirteens insist on recognition. This underlies their daydreaming and their emotional need to be a heroic person. This leads naturally to hero worship and a love of adventure tales.

These children are physically aware, and this becomes an emotional outlet as they run, swim, slouch, fight, or compete at sports. They tend to assert themselves through physically difficult actions, or to withdraw physically when threatened. They always want to excel at one thing, whether it is a skill, a special knowledge, or some exploited talent. They will therefore tend to overdo that one thing. The readers will read continuously, the ball players carry their ball to meals, the socializing child spends every waking minute socializing.

The biggest problem facing this child is the acceptance of himself, especially at twelve and thirteen years of age. He needs to learn that others have the same weaknesses he does, and have survived them—even turned them to strengths. This age group reads more than any other, especially the elevens and twelves. They choose adventures and outdoor tales of difficult journeys. They also like natural history, humor, and suspense. Mysteries, and biographies of people who have surmounted obstacles to make real contributions grow in popularity during these years. Children from ethnic minorities like to read about heroes of their own sub-culture. Boys like science and sports stories, while girls choose romance and everyday life stories. Most studies indicate that girls will read "boys' " books more than boys read "girls' " books. Series books, such as *The Hardy Boys,* or *Nancy Drew,* have appeal at this level, and later, too. The child from ten through thirteen needs mainly to find examples of individuals who have won recognition.

fourteen through eighteen years old

The individuals in this category can hardly be described as children. They are teenagers trying to become adults. They are receiving more and more responsibility for their actions, and they need to develop self-discipline in order to handle it. They hate to disappoint their parents or peers, but hate even worse to be unable to accomplish all that is asked of them. They are as apt to use the unreasonableness of the assignment as an excuse for failure as they are to plead their own error or inadequacy. The preservation of face among one's peers becomes so critical that teenagers who lose it, or think that they do, are liable to retreat into overprotected shelters rather than lose status. Overeating and suicide are not uncommon teenage retreats from a fear of failure, especially if the peer or parental pressures—already magnified in their own minds—are serious in actuality. Although these youths still want to be recognized, they also need to accept the limitations of being human, of making mistakes.

They are forming philosophies and priorities at this age, too. Friendship, duty, honor, and success must all be weighed and ranked in order of importance. Interest in the opposite sex often comes along to disrupt that order as soon as it is decided. Notions of good and bad are being overthrown, and perhaps replaced by choices between two evils, or two goods. The teenager must learn that others are not all good or all bad; then he must learn that of himself. Not every adult is mature enough to accept the fact that a person may disagree with him and still not be "evil," but every teenager is trying to learn just that. "Right" and "wrong" become "right for whom" and "wrong for whom." The same action can be good and bad simultaneously.

In selecting literature, boys traditionally prefer adventure, mystery, science fiction, and humor—roughly in that order. Girls like romance, mystery, humor, and adventure. Both like to read about famous people, careers, and other lands. Magazines and newspapers are also read at this age, and seem to be increasing in importance. These young people are looking for examples of individuals who have accepted limitations, even made sacrifices. They also want to know the kinds of values and priorities that guided historical or living characters.

All of these age groups require a sympathetic understanding of their particular needs and frustrations. If the children's theatre is to become a significant force for guiding the growing child, it must relate to the specific needs of children at different ages; and also to the existing environments of children. The primary environment through which society impinges upon the child from five through eighteen is the school.

PEDAGOGY IN THE THEATRE

The liaison between the arts world and the field of education seems to run the gamut from disdain by the educators to disinterest by the artists. Somewhere in between is a narrow band of cooperation and mutual respect. In the quick tour of European children's theatres made in chapter three, it was apparent that some countries use the theatre deliberately to supplement the formal schooling of the child, while others regard it as a "frill," unconnected to the child's intellectual growth. Whether educators recognize it or not, the theatre *is* a powerful tool for pedagogy—especially when reinforced with high artistic enjoyment. In studying the development of children's theatre in each of the various nations, there seem to be many variables, but in some cases a sequence is discernible. This sequence relates to the theatre/school liaison. At first, the educators are not interested; they are cautious about "new" methods. Gradually, the theatre wins them over, demonstrating its usefulness in the total educational process. This evidence is often anecdotal or motivational, rarely concrete. Then follows a period of close cooperation between the two institutions, during which the theatre becomes more and more dissatisfied with the limits—real or imagined—placed on it by its relationship with the slow-moving educators. Often the theatre breaks the tie; and, having established itself over the years of cooperation, insists on an end to school-time performances.

Hopefully, there will be a new phase of cooperation in which both school and theatre help each other indirectly and share mutual goals, but in which the artists are independent. Such a sequence may take many years to work itself out. The Soviet theatre seemed to enter the final phase in 1968, after nearly fifty years of forced school-time attendance. Other theatres can remain in the intermediate stage of cooperation indefinitely, usually due to a fortuitous match of personalities on both sides. There is much that can be done at every phase to strengthen the educational impact of good theatre, and, fortunately, most of it requires only a minimum of cooperation between school and theatre.

the pedagogue

The "pedagogue" is an administrative staff member found in most Eastern European children's theatres, but only rarely in the West. Generally, his is a high-ranking position, sometimes equal in authority to the artistic director of the theatre. It is through the pedagogue that the Soviet government, for instance, ensures the proper educational use of the theatre. These individuals are usually trained as teachers, and serve as liaisons between the artistic and pedagogical functions of the children's theatre. Even where the position does not exist, the job of liaison remains an important one and must be performed by someone. The pedagogue primarily has three functions: to advise the artistic staff, to conduct research, and to coordinate activities with the community's young people.

As advisor, the pedagogue assists in choosing scripts and assigning them to the proper age level. He judges their psychological and content suitability. Often he, or the theatre's dramaturge, help rewrite new plays to make them fit a specific age group's needs. The pedagogue sits at rehearsals, advising directors and actors on the reactions children are likely to make to each moment in the play. As researcher, the pedagogue studies each production carefully, supporting his predictions regarding audience reactions, or modifying them for future reference. Often a whole team of observers is used to note the audience's responses to certain key stage events. These responses are compared with the hypothesized or desired responses. Changes are made in script or staging if the goal for each important moment of the play is not achieved. Often these observation reports lead to theories of audience perception or attitude change. In Eastern Europe, there are periodicals which often publish summarized pedagogical reports on significant new plays.

In arranging for liaisons directly with children, the pedagogue often supervises contests of essays or drawings based on plays the children have seen. Youths of all ages participate enthusiastically in such contests, and they serve to relate the theatre experience to the other arts, as well as to stimulate the creative expression and dramatic interest of the participants. Pedagogues also frequently organize theatre "clubs" for interested children. These clubs may meet for previews of new plays, to have discussions with the artists, or to try their hand at recreational drama activities.

In some places, such as England, the pedagogue's role may be taken even further, and he becomes an actual performer. His teaching background is paired with artistic training, and he becomes the ideal person to interact with the children in participation dramas, or he performs in short non-participation plays which lead to creative dramatics follow-ups using the audience. These pedagogical teams, the Theatre in Education units, generally tour directly to the schools, making personal contact with the children, but rarely presenting polished plays.

The pedagogue is also responsible for whatever liaison exists with the local schools. He translates the school's needs into a language artists can understand, and the theatre's problems into educational language. It is unfortunate that few American children's theatres have yet seen fit to hire professional pedagogues, as such an interpretive role alone may justify the expense of establishing such a position.

helping the schools

Most children's theatres, even when they do not play during school hours, are completely aware that they are, by their very nature, working with the schools. If nothing else links the theatre and the school, at least they are both dealing with the same children. The theatre is helping the schools merely by means of its production program. If the school's goal is education, and the arts help to educate, then any effective play the children see is a direct aid to the school's mission. Even in schools that regard the arts as non-intellectual, their value as recreation and stimulation is usually accepted. It is to the school system's benefit if the children with whom they deal can receive outside stimulation which alerts them to the structure and values of the social system, and the theatre does that merely by showing characters in action. European school officials concur on the incidental benefits obtained by children from going to the theatre during school hours. From the school's point of view, such an experience serves:

  to make school time relevant to the life of everyday;
  to provide an opportunity for socializing with other children in one of society's institutions;
  to give a school-time experience which is purely enjoyable;
  to allow experiences with the spoken language, both during the play and in subsequent discussions;
  to motivate essays, drawings, and other creative work;
  to let the child experience something especially made for him by adults.

All of these benefits are accidental as far as the theatre is concerned. There are other, more concrete ways in which lines of communication can be maintained between schools and theatre groups. The theatre can improve its impact on the children and its relations with the community by providing carefully-planned aids for the school, in addition to its production program.

One common cooperative method is the study guide. If the theatre will take the time to devise materials for the classroom teacher which explain the play or the theatre experience, the teacher can find a way to integrate the theatre adventure into his overall goals for the children in his class. Very often theatres duplicate and distribute a short synopsis of the plot to permit a brief preparation by the teachers. Sometimes they also suggest pre-theatre experiences of more scope, such as related reading materials, discussion topics on theatrical techniques, or projects in creating costumes or scenery for a well-known tale. Occasionally, they will also suggest follow-up activities: questions for discussion about the theme or plot, art projects, creative dramatics, further readings, or applications of the play to other subject areas in the classroom. There is no reason why an integrated unit on geography, history, science, math, and language arts cannot be motivated on the basis of a play the class has seen. If the teacher receives a guide suggesting appropriate directions to take, he is often appreciative, and that makes him enthusiastic about the theatre's contribution. The theatre with more resources might provide a full package of materials—recorded scenes and music, slides, films, workbooks, short texts on acting or design, and other aids—all to help the individual teacher take the fullest advantage of the fact that his children will see a play. Even when the play is not attended during school time, such materials can be used by a teacher if a portion of his class will see the play; and such use may stimulate the others to want to see it, too.

A simple study guide which could be sent to teachers whose classes were about to see a play might be evolved from an outline such as the following (see Appendix D for a sample application of the outline):

study guide outline

Statement of Purpose   What are the goals of the theatre? Why has it prepared a study guide? What should the classroom teacher's responsibility be in utilizing the guide?

Background Information   What should the children know about theatre, or this particular play, to help them understand and appreciate it?

    1. Plot Summary. What is the basic story?

    2. Cast and Crew. Who plays the roles? Who are the various artists who contribute from behind the scenes? What does the director do? the playwright? the designer?

    3. Style and Theme. What are the theatrical conventions of this production? What key moments should the audience anticipate as revealing necessary or provocative ideas for future consideration?

Classroom Activities   What can the teacher do to maximize the impact of the theatre experience?

    1. Before the Play. How can the teacher effectively present the background information above? How can the child be prepared to actively enjoy the play while also observing a necessary minimum of theatre etiquette? What artistic experiences—doing creative dramatics, making collages, designing scenery and cos-

tumes—will arouse the children's creative energies to be good audience members?

2. After the Play. How can oral or written language activities be motivated by the children's experiences at the theatre? How can they be guided to express their own feelings or judgments about the play's theme or plot? How can they be stimulated to seek further artistic experiences? How can the play's impact be utilized in teaching science, or social studies?

Bibliography   Where can the teacher find out more about this play, the theatre's operations, the period or content area of the play, or other techniques for fostering aesthetic education?

Feedback   How can the teacher help improve the quality of plays by passing on his reactions, or creative work done by the children, directly to the theatre pedagogue or director?

Another possible aid for the schools is the scheduling of productions by the theatre which match the school's curriculum. If tenth graders normally study a Shakespearian play, and the theatre can arrange to do that play sometime during the year, the English teachers' efforts can be enormously augmented. A play set in Japan is useful to a class studying Japanese culture and society. A play about Pasteur will probably fit in well with a science class. Of course, the theatre can teach generalities like patriotism or morality—this has already been discussed. But the theatre can also teach specifics, like health care, history, geography, art appreciation, mathematics, or science if plays can be chosen to meet specific curricular needs. Obviously, no theatre wants to do *The Life of Pasteur* every year for the science class; but if the school is a little flexible, and the theatre can find artistically worthy scripts of topical relevance, much can be gained by exposing the children to the life behind the subjects they are studying in school.

A final benefit for the schools is the actual visit of theatre personnel to the classroom. The local actors can make the school day exciting with appearances to discuss the recent play; or with a poetry reading program or a lecture on the drama, unrelated to a specific play. Once an actor becomes familiar to the children, they are extremely anxious to ask him questions about the theatrical process and his life in the theatre. Visits by playwrights and designers or technicians can also prove stimulating to the school program, especially in terms of motivating children to explore their own creative potential in writing or design.

helping the theatre

These liaisons help the theatre, too. The classroom preparation for the play ensures that the children will arrive at the theatre with some idea of what is happening. It helps to dispel their natural fear of something new and unknown. By introducing them to the way the theatre operates, the subject of the play, the basic procedures of finding a seat, applauding, etc., the school personnel help the theatre run smoothly, and they help the child to concentrate on the artistic experience, which gives the play a head start. Similarly, by following up the play with activities designed to let the child make active use of his theatre exposure, the school aids the theatre in producing its desired effect. The teacher who drives home the thematic aspects of the play—not by telling the children the moral, which will only stifle their retrospections, but by creatively drawing them out in discussion—also serves to heighten the theatre's purpose. This retrospection may be best stimulated through a divergent assignment such as "draw your favorite moment," or "write a story about what happens to the hero after the play ends."

Besides helping the theatre to make its point, the school also helps by collecting and interpreting the children's reactions to the play. Unless the theatre director has direct access to children who will respond honestly to him, he cannot easily discover what the play's long-range impact has been, or how the children think about it afterwards. Only an adult who has the child's confidence can extract the truth about his reaction. The classroom teacher is in the ideal position to gather data on the audience's specific response to the production. If the theatre pedagogue can arrange to attend a classroom discussion, and then have the teacher's help in interpreting each individual student's response, he may learn much of value to future productions.

The other way in which the school can help the theatre is financially. Often theatres receive direct subsidy from schools or school boards in order to do plays for children. In other communities, schools buy out performances or book-in touring plays, providing them free or at low cost to their pupils. Even when performances are not done during school hours, the school can be a big factor in selling the tickets. Some districts will allow tickets to be sold right in the classes by PTA representatives or theatre staff. Others will let the teacher make the sales. Obviously, the teacher's positive endorsement of a play is worth a lot of sales within his classroom. Probably the theatre has no more influential friends than the teachers, if they can be convinced of the theatre's relevance to the day-to-day learning process of the children.

formal vs. informal theatre

There is one issue regarding the educational experience of going to the theatre which remains unresolved among practitioners in the field of theatre for children. This is the question of the amount of formality desirable in the theatre experience. Should the child regard going to the theatre as something very special? Should he be on his best behavior? Should he dress up specially? Is the theatre a holy place where the everyday affairs of life are taboo, and only the emotional heights are permitted? All this would make the theatre a very formal occasion. On the other hand, the theatre could be treated quite casually. The audience could "drop-in" for idle relaxation. They could come dressed quite informally; they could eat popcorn, and talk to their friends between scenes. This would create an informal atmosphere, an everyday kind of feeling about the theatre. It is important to realize that the pattern for the individual's relationship to the arts is being set when we first invite him to a play, and such a pattern can last a lifetime.

There is merit and custom on both sides of the issue. Both attitudes have prevailed historically. The Chinese Opera and Shakespeare's Globe both had food vendors; and other cultures permit open conversation in the theatre with one's friends, or even with the performers. Our own customs tend toward regarding the theatre as a place for black ties and rapt attention. There is little doubt that the formal approach shows more respect for the actors. My own preference, which is certainly not dogmatic or conclusive, is for informality. I feel that the theatre is in danger of becoming too rarefied to compete for attention with the mass media. Perhaps casualness and popcorn—as well as "popular" plots and themes —will help the theatre attract a wider audience. The children's theatre attracts a cross-sectional audience. It is the ideal place to introduce the concept that the theatre can be informal and fun—and also stimulating.

PSYCHOLOGY IN THE THEATRE

It has been generally asserted that the theatre makes a psychological impact on the child viewer—or upon any viewer. Throughout this text such an assumption is made often. There is, however, no *scientific* proof that the arts can change our perceptions, attitudes, and behaviors. Therefore this section should be regarded as philosophical or theoretical, rather than factual.

The child develops through a series of ego problems and psychological crises. In the following chapter, that sequence will be related to his developing aesthetic awareness. But before tracing this development, it is necessary to delineate the major psychological issues which seem to occupy children's theatre practitioners with an inclination towards psychology.

Pedagogues, directors, managers, teachers, and occasionally actors and playwrights concern themselves with the needs of the child for positive models, optimism, realism, resolution of fears, or catharsis of anxieties. Whether they realize it or not, these questions are really psychological ones. What is the process by which the child internalizes the theatrical experience, so that it somehow changes him? Even a fleeting emotional contact with another human being—real or fictional—can change our lives. If the theatre is set up to produce emotional contacts with characters, then it surely has a real potential to affect lives. How does it do so? And how should it be used so as to maximize the chances that its effect will be an "improvement," since the reverse could also be true?

identification

If we accept the validity of the assumption that the theatre does affect the child, the most immediate process by which it does so is through identification. This can be defined as the development of an empathic bond with a character on the stage due to some perceived relationship between that character and the self. We do not have to admire the character we identify with, nor identify with the character we admire. The key to identification is a perceived relationship to the self. The theory of identification further assumes that we tend to imitate the character we see as being somehow like us. In other words, when we see someone who reminds us, perhaps unconsciously, of ourselves, we form an attachment to him. That attachment causes us to see things more or less through his eyes. We take his part and defend his actions. Since it can easily be shown that we tend to believe in what we defend, we end up accepting the identification figure's actions and attitudes as our own desires. This onstage figure is usually referred to as the "model," because the audience member changes his behavior to become more like him than he was. For example, if we see ourselves as being like Androcles in that we, too, are controlled by greedy adults, and not allowed to be ourselves—just like him; and subsequently we see him being compassionate; we will tend to become like him in that regard, too. We identify with Androcles for one reason, experience the play through his eyes, and then become like him for additional reasons.

If this process is, indeed, an accurate description of what happens in the theatre, it can be seen that identification is a powerful device. By discovering what makes children identify with a particular character, one could write a play with a model in it who performed the actions which the playwright would like to see imitated. A revolutionary who wrote an effective play with a model close to many children could have this model defy authority, protest, and plant bombs, and the children would tend to change their *perceptions, attitudes,* and *behaviors* in the direction of the rebel. They would tend to be more aware of revolution; they would tend to think of it more positively; and they would tend more towards participation in acts of revolution. Obviously, the important phrase above is "tend to." There are so many influences on our lives which "tend to" change them, that no single increment of change is likely to be noticeable. Identification gives us a *direction* for modification, but it does not tell us the amount or *strength* of the modification. The influence of the theatre may be so small as to be negligible.

However, it occasionally happens that a single event can dramatically change a person's perceptions, attitudes, or behaviors. Such an event is defined as "traumatic." A sudden confrontation with death, or love at first sight can be such a traumatic experience. It is always an event highly charged with emotion, usually strong emotions as hate, or love, or fear. Traumatic events can cause obvious personality changes, or subtle psychological ones which may lead to eventual mental disorder. In theory, the more an event is charged with strong emotion, the closer it comes to being traumatic. Therefore, if the direction of audience modification in the theatre is determined by identification, it is quite possible that the strength of the modification is directly related to the emotional arousal of the audience at the moment when the model performs a key action. If the audience is calmly attentive as Androcles acts out compassion, or the anarchist throws his bomb, their change to become more like the model is, on the average, likely to be too small to notice. However, if the audience is wildly fearful or excited as Androcles helps the Lion, or the police station is bombed, they are more likely to show demonstrable evidence of altered concepts after the performance. This is an unsupported theory, however. In any case, it is worth considering tentatively, as it holds the key, even if partially, to behavioral manipulation and psychological modification through the art of theatre.

The question which requires answering before the previous hypothesis can be confirmed or denied is "What causes identification to occur?" Discussion of this topic rests on the idea of a perceived similarity between the self and the model. There are two sides to the problem: how does the child perceive himself; and how does he perceive the model? It is possible to give personality questionnaires and inventories to individuals for a response. They will usually reveal the way they feel about themselves at the time they take the tests. Let us call this description of personality the "perceived self." The same individuals can then be asked to complete the same tests, but this time responding as they would *wish* they were. Such a set of responses defines an "ideal self." A third set of responses can be obtained, all differing to some degree, based on the way the individual thinks other people would rate him. This might be called the "projected self." Generally speaking, the more these three "selfs" correspond to one another, the more healthy and happy the individual is. However, there will always be some discrepancies between the way people think they are, the way they want to be, and the way they think others see them. In identification there is a perceived similarity between the self and the model, but which self? Most theorists who have considered the matter, particularly Christel Hoffman, of the East Berlin Friendship Theatre, believe it is the *ideal* self image which determines identification. In other words, we identify with the model who is most like the way we want to be, not the one who is like we think we really are, or the one who is like others think we are. We identify with the strong and good, even if we secretly think we are weak and bad, as long as we have a personal goal to be strong and good. If this is true, it simplifies the issue, for more qualities are shared as goals than are shared in reality among audiences. Many of us want to be brave, even if few really are. It is therefore possible to get large sections of the audience to identify with the same character.

Looking at it from the model's point-of-view, there are qualities which seem to be part of many people's ideal self, and therefore seem good qualities for a potential identification model to have. Not all of these could exist in a single real character; some are apparently contradictory. But, assuming that the artistic direction of the play highlights the model's character—for the children cannot identify with what they do not even notice—the following factors seem to be widely shared within children's ideal self images:

> power, strength, ability to manipulate others or control resources, like the Lion in *Androcles and the Lion;*
> weakness, lack of control of one's fate, like Androcles himself, especially when coupled with an expressed need to gain control of one's freedom;
> a high energy level, producing a lot of actions in a given time period, such as Reynard, or Androcles do;
> external qualities, such as age (slightly older than the audience is considered best), physique (healthy and vigorous), sex (male preferred, but this may be changing as sex roles become more flexible in our society), temperament (rational, excitable, outgoing, sincere), and apparent intelligence (bright, but not too brainy);
> understanding people, having common sense—Reynard's major strength, of course;
> simplicity and innocence, such as Isabella's, or the brave little tailor's;
> apparent good intentions;

relevance of the character's problem, as revealed in the play's action, to the child's own level of ego development.

There are no doubt many additional factors common to the ideal self image of large parts of the audience, but these seem to be the most universal. It is through identification that the subsequent issues discussed make their impact, so research clarifying this process is critical to the documentation of theatre benefits, or the augmentation of the theatre's effects.

good and evil

There is no denial of the fact that good and evil, or some other kind of conflict, are necessary to a play. Without conflict there is no drama; and the easiest conflict to write about is the one between something agreed on as good or right, and something similarly recognized as bad or wrong. Since the child under nine is still learning these values, as interpreted by his particular environment, such conflicts are interesting to him, and they are also easy for adult authors to depict. There are probably several considerations, however, which need to be examined and understood before we can be certain how exposure to good and evil affects the child psychologically. It is likely that young children need to see good and evil relatively clearly separated. It is thought by many—the pedagogical staff at the Friendship Theatre is again in the theoretical vanguard—that evil must be portrayed concisely and specifically, at least for children five through nine. There must be specific weaknesses of character which are labeled "wrong." These should be, not minimized, but not exaggerated either. Evil must be characterized sufficiently to make it clear, but not enough to make it frightening. Both good and evil must, of course, be defined by deeds visible to the audience, not by descriptions of offstage events or discussions of character.

For older children, it is probably not enough to show good and evil; these behaviors must also be motivated. Even the villain has to have a valid reason for doing what he does, so evil becomes an inference and a judgment, not an absolute value. For older age groups, the possibility of change is important, too. An evil character may change if his motivations change, or if he can be reformed in a way which does not shatter his believability as a character. A good action may lead to evil through misunderstanding, too. These factors break down the black/white nature of good and evil. Interpretation, intention, circumstances, and other variables make evil a relative concept. As the child matures, the representation of good and evil in his plays must mature as well.

Most importantly for dramatic effectiveness and for psychological impact, good and evil must be in balance. The comic villain who trips over his own feet and bungles even his wrongdoing only serves to make the hero look ridiculous. Where is the merit in defeating the incompetent? Unless the danger is real and challenging there is no rationale for opposing it. Similarly, the passive hero who is saved from the clever villain by a trick or a *deus ex machina* at the last moment is an unworthy model. Vigorous evil should be met by vigorous righteousness. Passive goodness can only deal believably with passive badness. An imbalance on either side destroys all dramatic values in the play, and also diminishes any opportunity the audience might have had to manipulate concepts of right and wrong in a maturational way. Values can be learned and internalized from theatre, but only if good and evil are presented in ways which preserve dramatic balance, and are appropriate to the perceptual powers of the age group involved.

happy endings

Closely related to the portrayal of good and evil is the impact of idealism or realism on the audience. There is a continuous variable which has on one end the presentation of the world as it should be—idealized life—and on the other end, the world as it is—realistic life. Adults know that happy endings are often fantasies. Children are in the process of learning that unpleasant truth. Children's theatre leaders are not in agreement over which world is best to show the child. One group presents the philosophy that "children will find out about the world soon enough; let them enjoy childhood." This group feels that the audience should be sheltered from realism as long as possible. The psychological advantage to this position is that it teaches optimism. These children are probably more confident of success, more perseverant, and more positive about life when they grow up—provided they survive the mental and emotional shock of finding out that things don't always work out for the best. There is certainly an important advantage in inculcating an active, optimistic view of life.

The opposite argument is that children need to prepare for the real world. They must be realistic and practical. They must know that life brings limitations and disappointments as well as successes and surprises. This group of theorists would advocate occasional happy endings, but a healthy dose of realism, too. Many of this group, however, are willing to let the child start off idealistically, and then gradually expose him more and more to real life. The age division between "capable of handling realism" and "idealism only" is placed variously from nine to fourteen by different leaders in the field.

Of course, not all realism implies an unhappy ending. Plays for adults may end happily, or sadly, or happily for some and unhappily for others, or ambiguously for all or some of the characters. Realists advocate all these kinds of endings in plays for children; idealists limit them to the reinforcing happy ending. My own biases are toward letting the young child learn to be optimistic—but not to the point that such an assumption becomes automatic. Then, as the child matures, less and less attention would be paid to the play's ending in choosing a script, until there were no rules after the child reached twelve years of age regarding happy or sad conclusions. If the theatre is to be relevant to all, it will not be because it is a haven of escape and fantasy. That may make it valuable, but hardly relevant. In the last analysis, drama reflects human behavior, and the child should surely be able to learn about the range of human relationships and conflicts from the theatre by the age of ten or so, if he hasn't already seen plenty of "real-life" brutality and sadness on his television screen. It is of significance that the English word *happy ending* has crept into usage in many countries, perhaps as a result of the influence of the Hollywood film period.

violence

The psychological impact of stage violence upon the viewer is a complex issue, and one that has already given grey hairs to publishers of comic books and producers of children's television programs. Almost every few months some new research report is released which either "proves" or "disproves" a relationship between seeing violence in some media, and subsequent violent or anti-social behavior. There is little doubt that eventually someone will succeed in demonstrating a real relationship, but there will still be no way to be sure that fantasy violence is causing the negative behaviors, and not exposure to news programs or daily papers which report the actual violence in the world. Another possibility is that individuals with a predisposition to be violent also are more likely to choose fantasy violence experiences in the mass media.

Among the children's theatre theorists, most make the assumption that violence will always be shown on the stage, since it is one of the ways visibly to defeat the evil. If a villain uses violence, the hero must use violence against him. They believe that the child does not learn to imitate violence but rather to oppose evil. Two less widely held ideas about violent shows for children are: one, that children notice and imitate violence, and therefore it should be avoided on stage—the resulting plays are invariably dull, unless they can stand entirely on humor or circus tricks, and require no conflict resolution; the other position is that violence is noticed by the children and therefore should be included! By forcing children to consider violence as an alternative, they learn how and why to reject it, or else they *learn that it is sometimes justified*. Both the United States and the Soviet Union exist because violence was used to revolt against an outmoded governmental form in order to win new liberties. Some justification for that violence is permissible. In addition, one cannot teach the wise use and control of violence unless one is willing to deal with it as a subject. It is obviously an involved, psychological problem in American culture, and one that requires critical examination —not avoidance.

In dealing with moments of stage violence, however, it is fairly well-accepted that the unpleasant dangers of imitation are best reduced by *stylizing* the violence, that is, treating it unrealistically. Maturational concepts can be conveyed just as well by a theatrically staged fight as by a naturalistic one if the style of the play permits. In some cultures, all stage fights are done in slow motion and without ever touching the opponent. Cartoon figures slice each other to pieces and bounce right back —a stylization of violence which permits conflict but not unpleasant consequences. Even the Coyote, much mangled in his pursuit of the Road Runner, will always reappear in perfect health in the next scene. While it is not wise to teach that violence has no consequences, it is also not desirable to offend taste with realistic wounds and bleeding corpses all over the stage. The play's purpose in introducing violence must be carefully evaluated. If it is to provide excitement or humor, any fantastic approach to staging is permissible—even the cartoon format. If it is to resolve conflict, it is the respective attitude of the victor and the loser which communicates this to the children. The actual fight may be strongly stylized, but the consequences must never be glossed over. Only if the point of the play is the shocking brutality of a violent act is realistic violence artistically necessary—and such plays are probably not aimed at children. Stage violence is an area for extreme caution in the theatre's dealings with the public. But it presents an opportunity to deal with a psychologically relevant problem that is too important to allow the theatre to avoid by a retreat into "harmless" non-violent scripts.

conflicts with authority

At a certain age, the child begins to question the authority which has thus far regulated his life. As he becomes a teenager, his need for psychological independence becomes particularly strong. If the children's theatre is to be relevant to this need, it must deal with the difficult subject of conflict with authority. The stronger the authoritarian nature of the society, of course, the more difficult it is for the theatre to get public support to examine such conflict. What role should the children's or youth theatre play in easing, or augmenting "generation gaps"? There has been little theory promulgated relative to this question, but it probably is a potentially important one.

The problem also arises in plays for younger children that deal with negative characters in positions of responsibility—the corrupt king, the greedy minister, the lazy or stupid policeman. Difficulty with the public comes when a villainous teacher or parent is presented in a play. Adults who readily see and accept evil husbands and wives in murder thrillers can't stand the thought of their child exposed to a cruel parent figure in a fantasy. Whether harm is done to the children, or there is some benefit which results from seeing that even mothers can do bad things is largely undocumented. In line with current child-rearing practices, it probably would be acceptable psychologically for the child to realize that the adult has weaknesses and limitations. *Hansel and Gretel* is an old story, and usually popular among children. If parents don't like it, perhaps they, too, need to learn that actions determine character, not just titles. Nothing focuses the child's attention on the necessity of making his own judgments quite as fast as finding weakness or evil where one surely expected strength and goodness—in a parent. A more thorough analysis of the role of theatre in easing this particular transition awaits research, or at least more active theorizing.

ego conflicts

There is a sequence of psychological problems relative to the development of the ego in the normal child. An awareness of self comes before an awareness of family. The extended family, the neighborhood, the community, and the larger society all represent necessary adjustments of the concept of self held by the individual child. Each level diminishes the relative importance of self, and each puts pressures for outside recognition upon the child. Each new pressure is often in conflict with the preceding ones, as peers require different qualities of character than do parents. The next chapter completes the discussion of the child and his psychological interaction with the theatre by tracing his development in aesthetic sophistication as a function of his developing ego crises.

five

THE

DEVELOPMENTAL

THEATRE

To study an institution "developmentally" is to be concerned with the evolution of the institution, and also with the way the institution affects the individual, particularly if such effect changes or grows as contact is prolonged. For the student of "development," it is appropriate to consider the need behind the institution, its operating procedures, and research which reveals the precise way in which the institution makes its impact.

Every institution arises out of a need. Law evolved because people needed a way to enforce the social contract; the church evolved because they needed security; the theatre evolved because they needed to imitate their environment in order to understand or control it. Every institution also undergoes codification. In the theatre this refers to conventions and styles. Many different sets of conventions have arisen—some for arbitrary or trivial reasons, others for more practical ones. Next comes the study of operation—the organization of the institution, its procedures and practices. The developmentalist is especially interested in how the individual comes to know about these procedures and practices. Finally, a developmental study focuses on the changing relevance of the institution to its participants. In the case of theatre, this may mean asking questions such as how the theatre moved from being magic and ritual to being a social forum or an intellectual stimulus. In this chapter, only those aspects of developmental theatre concerned with the individual's growing needs and awareness will be considered, including a look at the research technology which may help to elucidate this process.

In many ways, the development of the theatrical sense in a child parallels exactly the development of the theatre in our society. Not only does his interest and acceptance of the theatre change as he becomes more sophisticated, but he proceeds through stages of ritual and role experimentation progressing to aesthetic pleasures and psycho-social concerns. By studying the children's theatre from this point of view, we can understand more about the way in which our adult theatre tradition evolved. The term "developmental theatre" is in some ways equivalent to "children's theatre," except that it does not define the age group of its audience. Development in the individual begins with his first need and lasts until full aesthetic maturity—at which time there may be a change or lessening of the theatre's significance in his life. It will be of special interest to examine the sequence of theatrical perceptions and relationships which take place in the individual who is regularly exposed to theatre.

In proceeding with this discussion, two assumptions are made. First, it is assumed that there is a single theatrical organization which provides or arranges the artistic experience of the growing individual. Let us call this agency the children's theatre. When maturity is reached, the choice of experiences will be opened to the individual, and he should want to seek out a variety of theatres. But while he is developing, we will assume that it is possible to talk about a "master plan" for his theatrical exposure. This guarantees a continuity, and also a freedom from outside sources which might speed up or slow down certain aspects of his artistic growth. The second assumption is that the elitist concept of theatre held in the Western nations is a result of an accident of social custom, and not any true requirement of the theatre. In children's theatres where school audiences attend, there is a complete cross section of the population, and it may be assumed that nearly 100 percent of adults would also attend the theatre if the motivation and habit were developed. Obviously, both of these assumptions—controlled continuity and mass appeal—are not demonstrable in this country; but they are or have been in the Soviet Union and elsewhere, and therefore could exist here, too. The attempt here is to talk about developmental theatre independently of accidental influences, such as no theatre for a certain age group or socio-economic group.

A SEQUENCE OF EXPERIENCES

If a person is an adult before he makes his first contact with the theatre, he may move rapidly through the early stages of this sequence. If he is only four or five years old, it may take him fifteen years. The sequence is based on a development from beginning to end, not upon age. In the normal individual, certain experiences will be impossible until a level of physical and intellectual maturity is reached. However, individuals develop at vastly different rates. Age groups are included in the following discussion only as a general guide, not as an attempted prescription. When selecting experiences for a large group, it is always necessary to be ahead of some of them and/or behind some of them. Extra activities to stimulate the advanced or encourage the slow are always a good idea.

natural play

We begin with the child who has barely developed the ability to communicate. Most of a child's play consists of experimentation with life. He practices sounds, movements, roles, and relationships. Before the acquisition of language we cannot say that any of these behaviors are motivated by an outside purpose; they are, rather, an end in themselves. He moves to practice movement, not to get somewhere.

The next largest percentage of his play activity might be classified as self-stimulation. He tries to find means of giving himself an experience—a visual impression, a repeated noise, an adult's presence, a physical stroke, or a psychological one. These behaviors do have a reward attached, and they therefore increase in proportion to the pure experimentation. By the time he is an adult, he will do little for the satisfaction of doing it, and much for external rewards (see Eric Berne's perceptive books, or others that deal with interpersonal "games"). What concerns us at this point is the initial stage at which the child takes on roles.

The drama begins—both in the child and in the society—with the imitation of animals and other people, but especially animals because they present totally different patterns for physical exploration. The beginning of the theatre lies in the primitive medicine man dancing out the fate of the antelope, generally as a magical device to attract antelope for the forthcoming hunt. The antelope was the major contact for early tribes with the animal world, and the essential element of their survival. For the American child, the major contact is with dogs and cats. My own daughter, before age two, was equally adept at pretending to be a dog as she was at walking upright. She assumed the name of our pet dog, his favorite spots to sleep or play, and even insisted on lapping up food from a bowl! Some time after this period, she began to imitate the humans around her, portraying the mother to her dolls or the father to an imaginary mischievous child. She was especially interested in playing out moments of crisis—the mother of the doll who would not take a nap; or moments of great comfort—the mother feeding her doll. The activities of imitating both human and animal are dramatic play. They are natural, and arise as soon as language is established—around the age of two. Physically different creatures and moments of high emotion, both positive and negative, are the most attractive materials for imitation. Note that the child is not really able to distinguish between pretending and reality for at least another year or so. He plays roles as seriously as did the medicine man—for magical purposes—long before he plays them to win adult praise.

At this age, the only "theatre" to which the child can respond is the adult who plays along with him. He cannot watch a performance, but he will welcome a fellow actor. If he is the dog, you can be the cat, or if he is the father, you can be the child. If an adult starts playing a familiar role he will not watch at all, but will assume a role and play along. Until he reaches the next stage of ego development, in which he can begin to distinguish himself from another individual, no other theatre is possible or necessary.

Note that this dramatic play is always both imitative and improvised. The child usually cannot invent incidents beyond his immediate experience, nor can he repeat his playing with any precision. Since he is not yet aware that he is creating a play, there is no reason to memorize an action or refine it—except for pure experimentation. Similarly, he cannot conjecture much beyond his experiences. "What if" sets in at about age four or five. At two years, he is limited to the dog he knows, the adults he sees, the children he plays with. If the children's theatre wishes to work with those under five, there is only one worthwhile activity—expose them to other live patterns of movement or behavior. Taking a group of pre-schoolers to a zoo is as much of a stimulus as any play could be. Showing them an Eskimo family in everyday action satisfies all the needs they have for something to imitate, especially if the actions are equivalent to some they already understand; i.e., an Eskimo child eating, or being put to bed.

Although this child does not need the formal theatre, it is important to understand him so that the transition can be made from this stage to the next one. A familiarity with pre-schoolers is helpful in dealing with the next older stage. It is also helpful to be familiar with natural play so that we, as adults, can allow it to continue, while also helping the child of three or four to learn to distinguish it from life.

participation drama

The next stage is the transitional one during which the child begins to delegate the responsibility of playing to another. As the medicine man developed because he could imitate the antelope most successfully, and the priest because he persuaded others he could perform the rituals best, so the actor develops because he is the cleverest at playing roles. The child of about five years to about eight years of age is ready to learn not to take a direct role in the drama, but to experience it vicariously. It probably takes the full four year period from five through eight before he can completely learn that lesson. The theatre for this age level must undertake the responsibility of teaching the child what an actor is, how he enacts roles for viewers, what some of the devices and conventions are which he employs, and how the child can still participate, but as an audience member instead of as a performer. During this period of transition, the child will be partly involved in playing, and partly involved in learning to be an audience. He will sometimes want to move and mimic, and sometimes be willing to learn about behaviors he has not seen before; he will sometimes insist on spontaneous but familiar actions, and sometimes be open to rehearsed and novel actions. The theatre for this age group should include an opportunity for the child to retain his natural play sense, while moving toward aesthetic distance. It must truly be a transitional theatre—sometimes the earlier kind of natural play, and sometimes the conventionalized formal theatre.

It is for this age group that the so-called participation drama described as a modern trend in chapter two is particularly suitable. Since these plays involve the child creatively, they contain chances for the child to take a role, but they also present him with adult actors who guide the play's development, and there are invariably sections of the play where the audience does not participate actively, but watches. The shape of these performances is usually in-the-round, which corresponds more closely to the child's natural play, and yet gives some focal point to the playing since there is a "stage" area and a "non-stage" area. Although the play structure is determined, and sections of it are well-rehearsed, there are usually flexible portions, where the audience can change the flow of the action. The child is both a player and an observer from moment to moment in this kind of play, and that exactly fits the requirements of a transitional style.

This kind of drama can do much, moreover, to introduce the child to the theatre as an art form. By having the preparations for the play worked into the play itself, the child can begin to learn the basic format of the theatrical event: scenery, costumes, props, a beginning and an end point, and an on-stage and off-stage for the actors. In my work for this age I try to do almost exclusively participation drama, and usually incorporate some kind of an interesting prologue into the play in which the children see the actors warming up, trying on costumes, arranging scenery, practicing characterizations, and, of course, opening up channels of communication with the audience for later use in the play. This prologue needs to be imaginative and filled with conflicts, or it becomes "teaching" and that is anathema. Having a character actor refuse to wear his ogre costume until the others persuade him that they won't be frightened unless he does, teaches the importance of visual elements of character, but is also good for a few laughs as the actor in question tries funny faces and noises in an attempt to scare his colleagues, but succeeds only with the costume piece. These kinds of activities cannot be sloppy or casual; they must be as rehearsed and focused as the story part of the play, and just as entertaining. When done effectively, the audience quickly learns all the components of a play without even realizing it, and then moves smoothly into an appreciation of the play itself.

Another benefit of such a prologue is the establishment of rapport between the *actors* and the audience, before the *characters* of the story are introduced. The actors are thus seen as people playing parts, which helps the child to distinguish reality from fiction, as well as guiding him to the delegation of acting responsibility to these actors. The critical ability at distinguishing life and art probably begins for children about four or five years old, but really is not absorbed fully until around seven or eight, or later. The rapport established by the prologue is also useful in helping the child to see the live performance as distinct from the filmed media. By the time the child is eight, if he has been exposed to theatre of this kind, he understands the basic conventions, the art of acting, and the concept of aesthetic distance. Although he is not sophisticated about achieving this distance, at least he can recognize it as a valid means of participation. Now he is ready for his first legitimate theatre experience.

stage tradition

The beginning of an appreciation for the stage play probably overlaps the last year of a need for transitional participation drama. The theatre experience prepared for the child from eight years through about eleven is designed to aid his development of aesthetic distance, to make him fully aware of the fictionality and conventionality of the theatre, and to introduce him to the primary clusters of theatrical practices known as styles. At the age of eight, or thereabouts, the child has completed the formation of his ego—he knows by now that he is a separate individual, with his own view of life and his own frustrations and needs. He psychologically is seeking a way to fit into the codes of behavior established by his environment. He has been learning values, but now needs to relate them to his own abilities. What the theatre needs to give him at this age is a chance at a large variety of experiences so that he may choose the values which best meet his needs.

For this age group one should do a large range of styles and kinds of plays. This child needs to see many different ways of life so that his impressions of right and wrong don't become too limited by his immediate surroundings. He needs to see many kinds of problems faced by means which better the self or the situation. He also profits from seeing many ways of dramatizing life: theatrical styles, from Oriental theatricality to Belasco realism, from Commedia dell' arte to romanticism. He can learn not only about the many approaches to life and living, but also about the many approaches to artistic exploration of life. Over two thousand years of stage history lie behind today's theatre, and the child of this group is ready to see the range of expressions which form today's eclectic heritage. He understands sets, costumes, and acting; now he needs to learn stylistic approaches to these and other components of the production. Even if the plays themselves do not come from different periods of theatre history, they should be explored carefully to see if they might legitimately sustain another set of conventions—merely as an excuse to challenge the child's mind with a new approach.

Aesthetically, the child completes his maturation during these years, assuming moderately continuous contact with the performing arts. By the time he is eleven, he no longer needs to meet the actors after the show in order to check out their reality. He can applaud the villain in the curtain call, and discuss intelligently a stage effect without it hurting his concentration during the performance. The plays, therefore, must give him a chance to suspend disbelief. He must not have only participation plays, or arena plays. He must have a chance to sit behind a "fourth wall" and watch a representation of life that does not depend on his active participation, but does depend on his aesthetic participation. Otherwise he can never learn the difference between the two. He must learn to accept the reality of fantastic events and theatrical wizardry—until the play is over and he can run on-stage to touch the costumes or inspect the machinery. Without spectacle, he cannot develop the correct attitude toward it, and therefore cannot develop the right attitude toward imagination which substitutes for spectacle. At this level, the boundaries of the theatre form should be explored. If the boundaries are too narrowly defined for the child, it will be difficult to move beyond that narrowness at a later stage of his development.

personal relevance

By the time the child is eleven, he understands the theatre. Now he needs to learn its relevance to his own life. The period from eleven through thirteen years of age is one of the most traumatic. He experiences the shock of being unable to be everything he wants to be, the bitterness of peer disapproval, and the frustrations of a developing sexuality unwished for and apparently uncontrollable. If the theatre is to do anything for this child, it must do it by showing him himself and his immediate concerns. At this stage the child needs to learn that the theatre can be a helpful device for projecting our problems, or, at least, for discovering that others have our problems, too. This is the period for plays about characters with the psychological problems of peer acceptance, tolerance, and a need to find their own limits and abilities. A play like *Servant of Two Masters,* in which the protagonist tries to serve two people at once just to see if he can do it, is tailor-made for this age group. Plays about historical personages, which show them passing through some personal difficulty, are usually aimed at this age.

These needs correspond roughly to the development of humanistic —even vulgar—characters in the early religious drama. When Noah's wife, in the Medieval cycle plays, became a common woman the drama was trying to become personally relevant. When stock characters evolved in Roman comedy, it was an attempt to guide behavior by ridiculing contemporary personality traits. Theatre as a behavioral model is a step beyond theatre as an abstract or magical ritual. For the child from eleven through thirteen, the theatre is no longer the imitation of roles, just to try them out; now it is the examination of roles in order to make choices about them. Cinderella is good because she is good, but Huck Finn is good because he cannot find it in his ethical awareness of the universe to be intolerant. He *chooses* an unpopular attitude because it is right *to him.* Note that the developmental sequence being described takes the five through eight year old child from his natural experimentation with imitative behavior, through a period from eight to eleven when the primary concern is on learning to learn aesthetically, and then back at eleven years to a behavioral concern. But now he is evaluating and choosing behaviors, not just learning to duplicate them. At eight years of age, the child learns to play the role, to follow the moral code. At twelve he learns why; and—perhaps—whether it is really necessary for him.

Obviously, most of the typical children's plays in which judgments are arbitrarily determined by fixed codes are of no interest to this age group. No matter how moral the resolution, the morality must be justified by a character's choice. They like adventure primarily because the hero in an adventure is forced to make up his own rules of behavior. He is off in deep space or dark jungle—away from society's code. He has to solve his inner conflicts to make his choices; as opposed to the fairy tale hero, who only has to obey the rules. Romanticism is the ideal style for the child of this age, and Robin Hood—who breaks the rules to follow his inner sense of justice—the archetypal protagonist. There are fewer plays written or performed for this age group than for any other. It is this factor which causes these children, even when avid theatre-goers at ten years of age, to turn away from the arts. And yet this age group is probably the most active of all—including adults—in terms of reading interest. The children's theatre must learn to serve this potentially avid audience.

concept formation

The youth of fourteen through eighteen years has, hopefully, developed an understanding and an appreciation of theatre and its traditions, the ability to participate aesthetically in a performance, and a sense of the theatre's potential as a guide for personal judgments. The final step involves his experiencing the theatre as a forum for philosophical concepts—without being turned away from it by an over intellectual snobbery. The mature adult in the theatre is capable of using the art form to explore the quality of modern life, and to make decisions about its assets and liabilities. While the theatre for this age group should certainly continue to be personally relevant, as the teenager copes with his aspirations and the self-image of the adult he is becoming, it should also introduce him to the great analytical plays of our heritage—especially the ones with popular appeal.

Chekhov, for example, dealt with the details of life—with work, with disappointment. He raised questions about whether mankind was to be pitied, or to be loved. One can see Chekhov as a great believer in mankind, or as a chronicler of man's hopelessness. These questions can be raised by his plays without the necessity of morbid intellectual analysis—they are contained in the action of the dramas. Shakespeare also dealt with sweeping statements of the human condition—with concepts of order and disharmony, of sincere and insincere love, of the difficulties in human relationships. The great playwrights from Aeschylus to Pinter all deal with mankind as a whole, as well as with the individual's choices. All of these plays are of interest to the youth trying to decide what he believes the human condition is. At this stage, the classics should definitely be a part of the theatre's repertory.

Most adult plays are suitable for this age group. Of the least interest are those that are completely removed from the problems of youth. Those that combine an examination of philosophy with an example of a young person with a problem are the most relevant. At the end of this phase the youth is an adult. At the beginning he is still a child. Throughout these difficult years the theatre must gradually make itself more useful in the larger issues, as well as in the smaller. Interestingly, at this period there is often a rebirth of interest in fairy tales and other earlier dramatic forms—probably for their traditional value as allegories of man's value system. There is also a wide range of individual difference in taste and interests. By now, one theatre cannot fulfill the needs of the youth, and he must be introduced to the various adult theatres in the community, to stretch the range of philosophies to which he can be exposed. In all, if the developmental sequence has been successfully pursued, the result will be an aesthetically matured individual who uses theatre as he uses any recreational media—because it helps him to relax, or improve, or grow. The perfect man does not need the theatre, but he probably enjoys it anyway. The rest of us need it, whether we are aware of it or not.

family theatre

There is one kind of play that transcends all ages, or at least more than one of the stages listed above. It is the one kind of non-participatory play that I would do for children under eight. This is the *family* play. By this is meant a play which simultaneously appeals to many ages, including adults. In other words, the play must have something for every age group—but not always the same thing for each. *Peter Pan* contains participation, personal choices, and human concepts. It deals with many levels of theatricality—from spectacular adventure to fantasy and realism. It is an excellent example of a family play, if done in a manner which preserves its multi-level appeal. This varied appeal makes it a difficult kind of play to direct, since the attention of the youngest and the oldest groups must be captured, generally, by different kinds of stage activities. The family play is really several different channels of theatrical event, all related, all going on simultaneously, and yet all appealing to different segments of the audience. There are, naturally, few scripts that can sustain the interest of an audience that ranges from five years old to ninety-five.

The biggest reason for doing these plays, in spite of their difficulty and scarcity, is because they reinforce the concept that the theatre is not a set of separate kinds of plays for different ages, but a continuous art form, inviting an increasing sophistication, but still remaining the "theatre." Developmental theatre is a sequence of needs and awarenesses which overlap and extend well beyond the stage at which they are the dominant patterns. The young child has some philosophical concept of life, and the oldest spectator still loves to imitate and participate. The stages discussed above are not discrete stages at all, but only high points along a continuous process of artistic maturation. The family show reminds us that we can all enjoy the theatre in common, as well as separate ways. It also serves to dispel the idea that children's theatre requires specialists. If an actor can play Peter Pan well it is because he (or she) is a good actor—not because he is a "children's theatre actor." If the stages mentioned above are arbitrary divisions, so is the very title of this book. A family play—and several have been done on Broadway with no concessions to "children's theatre"—contains everything that any children's play contains, all packaged together with traditional adult values and appeals. The only difference in performing for a special age group is that we want to make sure that we emphasize the values most pertinent to that level of development. The theatre that cannot bring off at least an occasional family play, without compromise, probably has no business doing plays for *any* age group of children.

The audience at the family show also gains the advantage of exposure to an overview of the whole sequence of development. This is especially useful to the fast or slow maturing child who is not fully satisfied by the plays for his narrow age group. It also satisfies the older child who can see the reactions of his younger siblings and realize that he has matured from these reactions to his own. And, of course, all children can learn subconsciously what the adult drama values are by observing their parents' reactions to the play. There is a social benefit, too, from an activity which all ages can enjoy together, and yet each in his own way.

THE RESEARCH LABORATORY

Besides being a sequence of stages, the other implication of the term "developmental" is the idea of a process of awareness acquisition. This process is what develops in the mind of the beholder of a play. He somehow receives the play through his senses—a process of perception. The input he receives somehow affects him—either intellectually or emotionally. This may or may not produce a change in his attitudes or concepts—either of himself or of the world. And this, in turn, may change his behavior. In the child, who is absorbing impressions and forming patterns of perception, attitudes, and behaviors, we have the opportunity to study this developing process much more easily than in the adult, whose perceptions, attitudes, and behaviors are all fairly rigidly established. The children's theatre thus presents an ideal opportunity for research into the process by which the theatre affects man—if indeed it does. Research into any learning process is usually termed "developmental" by behavioral scientists.

Many artists instinctively challenge the assumptions of scientific research. There is a feeling that art is a fragile, creative event, which disappears if it is touched by the researcher. Fortunately, techniques have been developed which permit the study of experiences in their more or less "natural habitat," so that it is not necessary to bring the actor into the laboratory in order to study his impact on the audience member. The theatre, itself, can become a laboratory. Proper research design and statistical analysis provide opportunities to study the instinctive knowledge of the artist—to help him understand his power; but, as importantly, to help him explain and demonstrate this power to foundations and government agencies with money to distribute in a search for quantifiable benefits. Without the quantification, many of the funds will be unobtainable.

designs and methods

Three basic methods of research are relevant to the theatre: *artistic, demographic,* and *behavioral.* (This excludes non-developmental kinds of research which may be borrowed from the physical sciences; for example, the testing of new materials for lighting or construction purposes.) Every method suggests experimental designs most appropriate to it, and each approach is suitable for answering particular kinds of questions. The artistic method is the least precise, the least reducible to statistics, and therefore the least convincing to non-artists. It is really the technique used by all artists since art began: trial and error. In performing a role, the actor tries a series of interpretations or gestures for each moment in the play until he finds those which satisfy him. The director decides whether these are acceptable; if not, the actor experiments some more. Finally, both are satisfied and the performance is "set." The audience does not respond exactly as it was supposed to, so further changes are tried in performance. By the end of the run, the sequence of actions performed is, hopefully, the best one that could be found, in terms of achieving the responses desired. In scientific terms, the experimenter begins, as in all research, with a hypothesis. Probably this can be stated in terms of an audience response. For example:

HYPOTHESIS: *At this moment in the play the subjects (the audience) will laugh (or cry, or wince, or listen attentively).*

The experimental procedure consists of trying a series of behaviors until one is found that the experimenter thinks will achieve the goal. The experimental consultant (the director) assists by offering his prediction of success. Finally, the subjects respond and the experimental effect can be evaluated in terms of the prediction made. Further experimentation is possible with succeeding groups of subjects until the hypothesis is proved, or the experimenter admits he was wrong about his hypothesis.

The biggest weakness in this method of research is that no records are kept. Therefore, the body of knowledge which is accumulated cannot be shared; it only serves to enrich the knowledge and predictive capabilities of the experimenter himself, and his immediate associates. When successes are recorded or published (see, for example, Martyn Green's notes on gestures and business for all the Gilbert and Sullivan operettas), they usually are not trusted by subsequent experimenters, who may have different hypotheses about audience responses, or different kinds of equipment (i.e., bodies and voices) and so are unable to duplicate the recorded gesture. Or, if only the finished performance is preserved, without the myriad of discarded gestures, we cannot discover the process used by the good experimenter, nor indeed whether his performance behavior was the only set of gestures out of a hundred attempts which succeeded, or the first one he tried. Although such a research method collects data in a disorganized way, because of the sheer amount of data that would be available if all artists kept records of their trials and errors, it would still produce significant knowledge about what people respond to, if the data was subjected to computer analysis.

Demographic research is confined to the accumulation of factual data and the subsequent analysis of that data in helpful ways. Such data might include information about the theatre's patrons: ages, income brackets, frequency of attendance at plays, play preferences, and responses to questionnaires about reactions. Or it may be data about theatre operations: which publicity media are seen by most audience members, how many patrons come per car; how many check coats. Such research can help in understanding local customs, and the interests of the prospective audience. It is especially useful in that it can tell exactly how the audience is constituted; making it easier to decide where and on whom to lavish the strongest efforts at public relations or script selection. Demographic data is usually so peculiar to a particular theatre's community that it does not generalize to other localities, except as a means of comparing operations and audiences. Almost every theatre manager keeps data on ticket sales, attendance, weather factors, or times of day preferred by buyers, and thus is doing research, whether he calls it that or not. There are many problems involved in getting complete data on any group, as not all indivdual subjects can be relied upon to fill out forms and return them, and even when they do there are errors due to the imperfection of the human memory. There are many questions, however, which can only be answered by surveying the "population" which consists of audience members. In some cases a selection of subjects from the total audience is sufficient for obtaining reliable data. Every tenth person, or every twentieth, may be approached for information—usually with a higher percentage of return if a personal appeal can be made. Such information is generalizable to the total audience, provided that certain statistical safeguards are observed. Determining the percentage of an audience which falls into certain categories rarely requires the use of a computer. This research technique does not manipulate variables, as do artistic and behavioral techniques—it only measures existing facts.

Behavioral research techniques evolved in the social sciences as means of testing the effects of certain events or stimuli on human behavior. Education, psychology, and sociology make the most use of these methods, but other fields are becoming more and more concerned with experimentation. The basic assumption behind this approach concerns the existence of "variables"—stimuli or responses which can be changed, either by deliberate manipulation or by some unknown internal process. This process is often the very phenomenon the researcher is trying to investigate. By manipulating those variables within his control and measuring the resultant changes in the response variables, the experimenter hopes to form a theory of the relationship between these two variables. For example, if you deny someone food and that makes him respond more slowly on a physical task, the experimenter can draw conclusions about food deprivation and physical performance. He may find it helpful to create a *construct*—a hypothetical condition in the body which is caused by the controlled variable, amount of food given, and which, in turn, causes the measured variable, physical performance, to change. This construct might be called "hunger" in this example, and is useful if it relates to other stimuli or responses, such as malnutrition or loss of appetite. Most behavioral research is concerned with the identification and study of constructs.

Ideally, only one variable at a time is manipulated, and only one response variable at a time will change. Such pure conditions are rarely found in life. Early studies in behavioral science attempted to set up laboratory conditions where only one variable was changed. However, modern social scientists realize that such data is relatively meaningless, since the human organism is much more complex than that, and all constructs and variables are operating simultaneously in the real world. Often it is the interaction of constructs which shapes our behavior— such as aggression being influenced by feelings of insecurity or deprivation to produce violence. The approach to studying individuals in their real life setting, with many variables to be studied and controlled at once, is generally termed *organic*. Those variables which we manipulate are called *independent variables*. The resulting changes which we then measure are the *dependent variables*. The way in which we set up the experiment so as to distinguish between responses to various independent variables is termed *experimental design*. In the example given above, the independent variable is food deprivation, the dependent variable is speed of completing a physical task. A simple experimental design might have two groups, one with no food for twenty-four hours, the other with normal meals, thus:

Group	Speed (*In Seconds*)
Food	Task
No Food	Task

A comparison of the dependent variable for both groups will tell us if there is a relationship between these two variables—*provided all other variables are controlled*. If the "no food" group was also deprived of sleep, or stuck with pins, while the other group was not, our results would be contaminated, as we would not know which independent variable had produced the effect. We could, of course, test two variables with a more complex design:

Group	Speed (*In Seconds*)
Food, no sleep	Task
No food, sleep	Task
No food, no sleep	Task
Food, sleep	Task

In order for behavioral experiments to be meaningful, extraneous variables must be controlled. In life this is impossible, so a technique has been developed called *control group design*. The control group is a group of individuals, chosen in the exact same way that the experimental subjects were chosen. Since we cannot control all the variables, we make the assumption that the uncontrolled variables affect both groups—the experimental and the control—in the same way. Only the experimental group receives the independent variable manipulation. If the two groups are alike at the beginning of the experiment in terms of the dependent variable but different at the end of the experiment, it may be assumed that the uncontrolled variables were not responsible for the difference, but rather the variable under investigation was. All results are generally analyzed statistically to determine if the changes were likely to be produced by accidental chance. Statistics never tell us whether an independent variable is indeed functioning to change behavior. It only tells us the numerical *probability* that chance alone is responsible. The lower the probability, the more likely we have discovered a true relationship between two or more variables.

The preceding discussion is an extremely simplified overview of a complex field. A thorough understanding of statistics, research methodology, operational defintions, and complex designs is desirable for the behavioral researcher, or the theatre practitioner who desires to become sophisticated in the reading or discussion of such research. However, even simple experimental designs and basic statistics will produce results of great interest. For example, suppose you are trying to discover if seeing violence onstage produces violent behavior in children. This complex question can be reduced to a simple design. To start, you need two large groups of children. They must be large to make the statistics applicable to the total population. If the two groups are chosen in a similar way, you may assume that they are equal in terms of any variables you can think of: theatre experience, intelligence, aggressive tendencies, family economic conditions, etc. If you want to make sure they are equal, you can pretest the groups, but it shouldn't be necessary if the groups are large enough (several hundred children from the same general environment, less than a hundred if they are preselected to be matched in major categories, such as sex, age, economic background, and theatre experience). Then you introduce the independent variable—violence seen on the stage. You have to be careful that that is the *only* variable you introduce. Both groups must see a play, preferably the same play. But in one case a scene is staged with violence; in the other case, the same scene is slightly revised to remove all violence from sight. Then you test both groups in some acceptable way for violent behavior. Perhaps you test three levels of response—three different dependent variables: was the play *perceived* as violent by the group which saw violence (Group V) more than by the others (Group N)? was there a change in *attitude* to-

ward violence in Group V that was different from the attitude expressed
by Group N? and finally, was there evidence of more violent *behavior* in
Group V than in Group N? Perceptions might be discovered by asking
questions in an interview or paper and pencil test. Attitudes might come
from an adjective check list or other word value test. Behavior might be
observed on the playground, or inferred from projective devices, like
pictures drawn afterwards. Whatever the measurements are, they must
be reduced to numbers that can be compared statistically for both groups.
A third control, Group C, that saw no play at all might also be used. The
design might look like this:

Groups	Independent Variable	Dependent Variables		
		Perception	Attitude	Behavior
V	Violent scene	Question-	Check	Playground
N	Non-violent scene	naire	list	observation
C	Saw no play			

In reporting such research, it is necessary to tell exactly how each variable
was measured (the operational definition) because your conclusions are
based, not on certainty, but on statistical probability. Subsequent readers
of the study must be free to draw their own conclusions based on your
methods as well as your results.

Behavioral research is less complex than many people believe. It
can involve huge computer analyses and multi-group designs or be as
simple as a situation involving one independent variable, and one dependent one. No artist should dismiss it as irrelevant until he has at least
learned its potentialities and limitations. The interested reader is referred
to any basic book on experimental design, or behavioral research, such
as Fred Kerlinger's *Foundations of Behavioral Research,* which also contains a helpful bibliography.

benefits

The use of research in the theatre laboratory will, hopefully,
answer questions for many groups of people. The sociologist is interested
in why people go to the theatre, what the relationship is between the
aesthetic experience and the political one, how the theatre expresses or
molds public opinion, and many other similar questions. He uses demographic data and behavioral research to study the theatre as a social
institution. The behaviorist, or psychologist, investigates the ways in
which we learn, interact, seek happiness, or otherwise develop and func-

tion. He wants to know how man operates. Information about what causes identification, violence, or grief can be used to make the human condition better—or, of course, it can be misused. The scientist is only concerned with knowledge—not with application. But educators *are* concerned with application, as they try to use behavioral discoveries to increase learning ability and to choose worthwhile traits for augmentation in their individual pupils. They allocate huge sums of money for research and upon their findings they base many of their classroom activities. This trend increases every year. The educator's function is to change attitudes and behaviors, or at least guide their formation, and he will make use of whatever knowledge he can find. Whether the educator's goal is to preserve the present society, or to help it evolve, he still uses research findings as the basic guide in his search for teaching methods.

The artist, too, has much to gain from research—both as an educator, and as he seeks to improve his aesthetic impact. Artistic techniques which are intuitively valuable and workable can still be refined by controlled experimentation. The issues raised in chapter four regarding the psychological impact of the theatre are only part of the unsolved problem. Color preferences, perceptual patterns, factors which influence identification, the creating of an increased dependence on aesthetic means of knowing, and many other hazily asked questions can only be cleared up by some research method—whether artistic or otherwise. How good young actors can be identified and trained is another area for potential investigation. Not the smallest benefit foreseen is quantifying the impact of the arts—in order to convince scientifically-oriented government agencies and private foundations that the theatre produces a measurable effect and is worthy of financial support. The possibilities in research are not magical or miraculous, but they are significant. It is hoped that more artists will find ways to understand and use developmental research for the benefit of all the arts.

part two

A METHOD

The theatre practitioner who is creative and conscientious will often confess that his largest reservation about children's theatre is the fact that he "knows nothing about it." Such a statement is unfortunate, for, although it is true that there are special considerations when it comes to an audience of children, the learning of these few considerations is minor when compared with the technical skills and creative expression which have already been mastered by this same artist.

The basic principles of theatre are identical for children and for adults. The need for adherence to high standards is, perhaps, more *important* for children's theatre—but the standards are the same. What is different is contained in the concluding section of this book: considerations, advice, observations, and intuitions which suggest a methodological approach to the production of plays for children. The assumption is that the reader is familiar with what the theatre is, and how it is brought to life. The following chapters deal only with what appear to be the relevant differences between the traditional theatre and the theatre especially for children. The differences are discussed according to profession: playwright, director, actor, designer, and manager.

six

PLAYWRITING

FOR THE

CHILDREN'S THEATRE

One of the most grievous errors perpetrated by well-meaning children's theatre practitioners in this country has been the overemphasis on writing plays specifically for audiences of children. It is not that it is wrong to know one's audience; nor is it a terrible sin to slant one's creative talents in a way that will increase the marketability of one's product—Shakespeare and Molière both "catered to the masses." What is wrong, in my opinion, is to allow one's conceptions of the audience to dictate completely the material and treatment of the play. Shakespeare had his *Troilus and Cressida;* Molière had his *Misanthrope.* Although both plays failed to reach a wide audience, both are essential parts of the authors' works. To the creative artist there must be a higher priority than pleasing one's audience. The creative artist's first duty, as anti-social as it may seem, is to himself, to his art. If he can please both himself and his audience, he ought to. But he can never please his audience and not himself without violating his artistic integrity.

There are undoubtedly playwrights with little integrity. Many potentially serious artists prostitute themselves to commercialism on a "temporary" basis, in order to survive long enough to accomplish their real

121

purpose—to write "the great American play." Others, more pragmatic, turn out what they think the masses want—regarding it as a paying job—no more, no less. But there are many who write honestly and sincerely what pleases themselves, and there are foundations and producing organizations dedicated to allowing these creative artists a chance—perhaps not to make a living—but at least to have their work done with the artistic integrity it deserves.

In the children's theatre the latter group has been long ignored. Most plays for children are written by amateurs who have no hope of financial return, but are merely turning out what they think will please an audience; or by would-be professionals picking up a little extra cash by turning out commercial "kiddy" plays according to a formula. And formulas abound on how to write for children. Charolotte Chorpenning lists twenty-eight procedures in her anecdotal *Twenty-One Years with Children's Theatre*. Most playwriting contests happily furnish useful hints, such as the number of characters desired, optimum age of protagonists and running time. Rules and formulas may be stimulating to a genius, but are usually stifling to anyone else. Their worst fault is that they lead to dreary uniformity. The rules dictate the plays. Gone is the unifying force of the playwright's vision. Substituted is an external judgment, applied *a priori* to limit or discourage innovation. Where are the serious artists who write to express their own vision; where are the experimental plays that explore the playwright's powers of communication; where are the honest dramas created from a playwright's imagination and tailored to a growing mind? For the most part, they are *not* in the children's theatre.

This is not to say that the goal of writing plays for children is unworthy, but merely that the emphasis is wrong. One should write "plays," not "plays for children." If it develops that the material and treatment seem to be suitable for children, the wise playwright will revise his product, slanting it specifically to a young audience and using whatever guidelines are useful to this tailoring. If, however, it develops that the material and treatment seem to be most suitable for off-Broadway, or television, or any other market, then the playwright can accentuate his marketability in these directions. The decision as to which audience is best-suited for which script is perhaps not even one that should concern a playwright. Let the producer and director make such a judgment. Let the playwright be most concerned with pleasing himself! Let the material and treatment dictate the audience, and not the reverse.

There are several implications of this point of view. To the playwright then there is no difference in writing for children and writing for adults—at least for the first draft of the script. In both cases he is initially writing for himself. The result of this is that, since few play-wrights will be naturally interested in fairy tales or adventures, there will be fewer traditional children's plays written. This in turn leads to two possibilities, not mutually exclusive. First, directors and producers must take the responsibility of interesting playwrights in material which, when developed, will be suitable for children. There are significant truths behind all folk tales which sometimes need only pointing out to stimulate an artist's allegorical mind. And second, we must all revise our concept of what is suitable for children to include plays previously thought of as adult plays. To recapitulate:

1. The playwright must write to please himself, letting the material and treatment dictate the audience.
2. Someone else, probably the director, must decide for whom the play, as he will interpret it, is suited.
3. Those who want plays for children must bear the responsibility of in-teresting playwrights in suitable material, and/or finding suitable material in the wealth of largely ignored adult drama.
4. Producing groups and foundations must recognize as great a responsi-bility to the playwright whose material is suitable for young audiences as they do to the traditionl "adult" playwright, including his creative need to experiment and even to fail.

Now, having made a strong commitment to the playwright's crea-tivity, let us explore the problems of that creative writer who finds himself interested in material which is suitable for young audiences, or at least potentially suitable. Among the guidelines listed by the various sources intended to help this playwright, there are many which are trivial, a few which are helpful, and some which are harmful. It is as necessary to dis-pel false notions about non-requirements, as it is to explore useful hints about what is desirable.

THE NON-ESSENTIALS

Four principles often advocated in writing plays for children are potentially destructive. Following them produces a bad children's play as often as a good one. These misleading guidelines are "the typical hero," "the shallow conflict," "simplification," and "morality."

the typical hero

There is a feeling among many children's theatre practitioners that the hero of a children's play should be young (slightly older than the children who see the play), virtuous (although not perfect), and male (because girls can theoretically identify with boys easier than *vice versa*). In chapter four similarity to the audience member's ideal self-image as a powerful force in determining identification was mentioned. Other factors which attract identification are an on stage model's energy level, sincerity, apparent intelligence, and ability to influence actions. While a character may be young, virtuous, and male and conform to the criteria which are actually thought to influence identification, this is not necessarily so. An old, evil woman may have qualities which cause deep identification as well. Fauquez' Reynard is male, but not particularly young, and certainly not virtuous. Mary Poppins is not obviously virtuous and certainly not young or male, yet children identify with her much more than with the passive children she instructs. It is probably ridiculous to feel that a play for children must have a child hero, and yet many sources so prescribe. Too frequently one finds young characters added to traditional tales merely to give the children an identification model—the Miller's daughter in *Rumpelstiltskin* gets a younger brother, or Cinderella acquires a set of childlike talking mice. This gives the children something to identify with besides an adult heroine.

The assumption behind these irrelevancies is that children love an instant visual identification, and can accept nothing else. The first half of this statement is true, but the latter half is not necessarily so. A quick and obvious visual hero is not to be scorned, but neither is an equally strong identification with a character for psychological reasons, or a slowly developing alliance based on behavioral observation. Ideally, the writer should take cognizance of all the factors that influence identification, not just the surface ones. Every play of merit has characters in it who arouse feelings of identification. It is not necessary that all the audience members identify in the same way. It is only desirable that the director and pedagogue are aware of the patterns of identification so that they can adequately predict the impact of the play on the child's psyche. If the playwright creates honest characters of the depth and variety required by the play's action, he has done his job. He need not be concerned with the young, virtuous male protagonist any more than with the necessity of having realistic characters speak in grammatically perfect sentences.

the shallow conflict

An even more insidious error is the belief that the audience requires a shallow conflict. "The villain must not be too frightening," some will say. Perhaps they prefer that there be *no* villain, no antagonist. As strange as this denial of the basic conflict inherent in all drama seems, it occurs over and over in children's plays. The antagonist is either weak, or incompetent, or never appears. I have seen *Pinnochio* scripts with a rather pleasant Fox and Cat, who were only having fun with Pinnochio. I have seen "original" plays that were merely travelogues, where the prime dramatic interest was the kind of dance that the local inhabitants would perform. I have seen comic villians defeated by their own ineptitude, which was fortunate because the simpering protagonist was too dull to wake up the audience. Such pampering undercuts not only the drama itself—as Saroyan says, "Drama is people in trouble;" but it also undercuts the protagonist's *raison d'être*. There would be no Huck Finn without prejudice, no Jim Hawkins without greed, and no Snow White without jealousy. Those who would remove examples of evil from the child's view must necessarily also remove examples of those who defeat evil. Alas, he will see the evil anyway—in life. The active defeat of evil he is less likely to run across.

The honest playwright must present a conflict which is balanced. The forces of "good" are barely strong enough to defeat the forces of "evil." Or sometimes they are evenly matched, and neither side wins a clear-cut victory. Or occasionally evil wins a temporary victory. But an overwhelming triumph for either side is usually not dramatically viable. The full realization of the conflict in the play requires only that the playwright ignore the child's supposed squeamishness and concentrate on the level of conflict necessary to develop the action. Gratuitous evil is uncalled for. "Grand Guignol" is not for children, probably. But neither is all "sweetness and light." The guideline should be to portray the minimum necessary extremes of good and evil. To much and too little are both offensive to the child audience. A play about subtle variations from social norms does not require a terribly "good" protagonist or a terribly "bad" antagonist. A play about violent human temptations probably does. Again, the material should indicate the necessary extremes, rather than rules about the child's tolerance of evil.

simplification

Another well-repeated dictum is that children's theatre must be simplified. "Children can't follow a complicated plot." "Children can't understand big words." "Children don't care about ideological conflicts." All of these statements are indeed true, but, again, they should not dictate to playwrights. The key is that children don't *expect* to follow complex plots, or understand big words, or get involved in ideological conflicts. They expect only to be entertained. As long as a play contains a level of enjoyment which a child can appreciate, he is perfectly willing to ignore what he doesn't understand. The child does not have to under-stand everything. The only guideline is that he musn't feel that he doesn't understand.

It is the director's job to find ways to translate complex plots, big words, and ideological conflicts which are essential to the audience's comprehension of the play into a language the audience can under-stand—probably a visual or symbolic language. It should not be a concern for the playwright. Of course, the playwright should never be deliberately confusing. He may offer explanations which are non-intellectual, or non-verbal, but he probably should not treat any audience with disdain, and certainly not a child audience. The point here is simply that it isn't neces-sary to confine yourself to a child's language or concepts to make a play for children. As long as the material explains itself and is entertaining, simplicity and complexity are irrelevant variables.

morality

The fourth of the misleading principles is that a children's play must be "moral." The object of a play for children, some feel, is to convey society's moral values to the child. An ideal play, to them, deals with learning to tell the truth, or to obey one's parents, or to brush one's teeth. Plays that have no moral value, or those that merely entertain, are un-worthy. Unfortunately, many potentially fine playwrights believe this rule, and restrain their natural instinct for fun, or even their opposition to an outdated moral code, in order to conform to parental expectations. Many a well-meaning parent has complimented me on a production I've directed by saying how much they loved it when so-and-so said something or other which every child "ought to memorize and follow." Or, "how important it was for the children to be like so-and-so."

If a play is moral, it's moral; but the playwright who sticks fine sentiments and exemplary behavior into an otherwise interesting play because he thinks it is expected is sadly misled. The children don't expect to learn anything; they don't want to be aware of learning anything; and they usually don't believe half of what anybody says anyway. In addition, they are perfectly willing to have their moral beliefs challenged or even superceded by a savagely ethical, but blatantly amoral character like Reynard. Perhaps adults resist an attack on their morals; children rarely do. In fact, they often welcome a chance to test their philosophies in new situations. This is not to advocate immorality, but it is to say that a play for children may be strongly moral, or it may not be.

All four of these principles—"the typical hero," "the shallow con-flict," "simplification," and "morality"—are misleading because they are not essential. A playwright need not consider them as rules at all. What, then, should a playwright consider—besides himself and his material?

PLAYWRITING GUIDELINES

The following points for consideration are also non-essential. There should be no rules between a playwright and his inspiration. The only relevant test is whether a director can be found who will undertake the work; or an audience to enjoy it. But for the playwright who has material which he feels belongs to children, and who seeks a way to bring it closer to them; and for those who read scripts and evaluate their suitability for the young, the following discussion may be of value.

respect

It seems continuously necessary, even for those firmly committed to work for children, to ask the repeated question, "Are we being sufficiently respectful of the child?" Respect for the child implies respect for many aspects of his tenderness and potentiality. But "respect" also implies respect for the director and actors, the playwright's interpreters. They must be viewed as serious artists worthy of the author's finest efforts. "Respect" implies respect of self as well. Because one finds oneself creating a product for the young does not invalidate the product, the process, or the creator. It rather congratulates him on his integrity—he did not abandon his ideals nor distort them into more lucrative avenues. He produced an honest play, knowing it was for children.

But the primary difficulty, of course, is making sure that the playwright has respected the child. What makes this hard to do is that the child shares so many ideas and qualities with the adults around him, and yet still has his own conceptions. He watches adult programs on television, but also those for children. He can understand most adult emotions, but also has his own immature ones. He must be approached both as an adult and as a child. Perhaps this is why it is so much harder to write well for children than for adults. That which is created especially for children must please both the adult and the child. That which is created for adults need only please adults. In fact, since much of adult pleasure can be shared by children, it may be easier to find an adult play which appeals to children than to write one specifically for a child audience. The passions in *Macbeth* are fully comprehensible to children over ten. How much more would they get out of a well-staged *Macbeth* than from a not quite relevant passionless travelogue? Of course, the greatest benefit would come from a tightly written play with all the passion of *Macbeth,* and a direct relevance to the child's own world—which Shakespeare's play obviously lacks. The good children's play is not less desirable than an appealing adult play for children—it is only more difficult to find. If, however, the playwright can stay in touch with both conditions of mankind—the mature and the immature, and if he can respect both his own aesthetic sensibility and the child's naive emotionality, he probably has the potential to write well for children.

It may help to gain some familiarity with that special children's sense. My students are always surprised when I ask them to watch a group of children on the school playground, or in the lunchroom. Few adults take time to look and listen to children, and it can be alarming when one does. There seem to be definite patterns of behavior, seldom revealed in adults, which erupt quite freely from children, particularly in groups. William Golding's brilliant *Lord of the Flies* is about children, not about adults; except in the sense that the adult contains the repressed and socialized child. This novel of mysticism, courage, and saveragery makes a good introduction to the respect children require. Perhaps "fear" is a better word to describe one's reaction to children upon reading this book. If one understands the child, one fears the child—at least a little bit— that makes it much easier to respect him.

There is a sense of wonder in the child, too, that is a thing apart from most adult lives. The child's capacity to believe is higher. He appreciates more deeply. He is less jaded, less inhibited. In him exists the primitive ability to accept purely, to hope unself-consciously, to participate unselfishly. Children in the grip of a good storyteller or an exciting play seem to absorb imagination—become truly one with the performer. This intensity and appreciation must also be respected.

Finally, one must respect their weaknesses. Their extreme involvement makes them vulnerable to manipulation. Their physical limitations make them reliant on adult care for their health and safety. Their capacity for acceptance makes them dependent on adult good taste to maintain a level of participation which will not prove traumatic. There are no safety valves to protect the child against his nightmarish fears, his self-deceiving fantasies, or his physical weaknesses. Making certain decisions for the child is part of respecting him. We can damage the child by expecting too much of him, as we can by expecting too little. Unfortunately, there are no rules to set the boundaries of "too much" and "too little." Only by observing children at the performance can we learn the success of our challenge to the developing human mind.

These considerations suggest the necessity of observing children, of conferring with experienced directors of children's plays, and even, for the brave, of attempting to talk to children. A special word is in order for these last-named daredevils. Remember you are seeking a conversation, a dialogue. Nothing is gained from an adult's convergent questioning of a child, or from an embarrassed silence. It is more difficult than many people believe to engage a child in real conversation. It takes a sincere interest in his point of view, and some care in phrasing open-ended questions that will not telegraph to him the response you expect—for he has been trained to tell adults just what they want to hear.

There are, fortunately, a few exemplary plays that respect both adults and children: *The Tingalary Bird* by Mary Melwood and Fauquez' *Reynard the Fox.*

ENTERTAINMENT

If a play is entertaining, it may also be uplifting, educational, didactic, moralistic, or anything else. If it is not entertaining, it is nothing. The question, then, is what entertains children, at least as far as the script is concerned? Assuming that the integrity of the play and the performance is preserved, children find certain things particularly enjoyable—more so than adults. The following is by no means a complete list, nor even an accurate one. But some of the things which can usually be observed that children like are:

Presentational Styles   Lacking in preconceptions about what the theatre should be, children tend to find presentational and theatrical styles more relevant to their own natural play than they do naturalism or realism. Direct address is particularly satisfying to them, if it is sincerely done, as it takes more account of their presence than does a "fourth wall" approach; and little is more satisfying to children than to have their participation acknowledged.

Non-verbal Communication   Mime, tableaux, elaborate stage business, character business, charades, secret codes, symbolic speech, and other forms of non-literary communication are more fun for children because they do not penalize them for their lack of vocabulary. Within the speech in the play they tend to prefer poetry to prose, especially onomatopeia, because of its added musical value.

Repetition and Build   The child likes repeated dialogue and repeated situations—provided they build somewhere—because he can have his expectations justified. The adult can have expectations justified by predicting behavior, but the child with less experience of life cannot predict as well unless there is a repeated pattern of behavior.

Slapstick   The child loves physical action and violence, provided it is sincere and in harmony with the production. He will accept slapstick even when it doesn't fit the production and isn't well-done, but he is then laughing at the clowning of the adult actors and not at the predicament of the characters. Chases, beatings, pratfalls, and other physical bits are stereotypic of children's theatre and some plays contain little else.

Childish Behavior in Adults   Perhaps this is the reason why children like slapstick. They love to see an adult brought to a child's level. It is a vengeful satisfaction to them to realize that adults can be silly, childish, or naive, and especially that they can be punished like children. This added enjoyment need not be humorous, moreover. An adult sincerely crying makes a very powerful impact on a young audience, since crying is thought to be a childish behavior. Any recognition of the child in an adult produces a heightened reaction.

The Antagonist's Realization of Defeat   Children are more cruel than adults. They take more pleasure from the villain's realization of his defeat than they do in the defeat itself. Justice must be felt to be appreciated.

Romanticism is funny or poetic to adults. Children accept it idealistically. Young lovers are beautiful to them, even when they are also recognized as silly. Noble thoughts are still valid to the young; Robin Hood is a juvenile hero, but an enemy to the adult "Establishment."

Physical Pleasures   Eating, drinking, having one's back scratched, and other everyday occurences which affirm our physical selves are most enjoyable to children. They love to hear tastes described, or watch a languid yawn. The humanity of the character is thus reinforced. The pleasures of the senses and appetites are all those which children can appreciate.

Besides these qualities there are many that children enjoy as much as adults do: suspense, the defeat of age by youth, cleverness, or beauty. There are also qualities which children enjoy less than adults: philosophical discussions, indirect motivations—such as prestige or money, or witty dialogue. A production is the only sure test of a play's entertaining ability, of course. The successful playwright for children is usually one who has watched a lot of young audiences responding to a variety of stage events.

contemporaneity

Children are most involved in a play when they sense its relevance to them. A play that deals with the problems of youth, of psychological growth, of the world as it is or is becoming, is far more interesting to them than a play about old age, or adult psychological crises, or the world as it was. This doesn't mean that a play must be limited to children's interests, but rather that it must include them. And above all it must be contemporaneous; it must be self-explanatory.

Adults have historical prespective. Children do not. Nostalgia, reminiscences, comments and "take-offs" on previous decades have no external interest to a child. A museum is of interest to the young only if the material preserved is of self-evident value. There are a considerable number of plays whose chief impact depends on an appreciation of an historical event—such as the musical spoofs of the Twenties. Children might enjoy such plays, but they won't enjoy them for their historical comment, only for what is actually in them. This is one reason why "in" jokes and "camp" are not very interesting to children. If they aren't familiar with the original material being spoofed, they obviously won't get the joke.

This caution also applies to acting styles and other theatrical conventions. If you want the child to understand it, it must be explained, subtly and artfully, in the play. The playwright should find a way to make all the devices necessary to the play's development self-explanatory. This isn't as difficult as it seems, since children do not have to unlearn conflicting conceptions of theatrical conventionality, but it does mean that the play must not rely on outside information—it must stand on its own and be relevant to the world of today.

action

Charlotte Chorpenning, easily the most influential children's theatre writer in the first half of the twentieth century, gave one piece of advice which is critical to success. She said, "Show it, don't tell it." Alas, she didn't always follow her own advice, but the words are true enough anyway. The essential meaning of "drama" is a "doing"; the essential meaning of "theatre" is a "seeing." Theatre is what is done and what is seen. Aristotle stated that drama was "an action—not a narrative." The child audience insists on a faithful adherence to this principle.

A play which depends on a narrator, or on dialogue, or on description of off-stage events may contain enough virtues to make it interesting to adults, but it will never make a good children's play. A piece like *Alice in Wonderland,* which depends so much on the humor in language, is suitable only for older children and adults. The scene in which a messenger reports the death of the villain in the next room is of absolutely no interest to most children, unless the messenger acts out the agonies of the death. The plot which involves a mistaken message will be missed by a young audience unless the message is a mimed one. In general, if the play depends on something which the audience must *hear,* it is not for children. The word most often used to describe poor children's scripts is "talky."

This does not mean that dialogue is unnecessary or unimportant, or that children don't listen at all. They do. But they simply believe the evidence of their eyes long before they accept the truth of what they hear. Children love clever dialogue, and verbal jokes, and even nonsense verse. They like the words in *Alice in Wonderland.* But they cannot follow a play which consists primarily of speech and only secondarily of action. The reason why *Alice* fails as a children's play so often is that most dramatic versions preserve faithfully Lewis Carroll's language but fail to add anything visual to match it. If a playwright could find a way to *show* Alice's adventures, in addition—not instead of—having her *talk* to the characters she meets, there is no reason why a good play would not result. But the writer who relies on wit and language alone will never succeed for children for more than an extremely brief scene.

The other implication of "Show it, don't tell it," is for the play's so-called "message." In too many plays intended for children the message is mouthed repeatedly and yet all to no avail, for the action of the play—what the children *see*—ignores or even contradicts the verbal instruction! When we see a villain, for example, enjoying vigorously the fruits of his wrongdoing, and then only mildly inconvenienced when he is forced to declare his reformation, the evidence of our eyes assures us that he is more content with evil than with good. His "turning over a new leaf" is obviously not sincere. If his suffering at being caught was visually more exacting than his previous enjoyment, then we can accept his conversion; but always what we *see* is more significant than what anybody says. If the play is supposed to be about "freedom," the audience has to see somebody who is free; and that sight must be compared to one of somebody not free. Then the child makes a judgment. To assume that a spoken goal is one worth fighting for is to ignore the entire point of the drama. No child will accept such an omission. The caution for playwrights is simple to state; Chorpenning did it with her five words.

But it is often difficult to know without a production if the action of the play is sufficient to hold the child, as well as harmonious with the playwright's intent. Unless both these conditions are fulfilled, the play will likely fail for children.

unity of organization

It is an often stated rule that in the children's theatre the story is the most important element and it must never stop. But this is not always true. How evident is the story in *The Tingalary Bird*? What about the many episodic plays with little story continuity and a strong character interest? *Reynard the Fox* comes to mind. It is true, however that *interrupting* a plot with irrelevancies is a great weakness in a children's play. What should be considered—not as a rule, but as a strong recommendation—is a careful adherence to whatever dramatic element it is which serves to organize and unify a particular script. In many cases, this will be the story; but not always.

The basic story-line play which depends on a chronological sequence of dependent events is the most popular kind of play for children, and in enacting this kind of play it is important not to distract the child. Once the play begins to unfold he will become very impatient at anything which does not appear to contribute to the plot's resolution. The same rule probably applies in mystery novels. The most common transgression against this principle is the musical interlude, with unnecessary comic sub-plots running a close second. Both kinds of interruptions may be well-done, but they belong early in the play, before the building of incidents to a climax begins, or else they must somehow be integral to the main story line.

However, this does not rule out plays where the story line is not the most significant dramatic element. In a character play like *Reynard* the guideline changes to, "Nothing must interrupt the character development once it has begun." In *The Tingalary Bird,* it may be the mood which holds the play together, and this mood then becomes relatively inviolable. The overriding principle is unity. Children are not as appreciative of diversions from the main road as are adults. They can be easily sidetracked, but do not enjoy having to sort out different directions that a play may take. They need variety, to be sure, but it must all contribute to a single drive. A play for children is often shorter than a play for adults, and yet always seems to contain as much action, or more. What is left out are the adult elaborations and diversions, the side-excursions. Many adult plays are perhaps only long one-acts with padding. Most children's plays retain the one-act structure. Whatever the play is about—a story, a character, or a mood—it should probably be about one thing primarily to make it more accessible to children. Other things add to the mainstream, and many techniques can be used to follow that stream, but nothing should distract from it.

age levels

Earlier it was said that age level concerns need not bother a playwright. The pedagogue and the director of a children's theatre should probably be the ones who decide on the appropriate age group for a play. It is useful to a playwright, however, who finds his play psychologically suited for eleven-year-olds also to be able to make the characters, language, and attention-span fit the eleven-year-old group, and such a fitting can often be accomplished through a minor revision of the script. Chapter four contained a discussion of the typical age divisions in a theatre for children. Other books on child development and psychology are also useful. Most useful of all are the experiences of watching children at play, and of talking to them openly.

Two principles bear repeating: the playwright must not forget to please himself as to language, complexity, and integrity of emotions; and he must also remember that the child does not need to understand everything, so long as he does not feel excluded by some part of the play. Any adult can find something new in a televised movie which he saw originally as a child. That doesn't mean he didn't like it as a child. The child simply doesn't notice what he doesn't understand unless nothing else is going on for a considerable period of time and he is forced to conclude that he is missing something. In fact, if we grasped all of an artistic experience the first time there would be no distinction between the ordinary and the classic.

Age level abilities vary so widely from region to region, and between various socio-economic sub-groups, that the best a playwright for children can hope to do is try for some consistency of appeal in his play. Then, at least, the director will not be forced to cut sections because they are too "old" or too "young" for the rest of the play.

variety and rhythm

If the would-be playwright will study the works of the more successful children's writers—an Aurand Harris or a Fauquez—he will perceive that they all share a remarkable ability to write to the child's attention span. They seem to be able to create a rhythm of short and long, talk and action, humor and seriousness, calm and tension, all of which combine relentlessly into a single dramatic action, but which, through their variety, keep the child attending long past the time when his teachers are sure he should be squirming. The normal principle of alternation of scenes to maintain interest applies even more obviously to children's audiences, with a special need being evidenced concerning the rhythm of visual activity. If the playwright can correctly time the inclusion of various shifts of focus, without violating his own sense of the play's rhythm, he will hold the child for long stretches. Among those events which never fail to secure attention, the three most useful are: a new character's entrance; a silence, especially if something is being mimed in the silence; and any kind of slapstick, violence, or large physical movement.

Knowing just when to introduce a physical action, just how long to prolong a discussion, and just when trained young nerves require a relaxation is a problem which is probably only solved by trial and error. The director for children must be extremely sensitive to this issue during try-out productions of the new script, especially as regards the length of time between key visual events. Cutting and rearranging scenes is a frequent necessity during this period of script polishing. Sometimes a director can solve the problem of a too long static scene by breaking it in half with a silent entrance and exit—perhaps the villain is looking for the hero, so he has to interrupt his planning scene by hiding while the villain passes across the stage. Of course, it is better if the playwright can anticipate such a need while revising his script to make it marketable for children.

Generally, the concentrated one-act nature of most children's plays, coupled with the range of episodes in most adventure tales and fantasies, force the playwright into a multiple short-episode structure. One of the dangers then becomes the audience's expectation of a short-episode structure. This makes it even harder to hold the audience when a longer, slower scene appears. This problem is complicated by the television-attention-span-syndrome. Blackout sketches on TV comedy programs, frequent commercials, and the normal cinematic shifting of focus all combine to *reduce* the attention span of the American public. The theatre must fight this problem or accept its limitations. It is probably wisest to do both. The playwright cannot afford to spend too much of his energy catering to attention spans, but he should be aware of the problem.

Besides their extreme need for action and their short attention span, children also like broad discriminations. A wide range of character types is easier for them to keep separated in their minds than a homogeneous group, and, although their ability for fine discrimination should be stretched by the play, it is desirable to avoid too similar characters or locations unless a special point is made of their subtle differences.

nutritional consideration

The analogy between a playwright for children and a dietician is a good one. A dietician has to provide meals that taste good so that people will eat them. They must appeal to eye, nose, and palate. He then has to pack into that menu as much as he can of a variety of health-giving nutrients—to provide energy, to build bodies, and to protect health and the feeling of well-being. He also should be building a sense of proper diet and culinary pleasures in those who eat the meals. Hopefully, he will not forget that children like and deserve candy occasionally.

The playwright must also provide a package that the consumer will accept. The child audience deserves its candy, too—pure taste pleasure with little substance. But the playwright must also be aware of nutritional requirements. Into that delicious-tasting play he should pack as much life as his artistic fabric will sustain—in order to cultivate sensitivity, to inform gently and painlessly, and to help the child grow both psychologically and socially. Like a parent anxiously trying to get his child to eat, the playwright must always be aware that threats, pleadings, and beatings will not teach a child good eating habits. Only cleverness, patience, an awareness of individual tastes, and delicious food will do that. Similarly, artistry, craftsmanship, an awareness of the child's world, and first quality entertainment are the only ways to build strong habits of theatre awareness, while—almost incidentally—giving the child his needed aesthetic vitamins.

seven

DIRECTING

FOR THE

CHILDREN'S THEATRE

The director in the children's theatre carries the major responsibility for communicating with the audience. One can write for children without understanding them, act for them without liking them, and manage for them without contacting them, but it is the director who mediates between the art work and the audience. He must know his audience. It has been said of Z.Y. Korogotsky, Artistic Director of the famed Leningrad Children's Theatre, that he always "has a serious talk with the audience" when he directs; and such an image may be a useful one to bear in mind.

The children's theatre director should have a belief in children's theatre, an understanding of the developmental process, and an insight into the child's interests, abilities, vocabulary, attention span, and humor. He ought to be able to accept the child's cruelty and his compassion. He must read children's books and watch children's programs on television, for these constitute the artistic background of his audience. He also profits by watching children at play, from which he learns the way their imaginations flow.

What is certainly necessary is that he *respect* the child and his milieu, or he can never successfully engage the child in the conversation which children's theatre should create.

As with all directing, the play should be only one-half of a dialogue. The mental and/or visible reactions of the audience are the important other half. The combination of the play as the stimulus and the audience's response is the experience that the child takes away with him when the play has ended. One cannot engage an audience in a dialogue unless one speaks their language. The technique of directing, then, is either to learn the language of the audience, or to teach them the language of the director. The good director probably does both, simultaneously, to doubly insure that the message is received. Learning the language of the children's theatre audience means knowing children, teaching them the language of the director means respecting their ability as one introduces the conventions appropriate to the specific play.

DIRECTING GUIDELINES

Nearly all of the real differences between the artistic production of a play for adults and the artistic production of a play for children can be discussed by examining seven directorial concepts. The ideas which follow are intended to be suggestive and thought-provoking, not definitive. Hopefully, they identify what should be the *areas of concern* to the director new to children's theatre. These seven aspects will be analyzed under the headings of *emotional truth, visualization, variety, multi-age considerations, casting and identification, audience participation,* and *theatrical magic.*

emotional truth

Children's theatre must be staged in a manner that is accessible to children. This means that adult logic, complex sociological imagery, and complicated plots are not desirable. But it does *not* mean that everything must be oversimplified. The greatest error in children's theatre is emotional condescension. There is a great difference between selecting material which is within the child's frame of reference and, on the other hand, simplifying life for the "childlike mind." The former is permissible, the latter is an error.

The child can probably comprehend the entire affective aspect of human relations from the time he is six months old. He knows anger, frustration, jealousy, love, fear, humor, friendliness, disagreement, peace, violence, boredom, and many other emotions before even that age. The child of five—generally the youngest age for formal theatrical experience—can read great subtleties in a parent's tone of voice, or bodily tensions. He knows when we are being hostile or uncooperative, when we are revealing unconscious prejudices, when we are playing social "games," and when we are striving for specific need-fulfillment. This receptivity to the affective domain is so strong in the child that he probably learns all about life through his emotions, long before his reasoning power ever begins to function. To eliminate emotional responses from a play is, therefore, to cheat the child.

Unknowledgeable playwrights, actors, and directors, however, often aim at over-simplified reactions. We see the stereotyped king who has only two emotions: pompous and loving; or the villain who is only mean. This treatment of the emotional life of the characters is worthless. The villain must try to rationalize his desires, as all humans do. The king must be trying to be a good father and king, as a king naturally would. Then we can judge his actions as those of a real person having real emotions. By giving him "cardboard" emotions, we tell the child only one thing: this is a puppet, not a person; he has no emotions, therefore he cannot be accepted as real, and, therefore, although we may laugh at him, he is not someone from whom we can learn. Charlie Chaplin, no matter how farcical the situation, has never cheated by reducing the complexity of his emotional reaction to what was going on around him. Any child would know that Chaplin is a real character, even though the situation might be grotesque. The reason is because the child learns *affectively first,* and logically, second (or not at all). Such a condition demands sincere portrayal of all emotional responses.

On the other hand, because children are so receptive to the affective content of the play, it is necessary to control the irrelevant emotions in the play, as these will tend to side-track the child and confuse him as to the issue in the play. In *Reynard the Fox,* one can notice the repeated pattern of the animals' greed, and Reynard's superiority complex, which tempts him to ridicule greed in others. That affective pattern constitutes the main plot of the play. The subsequent jealousy/friendship which the animals feel for Reynard is the emotional sub-plot, following logically on the dominant pattern. And these two patterns subsume all of the emotions which receive emphasis through the action of the play. Even Reynard's "self-sacrifice" at the end must be interpreted as part of his superiority drive, for to do otherwise will confuse the child as to who Reynard really is.

Consider *Macbeth* as a children's play. Ambition is the affective theme, and guilt is the counter-theme. In all their subtleties, these themes are accessible to children, provided they are sincerely portrayed. The witches enact the fear of retribution which brings on guilt, and this is accessible. But the porter scene is emotionally irrelevant, although it makes good theatrical sense. Children would probably be confused by it, and shuffle in their chairs. The same is true of the ironic scene describing Macbeth's peaceful castle. Irony and comic relief are not effective for children unless they can be made *emotionally* relevant to the play. The comic scenes in Marlow's *Faustus* are, for example, relevant emotionally to the main plot, dealing, as they do, with the affective pattern of a need for power. If done sincerely, children would probably accept them as relevant to Faustus' same emotional need.

Since the play should always challenge the audience, it is sometimes necessary to confuse part or all of the audience in an honest effort to raise their comprehension. The guiding principle should be, therefore, that it is always permissible to confuse the audience, provided always that they are being continuously entertained, that all emotional reactions are being handled with absolute sincerity, and that there is an *affective unity* about the production—even though the irony which unifies the affective elements, as in *Faustus,* may be temporarily above the child's understanding.

visualization

Probably the most successful children's theatre director is the one who, in his shows, excels in visual interpretations. The ability to make a theatrical experience fully visual is a useful one for any stage, but it is a *sine qua non* in the children's theatre. There is little doubt but that, to the child, it is the visual impression he receives which dominates the words of the play.

The adult in the theatre has the opportunity to learn from what he sees, what he hears, or what he infers from the unspoken ideas. He also brings his own experiences to bear in judging emotional states and ideological conflicts. The child has a surprisingly good understanding of emotional states, and is probably better than we imagine at inferring from actions. Where his lack of experience leaves him relatively helpless is in the areas of vocabulary, inferring from words, and judging ideological conflicts. He compensates by relying more heavily on what he does understand—the visual elements, including the decor. The emphasis placed on the visual increases the designer's importance in conveying plot outline and character.

The child relies so heavily on the visual elements that he simply refuses to believe anything he does not see. The weakest possible scene in any children's play is a messenger reporting an important action. He can report emotional consequences of an action by being, himself, moved

by the emotions he reports, but no description of an event has any validity to the children, especially under ten years of age. A good example
is the off-stage death. The child probably never accepts the villain's death
until he sees the body—preferably in the act of dying. Let the death take
place off-stage, no matter how thoroughly reported, and the actor's return in the curtain call will incite a storm of protest in the house—and
perhaps cause psychological fears to persist in the very young. If the villain is killed on-stage, however, and the actor manages a convincing death,
he can then pop right back up for the curtain call, where his presence
is accepted as a convention of the stage. (Nothing is quite so thrilling,
in any case, as the spontaneous applause that *always* accompanies the
convincing visible defeat of a sincerely portrayed villain.)

It is the director's responsibility to ensure that everything which
needs to be understood by the audience is clear visually, and likewise,
that the visual expression of the play is nowhere in conflict with either
the text or the conventions of the theatre. What is needed, in effect, is a
visual language. Almost anything can be communicated to the children,
providing that the director can find a way to translate the required knowledge into a visual mode. Not only dialogue, but the essential relationships
must be so translated. Upon the director's ability to find the right visual
symbol for the most complex concept depends the depth of understanding which the children will enjoy.

Consider the following relationship in Fauquez's *Don Quixote of
La Mancha:* Quixote has mistaken a servant girl for a fine lady. Visually,
this can easily be shown by his bowing and deference to her, when we
can see from her costume and posture that she is a peasant. But then,
through a series of episodes, the girl comes to accept Quixote's delusion
as a sign of his romantic faith. In fact, she falls in love with him. There
is no scene where she enacts her love, although she talks about it once—
no way to show visually what it is about Quixote that arouses her love.
The director must, therefore, find a way to translate this relationship into
a visual symbol. The possibilities are endless but one example will suffice:
in her first scene, the director could give the girl a dirty handkerchief,
into which she blows her nose. Quixote sees the object on the ground
and gallantly retrieves it for her. This creates a visual symbol whereby
the dirty cloth represents his gallantry. At first, she laughs at the handkerchief; later, she can regard it questioningly, hold it defiantly, or cradle
it lovingly, and the audience will understand, through the visual symbol,
that she is expressing her changing relationship with the Don. Such techniques are known to every skilled director. The difference in children's
theatre is that the search for visual symbols is absolutely essential if the
children are to comprehend the play's internal levels.

There is no easy formula to enable the director to learn this "visual language." Each situation requires a creative imagination and good taste, although considerable help can be found in a knowledge of the background of one's audience—as a rat can be something different to a slum dweller and a suburban pet fancier. There is, however, a test for the successful solution to the problem. In the words of Lucien Guitry,

> I have three spectators: one who is deaf as a carpet, another who is blind as a mole, and another who is intelligent—more than anyone in the world, fine, sensible, spiritual; but doesn't understand a word of my language. It's a matter of convincing all three.

In the children's theatre, it is the third spectator who most closely approximates the condition of the audience. If the play is comprehensible to an adult who does not speak the language, one may be assured it will be comprehensible to children. In my own directing I have often made use of the technique of asking the cast to perform a complete run-through of the play, but speaking only gibberish. This reduces the play to only its visual components, plus the vocal inflections which carry emotions. Whatever cannot be understood from this run-through will not be understood by the children's audience, and, if it is a necessary matter, I must find a way to add it visually.

A caution must be made regarding this "visual language," however. It must not become an excuse for a lack of faith in the audience, or an underestimation of the children's intellect. It is a mistake to seek the action at any price, because the play will then never stimulate the growth of the audience's verbal and social comprehension—which it obviously must do. It is easy to get so carried away with visual stage effects or dances that no depth of content is revealed; or no attention is paid to the language or ideas in the play. The essential point to remember is that the visual language is intended to make it possible to communicate deeper ideas; not become a substitute for them. It must not conceal a lack of sincerity, but rather permit the expression of complex relationships and ideas through an honest use of visual symbols.

variety

Variety may be the "spice of life" for an adult, but it is more like "bread" for the child. His shorter attention span and ever expanding curiosity make it essential that he continually seek new stimulation. Especially if we are considering the child under ten or eleven, it becomes an obligation of the director to find technical ways to change the focus of attention in a rapid pattern of alternating attractions. The child is also used to viewing camera-oriented theatrical events on television and in the films. The constant change of camera angle, the rapid montage of scenes, and even the frequent interruptions for commercials create a pattern of watching which serves to *prevent* the development of a longer attention span. The children's theatre should probably try to combat this unfortunate trend, visible even in adult TV addicts, which makes it impossible for anyone to concentrate for five full minutes on the same thing. Nevertheless, the director of children's theatre must be aware that this problem exists, both as a result of television exposure, and as a natural condition of the young mind.

One solution to this problem is termed *syntheticalism* by the distinguished Soviet director, Korogotsky. *Synthetical* comes from *synthesis,* a unifying of disparate elements. This means the staging of a play which includes a large variety of unified activities: song, dance, mime, puppetry, acrobatics, juggling, and magic. Syntheticalism also refers to the enormous variety of theatrical styles and genres which can be used to capture the children's attention—both within a single play, and within a season of plays intended for the same audience. Not only does this approach help to hold the child's attention, it also serves to introduce him to the scope of the arts available to him. Syntheticalism means, on a simple level, the use of variety as a technique.

In the chapter on playwriting, the need for a rhythm in the scenic framework was discussed: short scenes, longer scenes, fast scenes, slow scenes. The director must also be sensitive to this pattern, supplying it where it is not in the script. Use of mime, or other interpolations into the basic style of the play will sometimes prove useful. Finding actors who can sing, dance, or juggle will greatly assist the director's attempts at introducing variety, although one must be careful not to resort to variety for variety's sake. The integrity of the play must be observed. Extraneous dances certainly add to the holding power of a play, but usually at the expense of diluting the dramatic action. The proper way to employ this technique is with a sense of unity.

The two most important times to consider variety are when choosing a script, and when choosing a production concept. Many good scripts contain opportunities for synthetical staging *within* the developing action. The dance and puppet show in *Don Quixote of La Mancha,* for example, are thoroughly integrated. Frank Gagliano's *Hide and Seek Odyssey of Madeline Gimple* contains mime, magic, song, playground games, and other media—all contributing toward an artistic unity. Other good scripts, such as *Reynard the Fox,* contain no such multimedia treatment, but in the production style it is possible to choose an open, theatrical approach that will permit the miming of extended business, or the inclusion of short movement motifs for all the characters. Tumbling tricks can be quite correctly added to Reynard's character, if the actor is sufficiently skilled, and the production style is suitably presentational. In fact, an expansive production might even find the crow interpreted as an operatic bird who sings all of his lines! All, of course, provided that the artistic unity of the production does not suffer.

Another possible aid to meeting the need for variety for young children is the use of arena or three-quarter stages for the production of children's plays. The aesthetic requirements of the open stage usually demand a more cinematographic approach to blocking, and this provides more variety of focus to the child viewer, as well as being a more "natural" sort of space in which to play. The child's own fantasy enactments are spontaneously three-dimensional. The theatre is also three-dimensional, unlike TV or film, but the child is less likely to realize this fact if he only sees a proscenium production. Besides the increased movement on the open stage, and the increased recognition of the life-size action, the closer proximity and the relatively greater fluctuations in proximity which typically accompany arena staging add to the varied focus which helps the child to stay involved. As the child becomes older, of course, the importance of open staging and syntheticalism diminish toward an adult need for variety.

multi-age considerations

Throughout this book, "children's theatre" has been referred to as if it were a discrete phenomenon, separate and different from "adult theatre." Nothing could be further from the truth. Childhood is a continuous event, and the child of seven, although different from the one of twelve, is yet a part of that older child. Similarly, the adult retains some memories and behaviors of his childhood—and often many of his old dreams and fantasies. As long as this is true, there will always be a certain adult appeal in a good children's play—and rather than avoid a consideration of this fact, it is an important directorial technique to take advantage of it.

It is common to find children's plays done for "children of all ages." This usually means that pre-schoolers are brought by their teen-age sisters, or that grandparents bring all of their grandchildren—aged three through twenty-three. Obviously, in family productions of this kind it is necessary to provide something of artistic interest for each age level. The very young need the syntheticalism and visual appeal described above. The adults need challenges to keep them interested. Those in between need some of each. This means that the director of the "children's play" must find ways to create a compelling theatrical piece at *all levels simultaneously.*

Needless to say, the staging of these plays "for all ages" is extremely difficult and demanding. It is essential to start with a script that provides opportunities for syntheticalism, and, hopefully, exciting scenic effects. This means that the younger ages will be entertained, and that the director can concentrate on bringing out the adult aspects of the play and blending them with the theatrical exterior. If the play is all exterior, of course, it may fail to hold the older children and adults and may be artistically unsatisfying. If it is too conversational or involved it will keep the adults so busy disciplining their children that neither group will enjoy the production. The director must keep one eye on the children's viewpoint, and the other on the adults', trusting to his artistic judgment to blend the two. Good "multi-age" scripts, like *Peter Pan,* or Schwarz's *The Dragon* are hard to find, but worth the effort to do them well.

There is an important side-effect of this multi-age appeal—the benefit of seeing a play in an audience where all the different levels of the production are perceived directly by part of the audience, and indirectly by the others. The audience member visiting the theatre with his family always has other levels of understanding going on around him. He can note, perhaps unconsciously, that parents find such and such a thing amusing; or that his big brother likes such and such a comment; or that the baby loves such and such a kind of movement. The idea of "family theatre," where all ages can participate and literally share meanings, impressions, and emotional reactions is philosophically appealing, but it also raises technical problems for the director.

The alternative to the "multi-age" play, which aims at whole families, is the play set for a relatively narrow age range—such as seven through ten, eleven through thirteen, or, often, a single school class, such as the fifth grade. In these cases, it is easier to select a play that appeals specifically to the group involved. Chapter four contains a discussion of the specific interests of children at various ages, although local information can often supersede any general discussion by providing a knowledge of current specific interests—such as a Junior High group that has become involved in an election year project and would enjoy a play with a political motif. Plays for the eight to ten year range are probably the most numerous, but a few good ones exist for each age group. (See Appendix A for suggestions.)

When directing these plays, obviously the director must stress the particular level of appeal for the particular group which will see the play. *But it is still important to treat the play as though it were for the multi-age audience.* By forgetting the younger child within all humans, of whatever age, we rob the play of its unconscious appeal; we rob it of easy comprehension by the newly verbal child who still has his strong visual sense to rely on; and, we rob it of the cumulative effect, so necessary in the theatre, brought about when the spectator absorbs the same message through multiple channels of communication. It is not bad advice to instruct a director of an adult play to make sure his play is comprehensible to children, for this guarantees an imaginative appeal, easy comprehension, and cumulative understanding on the part of the adults. No matter how mature the individual, he still contains his earlier selves, and can be approached, especially in the aesthetic mode, by an appeal to these previous stages.

On the other hand, by forgetting to "play to the adults" with each production, we cheat the child of the challenge which is his right—the opportunity to grow up to a new comprehension and understanding. We also tend towards condescension by ignoring his adult potential. By saying, "I know your maximum level, and this is it," we insult his creative potential. Finally, by playing only to children, we bore ourselves—and who can remain a creative artist when his own work bores him?

All of these errors can be avoided by the simple trick of assuming the attitude that every play we do is intended for *all* ages. Such an attitude keeps us honest, and there is certainly a great deal to gain by creating a production that appeals to *more* people than are expected to see it.

casting and identification

Because of the extreme importance of visualization to the child, it is necessary to give some extra attention to problems of casting in a children's play. The child normally comes to the theatre with a few expectations. So does the adult, but the expectations are along quite different lines. In the child's mind, an image of goodness and an image of evil are evolving. Probably, by the time the child is seven, good is beautiful and evil is ugly. These are natural simplifications. The child's expectations may branch off in other directions, particularly if the play is based on a known story or book. In fact, he may have a complete visual image of the characters based on book illustrations, or a Disney version of the tale.

The director can take one of two approaches to this problem: he may fulfill the expectations, or he may challenge them. In order to satisfy the child's prejudices, many directors, in casting and instructing their designers, will slavishly follow an established model. Countless productions of *Alice in Wonderland* are based upon Tenniel, dozens of *Snow White* productions upon the Disney cartoon feature, and hundreds of *The Wizard of Oz* upon the MGM film production. In a more general

way, following the audience's expectations leads to the casting of stereotypes in traditional roles—the romantic type to play the Prince, a stout
funny-looking fellow for the King, and a lovely blonde for Cinderella.
There are certain advantages to this approach. The audience's sympathies
can instantly be directed. Cinderella's first appearance is sufficient for the
children to recognize her and become involved. The ugly stepmother is
so obviously evil that we immediately hate her. This instant identification is especially useful for very young or inexperienced audiences.

The alternate approach of challenging the audience's prejudices is
more risky, but perhaps, in the long run, more artistically satisfying—
especially for children ten and older. Many directors for children insist
upon casting a beautiful actress as the wicked witch, or the hero as a
meek, friendly type. This, they say, teaches the children to look beyond
externals in their future judgment of others. There is something naturally satisfying in immediately sensing evil when it appears; but the satisfaction is ten times deeper and more permanently rewarding if we are
able to deduce that someone is evil purely from our observations of his
actions. Presenting the child with a new set of characters for an old be-
loved tale can be a shock, but it can also serve to broaden his horizons,
to teach him that not everyone perceives every event in the same way.
Eventually, it teaches him an open-minded tolerance for the ideas of
others. For many directors, such a benefit outweighs the loss they must
suffer in capturing the audience's sympathies at the show's opening.

Upon analysis, the success of the second approach—challenging expectations—lies in the preparation of the audience. If the child can know,
in advance, that what he will see is a different interpretation, he will be
motivated toward understanding the new point of view. If he is caught
by surprise, however, he may be so slow to adjust as to lose most of the
benefits of the play. When performing for school audiences, it is easier
to achieve this preparation, provided that the teachers are cooperative in
the use of preview study guides. For public performances, however, unless a massive publicity campaign is done, or the play contains an artistically effective prologue which establishes a new point of view, it is
probably wiser to avoid well-known material, or to treat it traditionally.

Once the director departs from the stereotypic characters, he must
capture the audience's interest in the new image he will present. It is
commendable to try to stretch the audience's perceptual understanding,
but not if the children will totally fail to identify with the individualized
hero. Again, what factors seem to cause the child to identify with a certain character? How can the director cast so as to ensure the children will
like the hero, without the hero necessarily having to be a Prince Charm-
ing type? These questions are critical ones, but the answers await careful

research to determine the actual pattern of identification in children. One factor that attracts children to a particular model is probably simply the model's energy level. The more energetic the actor, the more children will like him. To repeat the concepts suggested in chapter four, other factors affecting this attraction are sincerity, physical beauty, apparent intelligence, apparent good intentions, and apparent ability to influence others. Similarity of the character's problems or ego needs to those of the individual child's is a most important concern in the director's interpretation of the characters. It will be noted that, except for "apparent good intentions," all of these traits may be possessed by the play's *antagonist*. It is fairly common to see a children's production in which the villain is more energetic, intelligent, and powerful than the hero. The result, of course, is that the child is more strongly attracted to the villain. This is not necessarily bad, but it is a factor to consider when casting a production.

Upon the child's identification will depend all of the play's subsequent psychological impact, so it is most important that the director consult his own instincts and the principles mentioned above while in the process of casting and interpreting the characters in the play. It is also important continually to observe the audience's reactions to the characters.

audience participation

Children are a volatile audience, easily moved to a noisy exteriorization of their inner feelings. They have not learned the politeness which requires that they moderate their reactions. They also are more inclined to participate on the side of their hero when he obviously needs some physical assistance. The director who works for a children's audience must prepare his production to capitalize on these factors, and protect it against their unfavorable intrusion. Earlier, a dialogue between the director and the audience was mentioned. The children's participation is the other half of the dialogue, and—unlike adult participation—it tends to be every bit as audible as the play itself should be.

The most important distinction the director must make, and train his actors to make during the production, is the difference between "noise" and "participation." If a child is commenting on the play to his neighbor, making an associated response, or even squirming loudly in his chair from delight or fear, that is not "noise," it is participation. It is a favorable response and should be both anticipated and enjoyed by the performers. When, however, the topic of discussion has nothing to do with the action, the response is directed at the actors instead of the characters, or the squirming is from uncomfortableness, that is "noise," and is an unfavorable event. The way to prevent unfavorable distractions, of course, is to do a good play. When the audience is unruly and non-attentive it is nearly always the director's own fault, assuming that a reasonable concern over the audience's safety and comfort has been shown by the house manager. I have directed touring plays for children in towns where the ushers would not allow the children to go to the bath-room—even during the intermission of a two-and-one-half hour junior high school play! Obviously, physical discomfort will produce non-attention that is beyond the director's immediate control. Teachers or ushers who too zealously prevent favorable responses will also eventually produce non-attention. The child who is repeatedly not allowed to express his natural response will, sooner or later, stop attending to the play, and thereby end his frustration.

With a favorable house staff, however, a good production that pays particular attention to sincerity and visualization will minimize the non-desirable noise. The director should be careful, however, to train the actors to expect some wiggling in any scene longer than a minute which is primarily dialogue.

Sometimes it is worth putting up with minor non-attention from the younger children in order to provide a scene of challenge for the older ones. In such a case the scene that immediately follows should be especially enjoyable on a visual level. The Father/Mother scene in *Hansel and Gretel* is usually more interesting to eight year olds than to five year olds. But it is followed by the action of chasing off to the woods. The lovers' scene which starts Act Two of *Androcles* also produces some restlessness in most younger children, but then Lion enters and the physical tension mounts. Both scenes can be sincerely done and quite effectively stretch the audience's ability to listen and sympathize—but because they are relaxed moments, there will naturally be a relaxation of the audience's "edge of their seats" concentration.

Great care should also be taken in the staging of physical details, both to avoid distractions and to ensure sincerity. Violence that is not stylized must be very carefully realistic, or well covered, as a glimpse of a faked sword blow or punch will cause an immediate noisy rejection. Care must be taken at beginnings, especially to avoid distracting from the world of the play—for example, a whistling entrance at the opening of a show may provoke eleven-year-old boys to start whistling in the audience.

The actors should also be trained in the techniques of recapturing a non-attentive audience by a sudden contrast of business, line delivery, action, tempo, entrance of a new character, or by the injection of a piece of pantomime which introduces a new, perhaps even irrelevant, idea. These tricks will also help to quiet an actively participating audience if some more subtle matter of the play must be considered. These techniques are discussed more fully in the succeeding chapter on acting. The principle of "pointing" is the same in the adult theatre, but in the children's theatre it occasionally must serve the extra function of re-capturing the audience's wandering attention, or calming their overly responsive participation.

Allowing for the desired participation involves considerable preparation and reassuring of the actors, as actors are inclined to assume that all exteriorization is "noise," unless otherwise alerted. It is also wise to prepare for cuts at high tension moments. If the audience has anticipated a reaction or an event, it is foolish to continue with it as rehearsed. The Lion's song near the end of Act One in *Androcles and the Lion* is usually drowned out by the audience's participation. The smartest move would be to be prepared to cut it entirely when the audience is so moved. If the children are less involved, it can easily be left in. A good chase should end just when the audience reaction dictates it—and this may involve considerable actor adjustment from performance to performance. The same kind of adjustments go on in every adult show, but the children's reactions are greater, and so the actor must be prepared to make equally greater adjustments.

The most effective use of audience participation comes about when the director has experienced sitting in the audience, surrounded by children, on numerous occasions. He learns then exactly what their reactions to a bit of action will be, and he becomes much more adept at directing the rhythm of the play so as to allow for the full reaction to occur, without slowing down the tempo of the play. More will be said about playing to the audience's participation in the next chapter, when we discuss the actor's techniques in the children's theatre.

There is also a type of play, recommended especially for children under nine, in which the audience is guided to participate creatively at certain moments; the technique of this style of play is discussed elsewhere, but there are additional hints that pertain to the director. The ideal situation when doing participation plays would be to cast actors trained in improvisation and creative dramatics techniques. When the moment arrives for the audience to join in, it should be a chance for each child to express himself. The actors must be able to reward unique contributions and adjust to suggestions made by the audience—if necessary changing the details of the story. The director must prepare for these events by testing the cast's ability to respond to bizarre suggestions without breaking character or interrupting the action. I often "torment" my cast during a runthrough of such a play by acting out the audience myself and trying to anticipate all possible reactions. If they can handle the "contributions" which I make, they can usually deal with those of the children. Since these plays are often created through improvisation in the first place, the cast needs only to remember the goals of the original scenario and they can generally find their way back to the rehearsed sequence.

An excellent guide for directors considering this kind of production has recently been published, entitled *Participation Theatre for Young Audiences: A Handbook for Directors* by Pat Whitton. This book contains a myriad of specific advice on rehearsal techniques and performance problems.

theatrical "magic"

Theatrical effects and spectacle are an important component of children's theatre. Elaborate scenery, splendid costumes, special effects such as disappearances, flying, changing size, transformations, and countless other magnificent magical marvels seem to be an expensive, but necessary, part of theatre for the young. Indeed, such techniques fit well with the need for variety and visualization, and, if well-executed, are always loved by the children.

Two words of caution are offered, however, to combat the feeling on the part of new children's theatre directors that their whole production is one special effect after another: first, it can be overdone. The children can become exhausted by theatrical magic. They require a considerable portion of relaxed concentration to balance the production. After having a series of mechanical marvels thrown at them, they can simply give up and refuse to watch more than they can comprehend. They can also be excited to the point where they lose sight of the plot and characters of the play. After all, the climax of a fairy tale is when the hero defeats the villain. If the transformation in the first scene gets more applause than the climax, the play, as a play, is a failure! Like all devices, theatrical effects must serve the purpose of the directorial concept of the production, or the artistic unity of the play is ruined. In most cases theatrical magic can contribute toward a building of excitement to the climax—as long as the director's good taste prevails.

The second caution is that we must not forget that one of the purposes of art is to stimulate the creativity of the spectator. By always being more creative than the child's wildest imagination, we dampen that same imagination before it can be expressed. Children enjoy using their own minds to create scenery, costumes, and effects, with only the director's suggestive powers to give them a framework to fill in. Research done in Russia by Lada Surina has even tended to indicate that some children *prefer* to supply the environment of the play with their own imaginations. Mrs. Surina studied the art work done by children after they had seen an extremely simplified setting for a play about a postman. The hero's car in the play, for example, is indicated by a tricycle. The audience invariably laughs when he refers to it as his "wonderful car." But when they draw pictures afterward, they furnish him with different models of real cars. In some of my own directing, I have tried productions which left things unstated, having the actors mime certain props, furniture, or even character transformations. I have noticed that it completely engrosses the children when an actor uses his imagination to fill in his environment, and they must do likewise. Nevertheless, there are productions which legitimately demand spectacle, and the children love these, too. The only essential is to make either elaborate effects or imaginative simplification serve the unified needs of the directorial concept.

LEADERSHIP RESPONSIBILITIES

Besides staging the play, the director in today's theatre also bears the primary responsibility for the total artistic creation. He does his own work, and also guides his colleagues. In addition, he is the unifying factor that mediates between the production and the audience. The children's audience and play involve the same responsibilities, but with special emphasis as dictated by the nature of the audience and the fact that it is generally considered a "different" audience by traditional theatre practitioners.

obligations to the audience

The director, along with the manager, is usually the individual who determines philosophy and policy in a children's theatre. For adults, it is generally sufficient to sell tickets and present a play. The adult is capable of protecting himself from ordinary hazards or undesirable confrontations. If he cannot drive, he will come to the theatre by taxi or bus. If he decides that the play does not interest him, he can leave, or doze. Most importantly, he chooses for himself whether he will come or not. If the show is advertised as a tragedy, he will not come expecting to laugh. If he insists upon laughing, he will go to a different play, or watch television.

The child audience is different. Most of the time, the decision whether to come or not is made for them by a parent or teacher. They must be brought to the theatre and then picked up. They often have no idea of what kind of play it will be; in fact, they may not even know what a play is, or what kinds exist. And if they do not like the play, they frequently have no choice but to sit miserably, or to seek to amuse themselves at the expense of the others in the auditorium.

To direct for children involves an obligation to make decisions for the young people whose hearts and minds are entrusted to the director's aesthetic control. The director must know and respect children. Imagine the scandal that would ensue if a school cafeteria manager was found to be feeding the children substandard food. No less a fate should befall the director of a children's play who fails to meet his or her responsibility.

obligations to his colleagues

When it comes to dealing with his theatrical colleagues, the director has an educational obligation. Most actors shy away from children's theatre, either because they instinctively know that it is more demanding, or because they feel that their talents will not be properly appreciated. Designers, on the other hand, love children's theatre as they feel it permits them to do all kinds of elaborate storybook decorations. Both must be guided to an understanding of the child audience. The director must impose a strong discipline on all his colleagues.

It is the director's job to train the actors in accordance with the seven considerations discussed earlier in this chapter, especially audience participation, syntheticalism, and emotional truth. The principle of visualization also requires that he take a firmer than usual grip on the external aspects of the play, since blocking, pantomimic dramatization, character business, costumes, scenery, or props are proportionally more important than are internal components of character or line readings. The director must shift his focus to a concentration on these visual components. In this sense, it is accurate to say that theatre for children requires stronger direction than does theatre for adults, because the picture is much more important than the word or idea, and the director is the only man who, theoretically, "sees the whole picture." The director who excels chiefly in freeing his actors' creativity, and draws deeply felt portrayals from them should probably avoid directing for children. If, however, this same director has a visual sense that is creative and artistic, he will probably be an effective guide for a children's production. One of the keys to his success, however, will be the way in which he meets the challenge of instilling in his colleagues at least a little of the interest and respect he feels for the audience of children.

obligations to himself

The most important obligation which the director has is to himself. The underlying usefulness of the director as an artistic force is served only when an integrated and unified aesthetic work is produced. The choice of scripts must satisfy his interests, and call him forth to interpretation. The characters and their conflicts must seem honest and real, so that he feels inspired to bring them to life. He must believe that his work is important, that it will be noticed, and that it matters if he does it well. He should have the same anxieties, obstacles, personality problems, and self-doubts to overcome as he would have in the adult theatre; and he should experience the same sense of accomplishment and reward when he succeeds.

eight

ACTING

FOR THE

CHILDREN'S THEATRE

It is hard to tell whether the child is more in awe of the actor he sees on the stage, or the actor is more in awe of the child. Just as a young child will hesitate to touch or speak to an actor he has appreciated, so most actors resist any confrontation with children—on or off the stage. This awe is understandable in the child. He is trying to reconcile life and art. He is unsure whether he is addressing the character or the performer. As he gets older, of course, he resolves this confusion and eagerly seeks autographs and conversations with the artists he admires. It is more difficult to understand the actor's shyness about children. Partly it stems from a valid fear of the child's intensity and commitment. As one actor voiced it, "Children gobble up actors." But a good portion of the performer's awe comes from ignorance. Not knowing what children are like and having only vague ideas about children's plays, he tends to avoid the whole experience of acting for children. And because extraordinary financial temptations and brilliant directorial guidance are rarely available to urge him to discover this audience, he usually doesn't know what he is missing.

Acting for children differs from acting for adults only in certain attributes of its public, and in the kind of opportunities available. The actual job of creating a role is no different; nor is the rehearsal process. But the importance of good acting is greater, and the performance situation can be both harder and more rewarding. There is good reason to be aware of the differences caused by performing for a child audience, and in the special needs created by the children's theatre repertory.

THE AUDIENCE

The audience for a children's play may be composed of adults and children, or it may be all children during school hour performances. There is a vast difference in response. But always one must play to both the adult level of appreciation and the specific response of children—the adult level for the integrity of the role, and the children's level for the success of the performance. The discussion that follows parallels much that was said in the preceding chapter to the director, but now from the actor's point of view.

the role

The characters in a play for children must be as motivated, as three-dimensional, as real as in any other kind of play. And, even more often than in the adult theatre, this means that actors and directors must flesh out a playwright's utilitarian creations. Most of the tales for younger children are filled with characters who represent broad human attributes, such as generosity or greed. It is this generality which makes the fairy tales so universal. But in translating the fable to the stage it is necessary to dramatize the character. He cannot simply *be,* and thereby represent a quality. He has to have a specific voice, a walk, and a physical carriage. The actor often has to supply these details of characterization with little help from the playwright.

The penalty for failing to achieve a believable human character is quite severe. Not having the patience of their elders or the manners to ignore their own boredom, children will destroy any performance that does not please them. If any detail of characterization strikes them as phony they will literally "turn off" that actor. If the slightest bit of condescension is detected, they will respond in kind, by ignoring the performer who is ignoring them. *It is absolutely essential that the actor be able to convince the audience that he believes in the truth of what he is doing.* The worst criticism that can be offered of an actor in a children's play is that he is "playing down" to the children. This attitude is easy for children to recognize. They sense immediately when any adult considers himself superior to them. They can tell when the actor simplifies or "indicates" his role to make it easier for the young "ignorant" audience members to understand it. Sadly, the actor is often unaware that he is projecting such an attitude. He thinks he is being noble and making great sacrifices to bring a performance to children that they can grasp. Unfortunately, he is defeating his intentions. If he played his part challenging the young to appreciate the depth of his portrayal, he would be far more likely to succeed. Again, there is a need for respect—respect for audience, respect for colleague-artists, and respect for self. The latter is the most important, especially to the actor, for he is seen directly by the audience while the playwright and director remain hidden. It is difficult to respect someone who does not respect himself. If the actor cannot believe in his character, and in the children's theatre there are many bizarre roles, than he must be so good at pretending he is believing that no one—child or adult—can tell the difference.

Moreover, this belief must be evident at every performance. Children don't read reviews which tell them that so-and-so was excellent on opening night. The only thing that matters to them is what they actually see. Consistency and concentration are particularly necessary in the children's theatre. The difference between an indifferent audience of children and an attending one is quite evident, and the difference can be caused by an actor having a "down" performance. Even the best professionals fluctuate from performance to performance—that is one of the things that makes the live theatre exciting. Typically, these fluctuations are overemphasized by the actors in an adult show. The show rarely changes as much as the actors think it has. But in a children's show, their worst fears are realized. A young audience is a too-faithful barometer of the level of the particular performance. On the one hand, it is a frustrating experience for the company to be found out in even their least lapses. On the other hand, it is gratifying to the honest artist to feel that the audience will know if he is at his best, and that it will let him know, too.

The characters in a play for children must, then, be approached with honesty and respect, must not be oversimplified or condescending, and must be played at every performance with consistency and concentration.

the response

There is an almost intangible skill, desired in actors, which is impossible to convey in a classroom or rehearsal hall. It is the ability to play *to* and *with* an audience. It consists of an almost subconscious control of timing, volume, energy, and other aspects of the performance in such a way as to take the fullest possible cognizance of the audience's responses. In a sense it is a kind of flexibility—allowing one's performance to be molded nightly by variations in audience responses. Experience in performance is almost the only way to develop such a skill, although, of course, rules can be drawn up regarding timing of laughs or entrances.

The child audience, especially the school-time, bused in, homogeneous age group, responds quite differently than does an adult audience, or a mixed audience of children, parents, and other interested adults at a week-end matinee. In the mixed audience, the children's responses are guided, at least partially, by the responses of the adults. Children are used to deferring to adult models of behavior. But when they are on their own their natural pattern of responses emerges. And these responses can be overwhelming to the unprepared. The absence of adult inhibitions makes the child much more demonstrative and exuberant than his quieter parent would be. Probably the biggest difference between acting for children and acting for adults is the need to become familiar with the response pattern of a school audience, and to learn some techniques of dealing with these vigorous responses.

The first thing to learn is the difference between a positive response and a negative one. The difference between restlessness and participation is readily obvious to the director sitting in the house, but to the actor on stage, the two reactions are sometimes hard to distinguish. Restlessness is usually caused by the poor quality of the play. To the actors it sounds, at first, like a vague shuffling or repositioning of bodies in chairs. Then one hears feet running up and down the aisles, and the slowly increasing general sound of an auditorium before the play starts. This constitutes noise and it is a negative or non-attending response. It means that the audience has withdrawn some portion of its attention from the world of the play. It may be caused by physical discomfort—too little air, too much time between intermissions, or too much heat; or by an overtaxing of the child's excitement which finally causes a breakdown of his ability to concentrate. It is most often caused by too little action on the stage, or by insincere business or characterizations. The only way to deal with this kind of response, if it is within the actor's power to deal with it at all, is by renewing one's concentration on the action, and trying to do one's subtle best with the character one is playing, perhaps slightly picking up the tempo of the scene—without losing any of the scene's depth.

A positive response from the audience can be just as loud, just as diffuse, and just as disturbing to the actor's concentration. It generally comes in one of several forms:

An answer to a rhetorical question in the script.

A warning or cheer for the protagonist, which is easily identified as a positive response; or a whispered warning or cheer to the child's neighbor, which is hard to distinguish from noise.

Repeating a favorite sound or funny line, perhaps elaborating on it. (This is especially common among younger children.)

Asking questions of one's neighbors or parents about the plot or characters.

Acting out at some physical level the action one wants the character to perform.

All of these responses are positive because they are sincere reactions by the child to the material of the play. If they become comments aimed at the *actors* they indicate a broken concentration, but as long as they are aimed at *characters,* or are comments about characters, they are legitimate expressions of the child's participation in the play.

The most difficult kind of positive response to handle is a suggestion for action, particularly if it is given out loud by a significant portion of the audience. The actors, assuming they recognize the positive nature of the suggestion, are at a loss as to whether to acknowledge it or not. To ignore the audience may cause them to lose interest in responding further. To accept the suggestion may encourage a flurry of further shouts which will totally disrupt the performance. There is also the problem of teaching the child about aesthetic distance. In an adult play we can rarely influence the action by means of direct suggestions. We must develop an involved detachment from the work of art. Should not the child begin to learn to dissociate himself? On the other hand, direct communication is one way to learn the difference between live theatre and television or film, and this is also something he needs to develop.

The answer probably depends on the specific situation. In all cases it is wise to ignore a response from an individual or two. Only if a significant portion of the audience in several sections of the house is responding should any notice be taken. Then the actor's procedure depends on the production style. If the play is very theatrical, with direct address to the audience, and especially if the audience is ever requested to participate actively at any point in the play, then the actors must somehow acknowledge the response. Not to do so would violate the internal validity of the style. How can the audience be asked to respond at one point, or be spoken to directly by a character, and then not have their response or their reply accepted at another point? However, in a moderately realistic style where no apparent notice is ever taken of the audience by a character, it would be wrong suddenly to break this convention and accept a direct response. Having made a bargain with the audience about a set of conventions, it is necessary to keep the bargain.

The audience response may be toward the play's development, or away from it. If the play is well-written the audience will probably only be anticipating the next action which is planned. In this case, the cast has only to speed through the intervening material—perhaps cutting some of it—and thus satisfy the audience that their suggestion has been taken. In the event, however, that a vigorous response leads away from the play's development, and the style requires acknowledgment, the actors should be prepared to acknowledge the response and then reject it, perhaps by indicating a reason why it won't work. This rejection of the idea is at least an acknowledgment of the response. The actors should immediately follow the dismissal of the audience's suggestion with a new action to prevent a repeated outbreak of the same or other suggestions (unless, of course, the actors are ready to abandon the script and improvise a new scene based on the best idea from the children).

Actually, there is a simple trick for controlling all audience responses. A noisy negative reaction can be halted and too boisterous positive participation can be quieted, provided the device is not overused. In both cases, the purpose should be to capture attention before introducing a necessary bit of the play's development. Otherwise, the trick is wasted. The hope is that this new development—when they see it—will recapture the wandering attention of the noisy audience, or refocus the energies of a loudly positive one. The trick is simply to *do something unrelated to the previous action, preferably in mime.* For example, take the moment when Androcles runs from the Lion. The children urge him to get away. Then the Lion steps on a thorn and moans in agony. Androcles overcomes his fear and returns. At this point, it is probably important that the audience realizes that Androcles is afraid, but conquers his fear out of compassion for the Lion's pain. But many audiences will not quiet down to listen if Androcles comes back and approaches the Lion. Unsophisticated children are particularly suspicious that the Lion might be faking. They scream at Androcles to run, and will miss the point entirely that he is coming back *in spite of* fear. The actor playing the slave wants the children to appreciate the struggle Androcles is undergoing within himself. He decides to use the "trick." He suddenly mimes the presence of a mosquito buzzing around his head. He brushes it off. The comic business develops with him anxiously trying to end the irritation. The audience gets quiet to absorb this new episode. As quickly as he can, Androcles shrugs off the fly and gets in a few key ideas of his inner conflict, which will hopefully have the result of involving the children in his decision to help the Lion. Without the "trick" they would surely have missed that particular point. Chasing a mosquito has nothing to do with the play—but at least it doesn't contradict the play's style, and, if it is done well, it can become a means to reveal a new side of Androcles' character, perhaps his tolerance of petty discomforts. Of course, he might have done something else—lost a shoe, found an itch, or dropped his moneybag. Something in keeping with the character is obviously the best choice, so long as it fulfills the criteria of being physical, unrelated to the previous action, and preferably mimed in a stage silence. In the same manner, a noisy audience can have their attention returned to the play for a new development which may get them interested, although this method won't work indefinitely if the whole play is dull or "talky." There are slow scenes in fairly good plays, however, and these are legitimate places for careful use of a visual "trick," when a key line is coming up. Obviously, if such needs can be anticipated, the attention-capturing business can be integrated into the character and plot development during rehearsal.

Of course, in a participation play, the actor's goals are slightly different. He wants the audience to participate, needs their help to do the show, and is prepared to improvise on the basis of their ideas. The participation play seeks creative responses, however, not just responses. Each child must be encouraged to respond in his own way. In *Hansel and Gretel,* when the children are asked to become berry bushes the actors keep insisting that they want all different kinds of berry bushes. If the children all imitate each other, Hansel may say, "Those are all the same. I want *different* kinds." Or the actors may take pains to reward the unique ideas: "There's a really different one, Gretel," or, "Look at this one, Hansel, it's so short," or "tall" or "prickly," or whatever sets a particular creation apart from the others. One reason for limiting the audience size at these performances is to give the actors a chance to be aware of all of the responses, and to reward the most creative ones.

To end a sequence of participation, the actors in these plays often use the device mentioned above. Gretel carries her apron full of berries to Hansel and dumps them in a basket very carefully. The audience quiets down to watch her concentrated pouring. Quickly she says, "Thank you," and nods for the kids to sit down. If necessary she might say, "That's all we need now; we have enough berries."

Creative dramatics training is particularly useful to the actor in a participation play, as it teaches him the techniques of phrasing questions so as to elicit a diversity of responses, and then helps him select the most creative efforts for praise and reinforcement. In more complicated sequences, where the children actually join in the on-stage action, it is an absolute necessity that the actors have experience at guiding this particular age group creatively. Otherwise the sequence deteriorates into instructions from the actors blindly followed by the audience—not the creative experience sought.

In any case, participation drama sets up the convention that the audience responses are a part of the play. This means that all responses by a significant portion of the audience must be dealt with. I have directed a participation version of *Rumpelstiltskin* where the children shouted out the antagonist's name in the middle of the play. The actor playing the part quickly responded, "That's right! But you also have to guess my *last* name," and the play went on. The actor who is not flexible at improvisation should stay away from participation plays!

the responsibility

Once the actor has learned to distinguish responses and control them, he will become aware of his power. To know that one can manipulate others is both an elevating feeling and a frightening one. When the group manipulated is as large, as diverse, and yet as unified as is the audience at a good children's play, the feeling is magnified. An Italian actor who had spent most of his career in the children's theatre once expounded to me on the "priesthood" of a children's theatre actor. The concept is a meaningful one. The child gives himself with complete faith into the hands of a good actor. In the primitive theatre, perhaps also in the early Attic tragedy, the actors were religious mediators—medicine men and priests. It was an act of faith to accept the meaningfulness of a dramatic performance. The child's response is similar to that of the primitive.

Needless to say, such faith confers a responsibility on the "priest." In a primitive dance/drama the performer who made a mistake was punished or humiliated. Those who performed well received the combined blessings of their audience/congregation. In the children's theatre, the actor who succeeds bears the credit for spiritual growth in his audience as well as other kinds of growth.

THE OPPORTUNITIES

One of the least attractive attributes of the American children's theatre is the extremely limited opportunity to create a career in the field. The children's plays done in this country have been amateur-dominated up until the early 1970s. Only gradually are professional possibilities beginning to appear. The roles and styles of many children's scripts are also limited in certain ways, depriving committed actors of a chance for personal growth. This rarely bothers the university or community theatre actor who goes from show to show as a matter of course, but it can become a real disadvantage to the professional under contract to a single theatre. Some of these disadvantages will probably remain in the field. Others, hopefully, are on the way out. Certain unique features of the acting opportunities in the area of theatre for children are worthy of some brief exploration.

range

Assume you were to find one of the relatively rare jobs in this country as a member of the acting ensemble of a children's theatre. What kind of roles could you expect? On the surface, a range wider than that in any other theatre. In a single season a character actor with juvenile features might play Androcles, Tom Sawyer, the Sailor in *Tingalary Bird,* and a realistic youth in a modern mystery play, such as *Emil and the Detectives.* If the theatre also plays for teenagers, he might add a Shakespearian or Sophoclean role to the list. All these are only levels of *human* characters—from Commedia dell'arte, Romanticism, Absurdism, Realism, and Classical Drama. But he might also play Reynard, Piglet, a troll, a dragon, or a talking tree within the scope of the theatre's repertoire. Since fantasy comprises a good part of every season, no conceivable kind of role is outside the realm of possibility.

Unfortunately, most of the roles in plays written specifically for children are somewhat one-dimensional. What makes playing the bizarre roles difficult is the extreme need for sincerity discussed throughout this book. It is relatively easy to flesh out an underwritten human hero. It is somewhat more of a challenge to the imagination when one is required to construct a serious biography or super-objective for a talking tree! Of course, the roles vary enormously in their problems. In the shallow scripts the actor has to be creative enough to provide the missing substance, while in other more complete plays he can concentrate on interpretation and interaction with his colleagues.

In addition to the many different parts, the variety of styles requires a multi-talented actor. In the previous chapter, syntheticalism was shown to be a useful device in the children's theatre. This puts added emphasis on the actor's other talents, such as singing, dancing, mime, magic, and playing musical instruments.

physical requirements

Due to syntheticalism and the extreme importance of the visual aspect of the play, the actor in a play for children often finds that the physical demands of the performance are his biggest problem. A great deal of stamina is required by plays with big action scenes, which are apparently unavoidable in scripts for the young. In fact, it is somewhat paradoxical that the audience of children requires sincere, controlled, and consistent performances—which usually implies mature representational type actors, while the scripts demand active, youthful physical bodies—which is more often associated with young presentational type actors.

Since mime and movement are so critical to the success of an actor in a children's play, it is essential that these abilities be evaluated before casting. I always require a prepared pantomime as part of my auditions for amateur productions, and try to insist on some physically expressive character when auditioning professionals. The deeply felt portrayal of a complex character is perfectly valid for a children's audience, but there should also be an aliveness in the portrayal and a readiness for non-verbal expression. The actor who can *only* talk well is not useful in a children's play. The actor who intends to work for children must therefore develop his expressive movement through formal training and a continual awareness that there is more to communication than words. The technique of "gibberish" is a useful one for supplementing language with gesture. The best description of this technique is to be found in Viola Spolin's *Improvisation for the Theatre*. The use of a mask may also be recommended as a rehearsal check for character business and the effectiveness of movement. By replacing the vocabulary with gibberish and the face with a mask, the actor is left only with inflection and gesture—two of the best ways to convey a character to a child viewer.

With all this emphasis on the physical portrayal, it is only common sense to insist on physical preparation. Warmups, exercises, frequent runthroughs to build up stamina, and outside training classes are all good ways to bring a company to a state of physical readiness during a rehearsal period. An external approach to the characterization, without neglecting the simultaneous development of the internal life of the role, is also highly recommended for the children's theatre.

the actor's growth

If there is ever to be a pool of talented actors working in the children's theatre in this country, there must first be an awareness of the naturally limiting aspect of *only* acting for children. In spite of the range and requirements of playing to children, there are still components of a performance which one finds lacking in a well-done children's play. One of the most noticeable losses is peer-approval. It is gratifying to be worshipped by a child, but it does not replace the adult praise which so many actors crave. Moreover, there are many roles and plays which simply are not suitable for children usually because of their emphasis on verbal or intellectual developments, but occasionally because the play is simply beyond the experience of even sophisticated children. Few children's theatres will stage a bawdy Restoration comedy—both language and subject matter are too remote for the child. Yet any good actor likes to feel that he can have a chance at all the roles in dramatic literature, at least occasionally.

It should be the policy of any children's theatre with a permanent company to *insist* that its actors play for adults as often as possible. The ideal, of course, would be to produce plays for all ages right in the home theatre. If publicity is carefully handled, there is no reason why two publics cannot be developed for a theatre, particularly since most children's plays are confined to matinees. For the actor (and the rest of the artistic staff) it would be an ideal application of the repertory theatre concept to perform in a play for children in the afternoon, and an adult play the same night. The most important thing to guard against in this connection is a too great separation between the adult theatre and the children's theatre. They are not two different phenomena which require two different sets of actors. They are both the theatre—merely with different audience orientations. The good actor should be able to switch from one audience to another.

If the theatre or the director is unaware of the actor's need to be a total actor, then it is up to the actor to insist on his right to pursue his own artistic growth. Any actor who feels he is being stifled by the limited opportunities available to him will quickly deteriorate as an artist. In order to ensure top quality performances for the children, everyone concerned must also work toward continually challenging the artists and providing them with a chance for self-fulfillment and growth. Besides roles in adult shows, this includes casting challenges within the children's theatre repertory, and a chance for continual development through the study of mime, voice, fencing, ballet, or other related skills.

the attitude barrier

The opportunity to make a contribution to the art of theatre, to arouse and excite an expanded audience for the performing arts, to help in the development of expressive and creative people, and to explore fully the limits of his own growth awaits the actor who can dedicate himself to acting for an audience of children. The only obstacles to these goals are the shortage of paying jobs and the actor's low opinion of the children's theatre. The job market is poor in all of theatre, of course.

Children's theatre is beginning to expand with the founding of several new professional children's theatres every year. Most of the new ones fail to achieve their highest potential, however, because they fail to find high calibre actors aware of the rewards to be found in children's theatre. It is up to the theatres to create the opportunities, but it is up to the actors to recognize and accept them.

nine

DESIGNING

FOR THE

CHILDREN'S THEATRE

Design in the theatre makes a narrative contribution to the story of the play. It helps us to know who the characters are, and where and how they live. We immediately recognize their social class by their dress, their life style by their possessions and use of space, and their cultural awareness by their choice of decor. The lighting tells us the time of day and the prevailing climate; the clothing tells us occupation, wealth, concern for self, and many other more or less necessary elements of the actual content of the play. But design does more than supplement narration. It also sets the mood and conveys a visual image of the play's basic action. It can create an atmosphere of despair or violence for a tragedy, or lightness for a comedy. In this sense, the design must be able to stand alone from the play. Every moment by moment "picture" in the drama could exist as a painting—apart from any narrative—and would convey a feeling, a visual mood, or a concept to the viewer.

These two functions of design—the narrative and the graphic— exist in the children's theatre as well. The child is capable of absorbing explanations from pictures, and also of appreciating the pure elements of visual art: form, color, mass, line, and balance. In the children's theatre the audience absorbs much of the play through the visual channels of communication. If the point of visual communication was stressed to actors and directors, how much more relevant it is to the designer, who communicates solely through the visual. The design component of the production is extremely important in the children's theatre. This is especially true of the narrative function of design. The graphic function is of about the same importance to children as it is to adults—both audiences need and appreciate it. But because the child's opportunities for plot comprehension are reduced by his lack of experience and vocabulary, all other production elements which help to explain the plot or characters should carry an extra share of the narrative communication. Therefore it is important for the design of a children's play to convey atmosphere and feeling, but critical that it correctly inform the viewer about who, where, when, and how the action of the play proceeds. A common design mistake in children's plays is to make everything look so powerfully whimsical that no specific information can be filtered out from the generalized saccharine coating. This does not mean that strong stylization, or even whimsicality, are impossible, but only that identification, discrimination of characters, and narrative explanations must not be neglected within the strongly stylized visual concept. This principle cannot be stressed enough, for although apparently obvious, it is still ignored by many designers of children's plays.

Because of the child's increased dependence on the visual, the director/designer relationship becomes much more relevant to success in the children's theatre than is, say, the director/playwright relationship. I have seen several fairly good productions for young audiences where the script was weak, but I have never seen a production work for children unless it possessed a creative and fairly well-realized design concept. A good director of a children's play will insist on the importance of effective design elements.

IMAGINATION VS. SPECTACLE

There is an important visual distinction which can be made between productions based solely on the variable of money spent. It is quite possible to design a production of any play for as little as $100. It is also possible to spend $1000, $10,000, or $100,000 on a production of the same play. Of course, there are some plays that require spectacle. *Peter Pan* calls for "flying" actors and several complicated sets—*Waiting for Godot* only needs a tree. Nevertheless, it is still possible to spend tens of thousands of dollars on *Godot,* or to do *Peter Pan* for less than one thousand. Generally, the less money one has available the more important becomes the creative selectivity of the designer and the use of imagination by the audience.

Children have imagination. They regularly create fantasies of their own, ranging from playing at "Mother and Father," to imaginary playmates and swashbuckling adventure tales. The medium of the animated cartoon is supposedly geared to the imaginations of children as it allows them to fill in the extremely simplified characters with details and elaborations of their own imagining. By being non-specific, the cartoon theoretically permits a vast range of interpretation. Each viewer can provide his own complexity while watching or subsequently imitating the behaviors of his cartoon hero. This simplification, or cartooning, is seen often in the children's theatre. A set may consist of line drawings, or simplified story-book illustrations. In a research project described in chapter seven, a study was done of a production which used imaginary locales and only suggestions of decor—a tricycle for a car, or a window-box and door for a whole house. Such studies generally show that children do understand the *where* of the play, and can explain it, filling in the details from their own imaginations. I have seen plays successfully done for quite young children with simple painted blocks as the only scenery. A cube can become a chair, a mountain, a table, or a fountain. Such productions substitute the creative use of details and imaginative design ideas for fully realized and expensive scenery. They obviously depend on the audience to provide the gaps in the visual world from its own limited but free-flowing imagination.

On the other hand, children also like spectacle. They love magical transformations, fully-realized fantastic scenery, bizarre and original costumes, special effects, lighting tricks, and stage machinery. They are used to the complete and instantaneous changes of locale which are so possible in the cinema. They like the excitement of being frightened by spooky noises or sudden appearances. Because they are so strongly visual, they can tolerate long complex visual sequences with little content— such as a choreographed set change or a ballet production number. Clever machines and mechanized costumes or scenery are particularly fascinating to children from about eleven through fourteen years. In general, children respond well to theatrical spectacle.

The problem, then, is to provide both the visual excitement of spectacle and the creative stimulation of suggestive scenery. The same play cannot easily do both. The designer of a children's theatre should probably be conscious of both needs, however, and try to use the widest extremes—from limited to elaborate scenery—in his productions during a season. It is a good idea to choose a sequence of plays for each age group that will expose them to the total range of design possibilities—from bare bones to super spectacle. The variable of money spent then becomes dependent on the requirements of the script, and not a decision based solely on the assumption that children need, or do not need, spectacle.

In the case of the theatre with limited funds, struggling to get every production mounted for the absolute minimum cost, my advice is to pool the budgets for an entire season. Then choose to do one of the most visually demanding scripts as an elaborate stage spectacle. Reserve only a tiny sum for the other productions—count on design creativity to make them work. It is better to do one big spectacle and a lot of imaginative simple shows, than to do a whole series of slightly under-realized productions.

DESIGN GUIDELINES

Having taken specific notice of the narrative importance of design in the children's theatre, and also having stressed the need for both simple and complex scenery, little else remains to be said to distinguish children's theatre design from that for adults. Basically, one finds that the most important principle is to interpret the drama, as guided by the director. Obviously, the visual world must reflect the play—no matter who is in the audience. The designer attends conferences where the director explains his concepts, then works to translate these concepts into visual means—costumes, sets, and lighting. He coordinates all three design elements with each other, and with the actors. He has to please his own tastes, and those of the director. The audience—even the child audience—does not come to the theatre to see scenery, but to see plays. The design must fit the production and enhance it. No other considerations really matter. There are, however, three problems which exist for the designer in the adult theatre but are potentially even more difficult for the children's theatre designer: the audience's expectations, their need for variety, and the extra concern indicated by the specific content of most children's plays. All three are worthy of brief special mention—not because they are different problems, but only because they usually acquire more emphasis in the children's theatre.

expectations

When the child comes to the theatre to see Peter Pan, he normally expects him to look like a peanut butter advertisement. Winnie the Pooh obviously looks like the cartoon figure copyrighted by Walt Disney Studios. Mary Poppins is a popular movie star, isn't she? Although it is possible for a designer to challenge these preconceptions, and many do, it is at least as difficult a proposition as it would be to dress Hamlet in any color but black, or put Titania in slacks. It can be done, but it must be done consciously. The guiding principle about shattering expectations is to be aware that you are doing it. Assuming the tale is a familiar one, as is true of many children's plays, the designer must be prepared to check literary and cinematic versions of the plot. Then, at least, he will know what the children expect to see. Deciding whether to give it to them or not depends partly on how close the play really is to the popular book or movie—it may be a vastly different interpretation. It also depends on whether the director wants to capitalize on instant identification or to present a different and challenging point of view to the youngsters.

If the play requires a different interpretation, it actually helps the child to focus on that difference if the visual impressions challenge his expectations. There are dramatic versions of *Cinderella* which try to make a modern and relevant point. To dress Cinderella in the traditional Disney costume would, conceivably, serve to hide the play's new twist. By changing her appearance, the designer calls attention to the fact that this is a different Cinderella, who stands for something different. This, of course, is done at the risk of offending the audience with a new Cinderella when they were set on seeing the old one. It helps to tell them, that this will be a *different* story, but it is also wise to bear their initial disappointment in mind when preparing for their reactions to the play.

If, on the other hand, the plot and theme are synonymous with a popular version, it probably creates needless confusion to design a new visualization. In order to be effective, the new concept must be a significant departure from the old. Then the point can be made that this is the same old story, but vastly different in appearance, hence, "There is more than one way to draw a cat." Unfortunately, this maxim is sometimes learned at the expense of the children not becoming immediately involved in the play.

When changing a visual tradition, it is important to consider the discrimination powers of the audience, and this, of course, is directly related to their age. Small changes may not be noticed by young children, just as characters who are too close in dress may not be distinguished. When I have changed an image, as I did in my own production of *Peter Pan,* I found it advisable to call attention to the change. In *Peter Pan* I asked for one of the other Lost Boys to be dressed as the traditional Peter, while Peter was dressed differently. Since we see Peter first, the

Pure Realism is rare in children's theatre. *My Little Boy* at the Erevan Theatre of Young Spectators (Armenian S.S.R.). Courtesy Soviet Center ASSITEJ.

Simplified Realism with fragmentary sets. The wall panels contain pictures of symbolic significance. *An Afternoon With Lewis Carroll* done by New York University. Courtesy Lowell Swortzell.

Realism treated to produce a fantasy impression for an absurdist play. The original set for *The Tingalary Bird,* Unicorn Theatre, London. Photo by Barry Griffiths. Courtesy Unicorn Theatre.

A "today" play in an expressionistic setting. *The Flight to Grenada* performed by the Moscow Theatre of Young Spectators. Courtesy Soviet Center ASSITEJ.

An interesting theatrical setting for *The Little Soldier Who Was Afraid* at the Teatro do Gerifalto in Lisbon. Photo by J. Marques. Courtesy Teatro do Gerifalto.

An expressionistic collage for a treatment of Hans Christian Andersen's *The Swineherd* at the Jiřího Wolkrá Theatre, Prague. Photo by Miroslav Tuma. Courtesy Jiřího Wolkrá Theatre.

A formal setting using photographic images. *The Return Address* at the Moscow Central Children's Theatre. Courtesy Soviet Center ASSITEJ.

A Kabuki treatment of another famous tale. *Sleeping Beauty* at the Minneapolis Children's Theatre Company. Courtesy Children's Theatre Company.

The participation play uses the audience as the locale. *The Bell* done by the Young People's Theatre of Toronto. Photo by Ludvik Dittrich. Courtesy Young People's Theatre.

A stylization based on a famous children's book illustrator—Maurice Sendak. *Peter Pan* at Florida State University. Courtesy Florida State University Theatre.

Stylized scenery using projections to comment on the action. *Appleseed: A Play of Peace* done by the Pickwick Players of Midland, Texas. Photo by Rubin's Studio. Courtesy Midland Community Theatre.

The simplicity of a touring production and the use of masks. *Just So Stories* done by the Asolo Children's Theatre, Florida State University. Courtesy Asolo State Theatre.

Traditional costumes for *The Wizard of Oz.* Note the influence of the audience's familiarity with the M.G.M. film version. Performed by Traveling Playhouse. Courtesy Kay Rockefeller.

The Bulgarian audience has less familiarity with the movie. *The Wizard of Oz* at the National Youth Theatre of Sofia. Courtesy National Youth Theatre.

audience probably barely notices the difference, which was not too drastic. However, when Peter later stood next to the boys, we saw clearly that Peter was wearing something different from his usual costume. (If the boys had been seen first, this approach would have been disasterous, for the children would not have known which one was Peter.)

Directly related to the problem of managing expectations is the one of teaching discriminations. The example described above actually taught the children to tell the difference between Peter and the other boy on the basis of costume. Similarly, costumes which are alike in every detail but one will teach children to notice that one aspect of distinction. But it must be something they can perceive as a difference. Don't ask them to make too fine discriminations of trim or hue—they simply cannot do it physiologically. And the director must also devise a means of drawing the different aspect to the audience's attention. Similarities of appearance are also discriminations which teach the children to relate certain characters to one another. The technique of color coding lovers, friends, and families is a fairly common one in children's productions. Again it helps if the attention of the audience can be focused on the match in the costumes. Then they become aware of design as a production element, instead of only subconsciously influenced by it. Obviously, style and interpretation determine the boldness with which such visual statements can be made. It is desirable to use the play as a means of teaching an appreciation of the visual arts; but not at the expense of the audience's involvement in the play.

the active set

The term "syntheticalism" was introduced in chapter seven to mean the use of a unified variety as a technique in directing for children. The same term should apply to the design elements. Within the basic interpretation of the play, the narrative requirements, and the graphic communication of the accompanying visual atmosphere, the designer must find a means of holding attention through the use of a variety of artistic elements—all contributing to a unified result. Especially in the one-set show the set, lights, and costumes must present different facets and different rhythms to match the changing facets of the play and to capture the shifting focus of the young audience. It is essential that the design become a *varying* element of the production through the synthetical use of all of the different components of the visual arts—from texture to line, from intensity to balance. The problem is no different from that in the adult theatre, only more critical in that the child's attention span is shorter, and his capacity for grasping complexities at once is reduced by his limited experiences.

The concept of an "active" set is useful—one that has a rhythm of its own, which complements and supplements the rhythm inherent in the script. Obviously, lighting plays a key role in changing the facets of an environment, but other things can contribute: differing treatments on the set, sequences of linear effects, the use of levels or varied surfaces, the actual movement of parts of the scenery. All these things help to change ratios and pictures and are useful devices for introducing variety. The designer with experience will already recognize that no one means of variety is sufficient to produce an active set. All the techniques must be used that are appropriate to the overall interpretation. An "active" set is not the same thing as a "busy" set, of course. "Busy-ness" is produced by a confused and overdone rhythm of impressions. "Activity" is produced by a rhythm of impressions which is harmonious with the total production, apparently presenting different components to the audience's focus as the actors move across the stage, as the lights shift, as the set itself changes, or as the audience's awareness of the play causes certain objects to change their symbolic relevance.

the material

To the designer, the most obvious difference between the adult theatre and the children's theatre is the range of material offered. There are fantasy kingdoms, weird non-human characters, and magical effects in plays for adults, but they are relatively rare occurrences. In the children's repertory they are common. The good realistic or naturalistic play for children is the rarity, fantasy and theatricality are the rule. This may mean that designers can experiment more than they could in an adult play. They can more easily create whole styles or periods from their own imagination. They can use color schemes as fantastic as the most imaginary land. They can make real the unreal, supernatural, and unconscious, drawing elves and dragons as though they were as common as dogs and cats. They can bring the non-human to life, devising foxes who exploit greed, or trees who give advice.

On the other hand, this diversity and freedom implies an increased need for self-discipline. Without the boundaries of an historical period, or even the limits of reality, the only unifying force on the designer's imagination is his own judgment and the director's. When creating a new style, it is necessary to also make it internally logical. When exploring color, and new combinations of colors, it is necessary to possess good taste. When endowing the non-human with humanity, it is necessary to find consistency and believability in the new forms. Although the designer's imagination is turned loose by the children's play, his responsibility for providing unity and interpretive validity are increased. The collaboration with the director becomes more critical the more the play departs from naturalism, and there are few naturalistic children's plays worth mentioning. Limits must therefore be set from within the script and production, and not externally applied from the real world. The nature of the material itself serves to stress the importance of a strong overall concept for the production, and of the necessity for the designer to challenge and please himself with his endeavors.

ten

MANAGEMENT
FOR THE
CHILDREN'S THEATRE

The manager's responsibility in the theatre is to ensure that the theatre continues to operate, and to establish policies and goals for such operation. Every theatre is organized somewhat differently, so these responsibilities may be vested in a board of directors, a general manager, a theatre president, an artistic director, a college department chairman, or any combination of these or other persons. Regardless of who carries it out, the managerial function requires careful consideration and sound training. Much criticism has been offered in recent years of the lack of competent arts management in this nation, and, although the situation is probably improving rapidly, there is still much to be said for the necessity of business-minded leadership in any field which must compete—as the theatre unfortunately must—for the time and financial support of the public. The situation is particularly complicated in the area of theatre for children for the obvious reason that its primary public—children—rarely has control of its own time or finances. Anything intended for consumption by children must be sold both to the children, and to the adults who control them, usually parents and teachers. Often these two generation groups have vastly different needs and expectations.

Occasionally they are in direct conflict. The manager's job is to make use of all the resources at his disposal—both economic and artistic—to establish goals, to communicate those goals to his adult public, to find procedures for the realization of those goals, and to do all this in a way consistent with good business practices. When one thinks of the obstacles, the kinds of personalities typically involved in theatres, the preoccupations of educational institutions and community organizations, the fiscal impossibility of the performing arts, and the general poor image of arts for children one cannot fail to be impressed by the fact that there is as much surviving theatre for children as there is.

ESTABLISHING POLICY

As in any other theatre, policies in the children's theatre are established in accordance with the philosophies of its leaders and the needs of the community. There should always be an attempt to find out what the community wants and what it really needs, and then determine how the theatre can provide both. Theatre personnel are hired, usually, because they are competent at meeting these needs, and working with the management. Harmony of operation is achieved only when the managerial goals are clearly understood and accepted, or at least tolerated, by the entire staff. Once goals are agreed upon by the key staff, priorities of goals must be set. It is not enough to know what you are trying to achieve; there must also be a relative importance attached to each separate goal. Every objective on the manager's list can be worked toward under ideal circumstances. But when the situation becomes less than ideal or when policies are in conflict, there must be a ready means for deciding which alternative is the most desirable, or which program the least essential. Obviously, such decisions should be made in advance.

The very act of stating goals and policies in the rank order of their importance, and having such a commitment available on paper for all new staff or community leaders to read, is an important step in obtaining the good will of both the theatre personnel and the public. Once operating policy is known, colleagues and supporters are able to interpret the manager's actions as motivated by the theatre's goals, and not by his own authority. In terms of operating efficiency and pleasant relations, there is an obvious preference for decisions made by following established policy, rather than those made by fiat. Regardless of who sets the policy or who serves the various managerial functions in the theatre, permanence can only be achieved by knowing where you are going, and letting all those who want to work with you know, too.

The policies involved in operating a children's theatre are varied. Some organizations produce only occasionally for children but have a full operation for adults; some only sponsor touring productions; some are committed to teaching; others only to performance. No textbook can possibly formulate ideal policies for all situations and individual managers. Nevertheless, two major considerations which should heavily influence the process of forming policy can be briefly discussed. These are the need for communicating artistic standards, and the principle of using available community resources.

artistic priority

Although goals such as "the development of personality," "aesthetic education," "the use of theatre to teach social skills," and "psychological acceptance of self" are all significant and worthy for a children's theatre, it is my own feeling that "enjoyment of the play" should always come first. For the manager who subscribes to my preference for artistic achievement over development of individuals or audiences there are certain implications, chiefly the need to spend money on productions. Unless the plays are competently done it is a waste of finances to provide elaborate educational aids, psychological consultants, and long-range research funds. Both the professional and amateur theatre manager should try to find a talented and strong artistic director, even if this means paying him 90 per cent of the production budget. It is far better to have a brilliant director for the children's theatre and have no money for sets, than mediocre talent and a lot of scenery. Next priorities go to actors and designers—get the best you can afford. Only when art and entertainment are guaranteed can the children's theatre become a force for education and development.

The problem facing the manager who accepts the premise stated above is quite simple—he has to sell that priority to the adults. He need not worry about the children, however, for every child would rather have fun than learn, especially when the fun contains a painless learning experience. But there is still an idea in some adult minds that unless medicine tastes bad, it will not work. It is extremely difficult to convince many principals, teachers, and parents committed to child development that their goal is best served by spending money from a limited treasury for a director and designer, even when this means less money for study guides, or teaching consultants. Many well-intentioned educators will fail to see why a delightful frothy script is a better choice than a dullish morally uplifting one. Too many parents applaud the irrelevant curtain speech about theatre manners, or the educational impact of meeting the friendly actors after the play, instead of the skill with which a professional actor reaches the child during the performance. The truth is that the children's theatre still projects an image of a social-welfare, educationally sound, "cultural" activity—generally with no mention of "artistically exciting." The manager should be aware of this problem and stress the priority of artistic concerns in his list of policies. Not every company can have a Laurence Olivier or a Peter Brook to guarantee artistic excellence. But every manager can order his priority of goals in such a way that high artistic standards are the most important concern for everyone connected with the theatre. He must also make the public aware of this focus. This does not mean the de-emphasis of developmental goals, but rather extra emphasis on artistic ones.

community responses

The leader who fails to consider the energies and abilities of his followers will quickly find himself leading a very small group. The teacher who fails to note the starting level of his students will soon leave most of them frustrated and floundering. The manager who fails to consider the needs, level of appreciation, and resources of his community—whether it be children, college students, or adults—will live to see his theatre cancelled for lack of interest. Any theatre, but especially the children's theatre, depends on good will. Relating the theatre to the community in which it exists is a two-way proposition. The manager must plan to give the community something for which it is ready, and he must be willing to take from the community the ideas and energies it can give.

One of the goals of the children's theatre should be to raise the artistic sophistication of the audience. This may pay off in increased appreciation of the adult theatre—in about fifteen or twenty years. It may also lead to the increased appreciation of challenging children's plays within a shorter time. But before the theatre can raise the level of appreciation, it must discover what level exists. An ongoing procedure must be established to monitor other artistic activities related to both children and adults. The relative success of different kinds of movies is an important clue to the tastes of the town. So, of course, are the reviews of artistic events in the newspaper. Neither are substitutes for a careful study of the theatre's own records. Which shows sell the most tickets? What kinds of plays, times of year, or weather conditions affect attendance and response? What about other theatres in the city? What kinds of plays do other local theatres do? Which ones succeed? How does your prospective public compare to theirs? What is the reaction of your audience and/or their parents to an amoral play, a weak or comical authority figure, violence, or unhappy endings? Until you know what people expect you to do, you cannot begin to teach them what you want to do.

As a technique for finding out what is wanted or needed, there are few methods better than asking, provided you know who to ask and when. The caution here is that you must remember to listen to the answer. If you ask people for advice or information and then ignore it, you do more damage than if you hadn't asked at all. At the same time, it is useful to let the general public know that you are guided in your policies by the opinions and tastes of the leaders of the community. Both of these ends—finding out what people want and letting them know you care—are served by the proper use of local human resources. Whether or not the theatre has an official board of directors, it is an excellent idea to have a regular consultation with a relatively permanent group of lay advisors, chosen carefully from the locality. In the event your theatre has a board, it still may be necessary to supplement this group with a less official advisory council, in order to make sure that certain elements of local opinion are represented. The existence of such a body can spell the difference between success and failure in any theatre not assured of governmental funding, and most publicly funded theatres are set up with advisory boards by law.

In creating such a group, it is wise to include several kinds of people, for different reasons. Financial advice and business suggestions are best obtained from businesspeople concerned with the public image of their own businesses. Bank presidents, lawyers, doctors, department store owners, and some car dealers are always good bets. They must, of course, be well-known to assure the community that it is represented, and they must be interested in the goal of good children's theatre, or at least susceptible to being educated to the possibilities. If the individuals or businesses represented have money available for philanthropic causes, they are even more desirable as advisors. Community organizations, particularly women's groups, are also "musts" for representation. Junior Leagues, Service Clubs, and women's auxiliaries are often deeply involved in cultural projects, and can provide a different point of view for your board. Those groups with a strong commitment to children's theatre, like the Junior League, should be made permanent members. Business and community leaders are particularly good on an actual board of directors, as they will then be fiscally involved in the survival of the theatre. An advisory board can be somewhat different in structure. Here one wants local educators, psychologists, recreation directors—professionals who work with children. Their consultations on scripts, age groups, recreational activities, and liaison with schools is invaluable. It may be desirable to have these individuals on the board of directors as well, but they should also form a subcommittee for pedagogical advice. Obviously, all these people should be thoroughly and publicly recognized—as a reward for their services, and as a means of letting the public know the calibre of the theatre's advisors.

The creation of such a community resource is good public relations, good business practice, and good for educational liaison and continuity. Unless it is used, however, it fails all three functions. This group is the first group that must be educated by the manager and director as to the potentials in children's theatre. From them the enthusiasm and support will hopefully spread rapidly. They must be given sound reasoning, well-thought-out philosophy, and artistic excellence. The manager should establish as a high priority the goal of an aware and responsive community advisory group. With them, further policies are set and the means of implementation are reviewed.

ESTABLISHING PROCEDURE

Certain procedures in the operation of a children's theatre are so common—either to the operation of an adult theatre, or to any business concern—that there is little point in discussing them here. Obviously, theatrical materials must be purchased with care and economy. Necessarily, accounts must be kept and bills paid. Depending on the kind of theatre and its financial position, staff or volunteers must be recruited and supervised. A chain of authority must be formulated, delegating responsibilities for both artistic and maintenance operations. The job of the manager is most complex, and varies enormously from college theatre to community theatre to professional theatre. The differences between operating a children's theatre and an adult one are small, but significant. The limitations of the child audience—both physical and economic —and the existing artistic conditions in the field are the two major causes of the differences. Several procedural decisions which must be made will vary as a direct result of one or both of these situations.

sponsorship vs. production

It is hard to imagine a successful theatre with a financial surplus and a high artistic reputation that never produces a play, but such theatre programs exist. As we have seen in chapter two, there have been definite trends among community groups away from amateur productions and toward sponsoring professional or semi-professional touring companies. The sponsoring theatre has a manager, but no artistic staff. A season of theatrical presentations is offered, tickets are sold, a reputation is built, and an audience is entertained solely on the basis of productions which are hired from outside. In many ways this kind of operation resembles exactly a college's artist's series, which attempts to provide a college community with a variety of artistic experiences beyond the production capabilities of most small colleges or communities. Seattle Junior Programs, our example in chapter two, has been able to offer annually four different professional companies ranging from ballet to drama. They have sponsored groups from the local University and from New York. They can contract for a single show, or several, from the same company. They bear some artistic risks, but few financial ones, since they can know from their advance season sales exactly how many performances of each show to purchase. The obvious advantage is the variety of experiences which can be offered. The disadvantage is the somewhat uncontrollable variety in artistic quality.

The producing group, on the other hand, has its own production staff, an artistic unit. It chooses a season not from available touring shows, but from all the suitable scripts which can be bought or commissioned. It hires or recruits actors, builds scenery, and mounts the play on the most desirable dates. It is free of conforming to the touring group's calendar, choice of scripts, or production style. It has full control of artistic excellence—and bears full responsibility for failures. It is, however, limited to talent it can attract or afford, and it is committed to a production budget that is relatively insensitive to the number of performances desired. There is the further possibility of combining the two approaches. Some theatres produce one or more plays annually, and then contract the remainder of the season. Such an approach is useful to the theatre group that wants to broaden its audience's exposure to the arts in general. Ballet groups and puppet shows are good "added attractions" in a season of straight plays.

The critical procedure in sponsoring productions from outside is to preview everything possible. The manager and a group from his advisory board should spare no expense to travel to the home of the company under consideration to see their work. If possible, the play or program to be contracted should be seen. If this is impossible because the season announcements are made before the desired production is mounted, a previous production by the same group should be seen, preferably one by the director who will do the new show. Certainly the prospective script should be read, and the design inspected, if finished. Most professional touring companies are aware of the sponsor's need to preview and will gladly lend scripts, designs, production plans, or even provide a specially staged scene from the work, if the total production is not available. The manager should be suspicious of those producers insensitive to this need.

Of course anything can happen in the theatre. An actor can break a leg, a director misunderstand a script, or an ensemble's morale be in a slump. The same problems can occur when the theatre produces its own plays. No amount of previewing, even the day before, will guarantee a great performance. But not to preview is to invite disaster. There are enough good companies available for touring so that a little expense and care in selection will pay off in excellence of the program with fair regularity.

The only other obstacle to a successful sponsorship program is its expense. Good professional productions are more costly, naturally, than do-it-yourself amateur ones. You will have to decide whether the difference in quality is worth it, based on the talent of your amateurs and the size and potential income from your audience. It is very hard to beat the best professionals, but there are also many amateur groups that can easily outdo the worst professionals. Expenses of sponsorship can be greatly reduced, particularly if distance from the producing group is large, by getting together with neighboring communities and arranging consecutive dates. Every professional touring theatre gives discounts for long runs, and most are willing to consider a circuit of nearby towns arranged in a single tour as a single booking for discount privileges.

For the manager of a group which hopes to tour, and thereby be the producing company for a series of sponsors, a whole set of problems exists, which are beyond the scope of this text. The problems of touring are not different if the play is for children rather than for adults, except that it is necessary to find a company that wakes up early—as most children's performances are given during school hours, and that may mean a set-up as early as 7:00 A.M. Another concern is to be aware of the needs of the sponsoring theatre's managers, particularly their need for some kind of preview or sample of your work.

the season

In selecting a season of plays for children all the usual criteria apply: variety, technical feasibility, casting problems, suitability for the audience, publicity value, artistic challenge, and many others. In addition the children's theatre manager needs to consider age groups. Are all plays done for all ages? Is there a separate season for the very young children? Are there plays for different age groups, but all in one package? The ideal situation is to separate the audience if possible. If school groups come, it is easy to say one play is for the fifth grade, another for the second, and so on. But if tickets are sold to the public, some notification of age suitability must be given in all advertising and when the tickets are sold. It is better to do two sub-seasons, one for younger children, one for older— or even three, if possible. Even if there are only two plays in each of the

sub-seasons, you will have a much better response to all of the plays because they will be more closely geared to their audience. Perhaps a full
season could contain seven plays: two for the under nines, two for ages
nine through twelve, and two for the teenagers, plus a family show that
all could enjoy. Each child would see three plays, two with his peers and
one with his family. This is probably the most desirable combination of
experiences to ensure continuity without sacrificing specific appeal.

Play choice is usually within the province of the artistic director but
certainly strong recommendations and a veto power should reside with
the manager. In addition it is wise to use the advisory board to make suggestions, particularly if it contains knowledgeable educators or developmental specialists. Some large European theatres for children have a staff
member responsible for script development—the dramaturge—but his
function can also be carried out by a volunteer committee. New sources
of material must be explored; thousands of unpublished scripts must be
solicited and read; and promising playwrights must be developed and encouraged by the individual theatres if the children's theatre repertory is
ever to rise to the desired level. Although there are several fine plays for
the young, they will quickly be exhausted by a theatre with a long and
varied season. When you add the limitations of a small cast, or touring,
or a wide age grouping, the stock of worthwhile scripts dwindles alarm-
ingly. A conscious effort toward the development of new material is therefore an essential procedure. If one hundred theatres in this country (there
were over 700 doing plays for children in 1970) each developed one good
play every five years, the situation would certainly be vastly improved, assuming a means existed to publish and share these scripts. Improvisation
of material, with a trained playwright to coordinate final selections, is a
possible method of creating new material. Talking to children is a good
starting point for plots or characters of interest. Play contests and commissions theoretically attract top script writers, but only a producing theatre can fully develop a script through the preliminary stages and into a
new play of merit. Contests and commissions which are connected with
a good production are of more value to the playwright and the children's
theatre repertory than are prizes or an advance on royalties.

facilities

Those children's theatres with homes built especially for them are
as fortunate as they are rare in the United States. There is something exciting about having your own building, particularly if you are a child in
an adult-dominated world. A building belonging collectively to the community's children is a source of pride for both the children and the community. However, it is unusual. Most theatres borrow space for children's

productions from an adult theatre, or use a multi-purpose auditorium or gymnasium. Theatres that play to both adults and children and have permanent control of their facility may be able to satisfactorily solve the space-sharing problems.

If the manager has to locate a separate playing facility, he begins with the disadvantage that few existing auditoriums are geared to the dimensions and sensory capabilities of children. Some theatre seats will not even remain in the sitting position unless a certain amount of weight is placed on them. It is a little disconcerting when the child audience gets excited, forgets to push down, and folds up into the lifting jaws of their chairs. If children in the second row have to sit on their knees in order to see because the slope of the house floor is based on the adult's eye level, there is a certain amount of discomfort—which is apt to produce enough non-attention to destroy a production. If a building must be borrowed for a child audience, at least try to find one that has non-collapsing chairs and a high stage.

Also, many theatres are too big for the child's wandering attention. For young eyes, as the proscenium opening shrinks in apparent size, identification and discrimination also tend to diminish. The child more than fifty or sixty feet from the action will not be as involved as he might be if he were closer. One can sense the differing reactions in a large house. Those in front are with the play completely—if it is good—while those in back are detached, as though they were watching television.

The ideal conditions are a maximum distance from the stage of sixty feet, a seating capacity of 450 to 750 (150 to 250 for arena audience participation plays) and a high stage with a fairly well-sloped house floor. The full width of space between rows is not needed, as young legs are shorter, but the full aisle width is a necessity. Of course, if the theatre also attracts teenagers or adults, you will have to make sure there is leg room for them. Try to minimize maintenance problems, providing a pleasant, durable atmosphere which will not be ruined by chewing gum and scuff marks. Of course, adequate bathrooms and an excess of fire exits are desirable. It is difficult to build a regular clientele unless the building is also one that can be used regularly for all your productions. This helps the image of the theatre as well as the technical aspects of production. Of course, many companies struggle successfully without an ideal building, and some even turn the lack of a permanent home into an asset by touring schools or neighborhood parking lots.

In existing buildings there is also an impossible range of backstage conditions—from nothing at all to too much. Consider your company's capabilities first. There is little point in having more stage than can be used effectively. It is wise to consider flexibility, as the trend toward eclectic theatre styles is likely to continue for many years, and hopefully will increase in the children's theatre. But stage equipment and expensive machinery are only useful if your technical staff is challenged by them. In many amateur children's theatres the ignorance of the crew makes such technical aids a waste of time and money. It is far better to bring in an expensive designer and tell him there is no backstage equipment, than to have elaborate machinery and use it badly. The children's repertory does require a lot of spectacle, however, so that if you can find the right kind of staff to make it work, a completely equipped stage will be an asset. But get the staff first, and the equipment afterwards.

If you are fortunate enough to be able to create your own facility, even if it is only adapting a warehouse into a permanent home, you should consider the thrust or arena stage—especially if you play to younger children. The more three-dimensional the acting space, the more it corresponds to the child's natural playing area. Primitive theatre is always in-the-round. Open staging is more conducive to rapid action and syntheticalism. It also saves money, putting the emphasis on actors and costumes instead of on scenery and effects. The open stage is limited, in that true spectacle is hard to achieve, so if your theatre is the only theatre available, and you play to all ages, perhaps it is an economy that you cannot afford philosophically. If you can consider it, however, do, as it provides a more intimate, compelling experience—if the artistic use of the stage space is satisfactory.

The most important thing when building is to create a home for your company—one that suits its style of life; one that children will feel is especially theirs and adults feel invigorated to visit. Try to establish a feeling of permanence about your company, and adapt your productions to the environment in which they take place.

publicity and public relations

If there is to be any permanence or continuity in your operation, it will easily be worthwhile to engage the services of a specialist in the areas of publicity and public relations. Our lives are filled with demands for our dollars or our energies. These demands are all managed with professional skill by the advertising agencies and public relations firms of the nation. Even safety reminders presented by the mass media as a public service are produced and managed by professional publicity people. It is almost impossible for an amateur to compete for our attention—no matter what cause he represents. The larger and more diverse the community, the more difficult the problem becomes. To attract the attention of the public to a children's theatre program requires the fullest exploitation of personal contacts, public campaigns, and the use of the public news media. Liaisons with schools, parents, businessmen, and community organizations require a careful analysis of the needs of each group, and a strategy aimed specifically at convincing each segment of the public that the theatre can meet certain of its needs. If the sales of tickets are made indirectly, through schools, it is wise to build an image in the public eye that will guarantee the approval of the school's participation by the taxpayers. All of these problems require the services of a specialist in the area of public relations.

In securing the cooperation of the schools it is important to appeal both to the local school administration, which must usually approve any school-time activity or solicitation, and to the classroom teachers, who have a direct influence on the motivation and interest of the children. The administrators must be convinced of the importance of aesthetic education to the development of a citizen, the *measurable* changes in perceptions, attitudes, or behaviors which result from exposure to good theatre, and the effect of artistic experiences on language skills and individual creativity. Some of these arguments are lacking in statistical support, but, hopefully, such evidence will be forthcoming in the near future. Private investigators and research groups such as the Central Midwestern Regional Educational Laboratory (CEMREL) are conducting studies to determine the impact of theatre on the child audience. CEMREL is also developing packages of classroom materials which will aid the teacher in aesthetic education. Such materials are carefully sequenced so as to provide a full curriculum in theatre, or other arts, for the elementary grades.

The teachers are less interested in the theory and more interested in the mechanical use of the theatre experience in the day-to-day classroom situation. If they can be shown how to integrate social studies or language arts into a trip to the theatre, or how to capitalize on the class's artistic motivation to boost their scholastic motivation, they will be supportive. They also respond, sometimes with surprise, to the fact that the children like the play and demonstrate greater emotional capabilities than the teachers have expected from their daily work with the children.

Parents, businessmen, and community organizations are approached more easily with appeals which stress recreational benefits and enhance the community's image as a place to live and relax. They are also interested in child growth, but more in terms of social graces than in terms of language skills. The concept of "culture" is probably poorly understood by many. It is important that parents and other citizens be made aware of the relationship between "culture" as a goal, and the ability to enjoy and learn from our aesthetic experiences—which is probably what "culture" really means. Such insights should make them more aware of the need to enjoy art, rather than to sit painfully and endure it like cod liver oil for the health of the soul.

Depending on the exact goals of the theatre, the public relations specialist will possibly also be the person to create a liaison between the theatre and the private and public sources of funding, although the manager may also assume this function. These contacts may be for the purpose of providing a fund to buy tickets for underpriviledged children, in which case community service clubs or local businesses are the best source. Contacts may also be with national or local foundations for the purpose of obtaining major operating, expansion, or experimental grants. The situation of grants is continuously changing, and different foudations become interested in supporting activities for the benefit of children at different times. The maze of guidelines and application procedures requires the talents of a specialist. The only difference in applying for a grant for a children's theatre than for any other project is to know which sources of funds are interested in aesthetic education. Research in children's reactions to violence onstage might appeal to one group; touring a play to rural, culturally isolated areas may appeal to another. As with every other aspect of pubic relations, it is necessary to gather data and information from outside sources before attempting to dispense information. The manager who is forced to handle all the various aspects of the operation of the theatre without the services of a specialist in the area of obtaining public support will find it wise to distribute other responsibilities to assistants so that he may become, himself, a specialist in developing relations.

the box office

Certain basic decisions relative to ticket sales are influenced by the fact that a theatre is for children—for example, the actual prices to be charged. Some theatres are funded in such a way that no charge is made to the audience, but such a practice is undesirable from a philosophical point of view, as it teaches the child that the performing arts are free—an untruth. Other theatres need every penny they can bring in from ticket sales, and are forced to wrestle with the dilemma that the higher they put the cost of admission, the more children for whom the price becomes an economic barrier.

Adults do not pay full prices for their children in our society. Children's portions are served in restaurants, movies sell cheaper tickets to youngsters, and mass transportation fares are usually much lower for a child. There is no good reason to expect this custom to be different in the performing arts, except that the economic situation of the arts is based on rising costs and limited production, as has ably been attested to in recent publications. (For one of the best, see Baumol and Bowen, *The Performing Arts: The Economic Dilemma*.) To add to the problem, children's plays usually require *more* in the way of expensive costumes and scenery than do their counterparts in the adult repertory. It is true that these added costs can be partially offset by the possibility of extra performances per week, as the plays are shorter and two or three matinees could be scheduled each day with appropriate school support. However, even this practice rarely enables the children's theatre to be economically self-sufficient.

The ideal is to set prices as low as possible, consistent with the idea of teaching children to place an economic value on the arts experience and with the financial realities of the situation. Probably the price should not be lower than a high quality candy bar, and it is unrealistic to expect more than an adult pays for a first-run movie. Within these two extremes it is permissible to scale a house so that some seats are quite cheap, and others more costly. It is also reasonable to charge more for an older age group's season of plays than for those intended for the very young, as their control of financial resources is usually higher. I have often been tempted to try to enforce age group attendance at plays by raising the price exorbitantly for all children *under* the minimum recommended age for each play; however, I have thus far lacked the courage. The price charged to the adults who attend is sometimes the same as that charged the child, and sometimes more; it varies from theatre to theatre. It probably keeps adults away, who might otherwise have come, if they have to pay much more for their seat. It is probably best to charge adults the prevailing children's price.

Ticket sales in the adult theatre are almost always made directly between the box office and a customer—through a personal contact, a telephone call, or a mail-in order. Occasionally, the theatre for adults sells through a deputy, such as a department store ticket agency, or a travel agent. Sometimes, a sale is made to a group—perhaps of all of the seats for one performance—which then takes charge of further distribution of the tickets. All these methods are used in the children's theatre, plus the common one of selling an entire performance or run to a school group. The school group then arranges all the details of attendance, and either passes on or absorbs the costs of the individual tickets. This indirect method is used exclusively by some theatre operations, which never put a single ticket on sale to the public but deal exclusively with school-time performances. Others use the method of selling tickets to individuals, but arranging to have the sales completed and the money collected by the classroom teacher or class PTA representative. Such a system has the advantage of a captive public, but depends on the good will of the teachers and the school board. Other theatres combine sales methods—selling some performances publicly, and others exclusively for school attendance. The more methods used, the more complex the box office management, and the greater the need for a trained specialist.

Another common method, particularly in Europe, is to sell memberships to a theatre "club." Members get the theatre's publicity, and then buy their tickets to the shows. Often non-members have to pay more for an individual ticket, and sometimes they cannot attend at all without joining the club. This approach is similar in operation to the season-ticket system, whereby a discount is given for purchasing tickets for the whole season of plays. The season ticket campaign usually results in a good mailing list of loyal supporters. Some theatres do so well on membership or season sales that there is no room for individual buyers at performances. It is obviously a scheduling advantage, particularly for sponsoring groups, to know at the beginning of the season how many members or subscribers are likely to come to each show. This means that they can schedule exactly the right number of performances.

Whatever methods of ticket sales are used, good accounting procedures and accurate records must be kept, not only to guarantee honesty in box office personnel, but to provide data on how the theatre sells its tickets, which agencies or methods pay off the most, and what times of day or periods of the year are most desirable for performances. If there is any complexity to the sales procedure at all, the services of a box office manager—whether paid or volunteer—become essential.

house management

A critical responsibility in the children's theatre falls on the shoulders of the house manager, for the problems of audience comfort and control are not always closely comparable with those in the adult theatre. For the sake of assigning responsibility, let us assume that the house manager is directly in charge of the audience, from the time of their arrival in the vicinity of the theatre, to their departure from that vicinity. Traffic, parking, seating, coat-checks, refreshments, programs, ushers, bathrooms, safety procedures, and sick children all come under his consideration. To the extent that the children in the audience come unsupervised to the theatre, the house manager becomes the adult responsible for their welfare, safety, comfort, and emotional well-being. He also influences their artistic appreciation by the level of participation which he allows them during the performance. The success of the total theatre experience, assuming the play is good, and the avoidance of volatile situations which could lead to tragedy or lawsuits, depends on having a mature, calm adult in the lobby at all times, with a disciplined staff of ushers under his control.

Since children never drive themselves to the theatre, and rarely come on foot, it is safe to assume that most of them will be brought by adults. These adults will either accompany the children to the play, in which case they assume some responsibility for them, or else they will drop them off. Someone must be on the sidewalk to supervise the inevitable traffic congestion caused by parents dropping off their children. Questions such as, "What time should I pick them up?" can be answered in front of the theatre, saving the added congestion of cars waiting for the children to return with instructions. It also comforts the parents to see that the theatre has staff on duty to care for their children. Some kind of costume or uniform to set off the house staff is useful in this connection. School bus drivers also need to know where to unload, where to park, and when to return.

If the performance is for school groups, ticket office lines are usually eliminated. Someone must simply show the groups to the areas reserved for them. It is essential to know in advance the approximate number of children in each group and the age levels represented, so that the younger ones may be placed down front, and classes may be kept together with their teachers. Otherwise, bad sight problems or unsupervised children become sources of confusion. If the audience is a general public, the seats are allotted either on a first-come-first-served basis or by reservation. The latter method requires more ushers and is more costly to the theatre when buying and selling tickets. But it is preferable because it avoids the serious difficulty of children coming too early to the theatre to get a good seat, and then being totally exhausted from waiting for the play to start. In either case, the ushers must be taught to be relaxed and tolerant, particularly with preadolescent children. The staff's desire should be to let the child feel at home and free to respond. Condescension from an usher sets a tone for the theatre as a whole, and prompts a feeling of rebellion in some age groups. Too much discipline inhibits their participation in the play. Too little evidence of potential supervision leads to chaos during the production—especially if it is not up to standard. The correct balance of firmness and tolerance, of presence and invisibility, should be the goal.

Most theatres do not issue programs to school groups, counting on the study guide sent to the teacher to inform the children of the play's background, cast, and setting. Many theatres do not give programs to public groups either. In both cases, the expense and the fear of paper airplanes and huge cleaning costs are the reasons given. Some theatres issue programs as the children leave, feeling that in this way they can give away a souvenir with no danger of noisy paper rustling or shredded programs to be cleaned up. Children, of course, can make plenty of noise and mess without programs, and if the play is boring they will. Most children do not understand the program anyway, except as a souvenir, or as something to play with while they wait. Hence, many theatres try to include in their program some kind of game, or at least a visual introduction to the play's theme. Children do like to collect autographs, and many use the program for that purpose after the play. There is, of course, an excellent reason to give them a program: it teaches them to expect a program, and to use it to prepare themselves for the play.

If the play is long enough to require an intermission, there will naturally be some confusion, as children try to find the bathroom, buy refreshments, get some exercise, or act out the first act highlights. Some theatres attempt to hold the interval to a short exercise time, with no one leaving the area of their seats. Others try for concessions sales which bring in a little extra money, but can lead to tripled maintenance costs unless all food and drinks are kept out of the seating area. With school groups it is best to sell nothing. If the school officials choose to furnish the whole group with a candy bar or a container of juice, these arrangements can be made as part of the purchase of the performance. If every child in the audience stood in line for something different, the interval would easily last longer than the second act. With the general public you have to make a decision based on length of the show, ease of setting up a canteen area away from the seats, maintenance costs, and local custom. Any kind of an interval is a headache for the house staff, and a problem for the cast when the play resumes, as youthful energies which have been botttled up by an exciting play will spontaneously erupt if the play lapses, and may be hard to rebottle.

The house manager must make sure, above all, that his staff is equipped for emergencies. Fire preparations, first aid training, and emergency clean-up equipment in case of a sick child are obvious precautions. Less obvious, but more frequently needed duties are as counselors for frightened children, bathroom helpers for the very young, or telephone operators for the child whose pick-up ride is late. After the performance, many theatres allow the children to meet the cast in the lobby. Often children will go backstage for autographs even if no arrangements are made. The house manager should remain on duty to help the actors get politely and safely away from the theatre, and to make sure that every child is off for home. The parent who is running late to claim his family must feel the theatre staff is functioning right up until the end to guarantee the safety, if not enjoyment, of his children.

image nurturance

An overall concern of the manager is the image which his theatre evokes in the minds of many different people: his own company, other theatre people who might want to work there, the governmental sources of funds, the private foundations, the audience, the school board, the parents, and the general public. A high positive image is created by a high quality product, a concern for the growth and development of the individual artists, and a professional method of operation which makes use of every technique of public relations and theatre operation to convince the public that this theatre is a place where good work is done, where children are respected, cared for, and given material to help them develop, and where every precaution is taken for the health, safety, and happiness of the children of the community. To build such an image takes time. No one with any knowledge of the theatre would expect a new adult theatre to play to 90 percent capacity in its first season; or to find the best actors from around the nation for its ensemble in its first auditions. The same process of slow development occurs in the children's theatre—perhaps slowed even further by the scarcity of critical notices for children's productions, and the poor economic power of the young audience. Patience and a commitment to ideals are required managerial attributes.

This book has presented a statement of the philosophical motivations behind the children's theatre movement, and given some suggestions of a methodology for implementing these philosophies in terms of artistic practices. The future of the movement depends on the acceptance by the public which supports the theatre of a set of principles—either those advocated here, or some others which fulfill the needs of both the children and the artists. Perhaps the most important job of the manager (or anyone) in the theatre for children is to communicate these principles to all.

appendix a

SOURCES OF

CHILDREN'S PLAYS

For the benefit of the student or director interested in scripts for children's theatre, the following list indicates the major American sources and one guide to foreign plays in translation. For some of these publishers a few of their most highly regarded titles have been added. An age group suggestion for these plays is also indicated, when obtainable. This list includes only plays specifically intended for children. Many other good plays for young audiences can be discovered within the traditional adult repertory. In addition to the single plays below, several good anthologies of children's plays are listed in the bibliography.

1. Anchorage Press (formerly Children's Theatre Press)
   Cloverlot
   Anchorage, Kentucky 40223

   Many fine scripts; see especially:
   Androcles and the Lion, Aurand Harris (ages five to ten)
   Big Klaus and Little Klaus, Dean Wenstrom (nine to twelve)
   Don Quixote of La Mancha, Arthur Fauquez (nine to adult)
   The Great Cross Country Race, Alan Broadhurst (five to ten)
   Huckleberry Finn, Frank Whiting (nine to twelve)

Indian Captive, Charlotte Chorpenning (nine to twelve)
The Land of the Dragon, Madge Miller (seven to ten)
Livin' De Life, Ed Graczyk (five to twelve)
The Man Who Killed Time, Arthur Fauquez (nine to fourteen)
Niccolo and Nicollette, Alan Cullen (eight to twelve)
The Prince, the Wolf, and the Firebird, Jackson Lacey (seven to adult)
Punch and Judy, Aurand Harris
Rags to Riches, Aurand Harris (nine to adult)
Reynard the Fox, Arthur Fauquez (nine to adult)
Trudi and the Minstrel, Alan Cullen (seven to adult)
Two Pails of Water, Aad Greidanus (eight to twelve)
The Violin of Passing Time, Aristide Charpentier (nine to fourteen)
The Wizard of Oz, Adele Thane

2. The Coach House Press
   53 West Jackson Blvd.
   Chicago, Illinois 60604

   See especially:
   Greensleeves' Magic, Marian Jonson (five to ten)
   Indian Captive, Gertrude Breen (nine to twelve)
   The Red Shoes, Hans Josef Schmidt (five to ten)
   Tyl Eulenspiegel and the Talking Donkey, Robert and Lillian Masters

3. Dramatists Play Service
   440 Park Ave.
   New York, New York 10016

   See especially:
   The Hide-and-Seek Odyssey of Madeline Gimple, Frank Gagliano (eight to twelve)

4. The Dramatic Publishing Company
   86 E. Randolph St.
   Chicago, Illinois 60601

5. Samuel French, Inc.
   25 West 45th Street
   New York, New York, 10036

   See especially:
   The Emperor's New Clothes, Charlotte Chorpenning (seven to ten)
   The Red Shoes, Robin Short (seven to ten)
   Peter Pan, James Barrie (five to adult)
   The Tinder Box, Nicholas Stuart Gray
   Toad of Toad Hall, A. A. Milne (seven to adult)

6. International Bibliography of Plays in Translation
   Michael Pugh, Editor
   10 Adamson Road
   London NW 3
   England

   Biannual publication of plays recommended by the various ASSITEJ Centers, which lists all plays that have been translated from their original language, together with synopsis, source of script, cast size, etc.

7. Involvement Dramatics (participation scripts)
   Oklahoma City University
   2501 North Blackwelder
   Oklahoma City, Oklahoma 73106

8. David McKay Company
   750 Third Avenue
   New York, New York 10017

   See especially:
   The Clown Who Ran Away, Conrad Seiler (five to nine)

9. Modern Theatre for Youth
   Department of Speech
   Kansas State University
   Manhattan, Kansas 66502

10. Music Theatre International
    119 West 57th Street
    New York, New York 10019

11. New Plays for Children
    Box 2181
    Grand Central Station
    New York, New York 10017

    See especially:
    Five Minutes to Morning, Mary Melwood (eight to fourteen)
    Hansel and Gretel, Moses Goldberg (five to eight)
    The Ice Wolf, Joanna Kraus (six to eleven)
    Mean To Be Free, Joanna Kraus (eight to twelve)
    The Tingalary Bird, Mary Melwood (eight to fourteen)

12. New Scripts Service (circulating library of unpublished scripts, sponsored by CTA)
    Beverly Sturgill, Editor
    567 Polk St.
    Twin Falls, Idaho 83301

    See especially:
    The Invisible People, William Lavender (nine to twelve)
    The Play of Innocence and Change, Jonathan Levy (nine to fourteen)
    Rumpelstiltskin and the Witches, Hal and Jo Todd (eight to eleven)

13. Pickwick Press
    Box 4847
    Midland, Texas 79701

    See especially:
    To Be, Ed Graczyk (eleven to fourteen)

14. Pioneer Drama Service
    Box 1420
    Cody, Wyoming 82414

15. Pittsburgh Playhouse Press
    222 Craft Ave.
    Pittsburgh, Pennsylvania 15213

16. Plays, Inc. (mostly non-royalty anthologies)
    8 Arlington Street
    Boston, Massachusetts 02116

17. Stage Magic Plays
    Box 246
    Schulenburg, Texas 78956

18. Tams-Witmark
    757 Third Avenue
    New York, New York 10017

19. Theatre Arts Books
    333 Sixth Ave.
    New York, New York 10014

    See especially:
    The Dragon, Eugene Schwarz (seven to adult)

20. Young Audience Scripts (primarily participation plays)
    9140-146A Street
    Edmonton, Alberta
    Canada T5R OX4

    See especially:
    The Mirrorman, Brian Way (five to eight)
    The Hat, Brian Way (five to eight)
    On Trial, Brian Way (nine to twelve)

appendix b

ASSITEJ CENTERS

AS OF

SEPTEMBER 1972

Austria

Peter Weihs
Austrian Center for ASSITEJ
Osterreichischen Jugendtheaterzentrum
Weihgurgasse 9,
Vienna, 1010

Belgium

Jose Geal
Belgian Center for ASSITEJ
Maison des Arts
147 Chaussée de Haecht
Brussells, 3

Brazil

Thais Bianchi
Brazilian Center for ASSITEJ
Rua Nascimento Silva 100, Ap. 101
Rio de Janeiro/G.B.

Bulgaria

Victor Georgeiev
Bulgarian Center for ASSITEJ
36, Dondukov Boulevard
Sofia

Canada

Joyce Doolittle
Canadian Center for ASSITEJ
Department of Drama
University of Calgary
Calgary 4, Alberta

Czechoslovakia

Vladimir Adamek
Czechoslovakian Center for ASSITEJ
Valdstejnské nam. 3
Prague, 1

England

Hilary Johnson
British Center for ASSITEJ
9/10 Fitzroy Square
London, WIP 6AE

France

Rose-marie Moudoues
French Center for ASSITEJ
98, Boulevard Kellerman
Paris, 13

German Democratic Republic

Ilse Rodenberg
DDR Center for ASSITEJ
Parkaue 25
Berlin, 113

German Federal Republic

Hanswalter Gossman
West German Center for ASSITEJ
Bücher Strasse 37b
Nuremberg

Hungary

Miklos Gyarfas
Hungarian Center for ASSITEJ
Bartok Gyerekszinhàz
Paulay Ede u.35
Budapest VI

Ireland

Mary Ann Gill
Irish Center for ASSITEJ
76 Northumberland Road
Dublin 4

Israel

Orna Porat
Israeli Center for ASSITEJ
Theatre Cameri for Children
101 Dizengoff St.
P.O. Box 3014
Tel Aviv

Italy

Benito Biotto
Italian Center for ASSITEJ
Piazza San Angelo, 2
Milan, 20121

Netherlands

Hans Snoek
Dutch Center for ASSITEJ
Hooftrstraat 55
Amsterdam

Norway

Bjørn Enderson
Scandinavian Center for ASSITEJ
Norsk Barneteaterunion
Rojaland Teater
Stavanger

Peru

Sara Joffre de Ramon
Peruvian Center for ASSITEJ
Los Grillos

Carabaya 719–116
Lima

Portugal

Lilia da Fonseca
Portugese Center for ASSITEJ
Rua Barao de Sabrosa, 309–2°, E.
Lisbon, 1

Romania

Ion Lucian
Romanian Center for ASSITEJ
Ion Creanga Theatre
O.F.P.T.T.R. 22, 3061
Bucharest, 22

Spain

Maria Nieves Sunyer Roig
Spanish Center for ASSITEJ
Almagro, 36
Madrid, 4

U.S.A.

Ann Hill
U.S. Center for ASSITEJ
Nashville Children's Theatre
201 Lynwood Blvd.
Nashville, Tennessee 37205

also contact:
Children's Theatre Association
1317 F St. NW
Washington, D.C. 20004

U.S.S.R.

Konstantin Shak-Azizov
Soviet Center for ASSITEJ
Central Children's Theatre
2 Sverdlov Square
Moscow

Yugoslavia

Ljubisa Djokic
Yugoslav Center for ASSITEJ
Maljenska 13
Belgrade

appendix c

SUGGESTED ACTIVITIES

In connection with a college level course in children's theatre, it might be desirable to involve the students, singly or in groups, in projects which would enable them to learn actively, as well as through the passive reading of a book or listening to a lecture. A number of suggestions for such projects are offered below, most of them tested with my own classes. Certainly, no one class will want to use all of these ideas; probably, the individual instructor will find other activities which could be profitably added to the list. The arrangement of activities corresponds, roughly, to the chapter divisions in the text.

chapter one

Individual Project Investigate the activities of the CTA in the immediate locality or region. Become an active member and try to discover all of the ways that such an organization concretely benefits the field of children's theatre.

Individual Project Observe a creative dramatics session in your community. Write a report stressing the activities you saw, and then draw conclusions about the value of creative dramatics. Do the same thing for a recreational drama rehearsal or performance, if available in your locality.

Class Project Attend a play for children. Do not sit as a group, and do not take notes during the performance—simply surround yourself with children and enjoy the play. Then get together as a class and share impressions.

Class Project   Explore introspectively all the members of the class to discover how they first became interested in theatre. Try to classify the early influences on the members of the group and decide, quantitatively if possible, what the most important factors were. Draw conclusions about the state of a "theatre tradition" in the United States.

chapter two

Small Group Project   Do research into the professed goals of the university system in the United States, and then prepare a report as to how the university system can best contribute to the growth of a children's theatre tradition. Do the same kind of study for a community service group, or a non-profit professional theatre. Report your findings and theories to the class.

Individual Project   Investigate your local children's theatre, if any. Analyze its growth, methods, and prospects.

Class Project   Write to active children's theatre groups around the nation. (You can get the addresses of member theatres from the office of the CTA, 1317 F Street, Washington, D.C. 20004.) Ask for their programs, publicity releases, photographs, etc. Make a geographical display of children's theatre activity throughout the United States.

chapter three

Class Project   Repeat the project above, for one or more of the nations listed in Appendix B.

Individual Project   If you can read a language besides English, write to the ASSITEJ Centers of those nations, and try to obtain good scripts for children which you might translate or adapt. Perhaps such a translation could be presented as a reading by the class.

chapter four

Individual Project   Arrange through a local school to observe a group of children at play, or in class. Choose one child and write a "case study" of him— his activities, language, interests, problems, joys, and fears. Try to talk with the child and include a sample of your conversation. Share your observations and impressions with the class.

Class Project   Spend some time in the children's section of the local library. Do a survey to discover the most popular books, or kinds of books, among children of different age groups in your own community.

Small Group Project Prepare and administer an audience observation checklist for a specific children's play, if one is scheduled in your locality. Attend rehearsals and predict audience responses to key moments. Then check your predictions by observing a series of audiences. Evaluate the success or failure of your predictions.

Small Group Project Interview local school personnel and prepare a report on their attitude towards children's theatre. Specify benefits which, in their opinion, the audience could receive from watching a good play.

Individual Project Using the sample outline on page 88, or an equivalent of your own, prepare a detailed study guide for one of the children's plays you have read.

chapter five

Small Group Project Design a simple behavioral experiment which might shed light on one of the psychological issues discussed at the end of chapter four. If resources permit, you might even carry out your designs.

Individual Project Interview a local child psychologist or pediatrician. Try to uncover his impression of the child's aesthetic development. Invite such a specialist into the class for general discussion.

Class Project Try to apply the principles of "developmental drama" to the adult theatre. For example, take the plays of Shakespeare and try to arrange them in order of their aesthetic sophistication. Which of his plays are most accessible to naive audiences? Which requires the most aesthetic distance or sophistication? What are the implications of this sequential arrangement for a children's theatre? for an adult theatre?

chapter six

Individual Project Create an index file of children's plays. Read a large variety of scripts, and then fill out a three by five inch filing card on each one. Data to list might include: title, author, publisher, cast size, technical requirements, brief plot summary, age group suitability, and an overall personal evaluation. Build this file up over a long time, and keep it for future reference.

Individual Project If you are interested in any particular story or book which seems to relate to childhood, and if you like to write, you might try to convert this material into a play. Then read it to the class and let them discuss its suitability as a children's play.

Small Group Project Confining yourself only to plays written originally for adults, choose a season of plays that might be produced by a professional children's theatre. Indicate age suitability for each suggestion.

chapter seven

Individual Project Direct a scene or play for an audience of children. Specify the age group you most wish to reach. Try to present your work to a group of children as well as to the class. If it is impossible to direct a fully staged scene, a staged reading, or even a detailed prompt script might be of some value.

chapter eight

Individual Project Perform any scene for children. After the experience is over, compare it with acting for adults which you may have done. If you can actually perform the same role for adults and children, compare their responses.

chapter nine

Individual Project Design sets and costumes for a children's play, basing your work on a valid and clearly stated interpretation of the script.

chapter ten

Small Group Project Assume you are the recipient of a grant totalling 500,000 dollars, in order that you may establish a non-profit children's theatre company. Prepare your detailed budget for the first five years. Make sure to include individual listings of all key salaries, and also show detailed awareness of production costs, operating expenses, maintenance, audience development, and all sources of further income. Be as specific as possible in defining your hypothetical conditions—location of theatre, physical plant, types of plays done, and other related activities of the theatre. Report to the class with your ideas.

Individual Project Map out a public relations campaign to introduce the new theatre suggested above.

appendix d

SAMPLE STUDY GUIDE

androcles and the lion
grades four through six
hereandnow children's theatre

Purpose   The children's theatre program begins on the primary level with a play that is toured to the individual schools, and which the children see in-the-round and participate in. For the intermediate grades, the theatre's goal is to help the child make the transition to the concept of aesthetic distance in the viewing of a stage play. To achieve this goal, the children are brought to a central theatre where they see a fully staged production, but one that still involves them to a certain extent, through audience identification. This year's play is *Androcles and the Lion,* by Aurand Harris. The purpose of this guide is to acquaint you, the teacher, with some background information on the play, and to list some possible ideas you might use with your class, either before or after they see the play.

Background Information   The play *Androcles and the Lion* was written especially for children by Aurand Harris, the foremost children's playwright in the United States. It is based on the Aesop's fable by the same name, although much elaborated, and, of course, greatly changed to make it fit the form of a play instead of a short fable. The script emphasizes the values of freedom and friendship won by kindness. The children can be alerted to watch for acts of kindness, to prepare them to discuss the consequences of such acts afterwards.

The play is interesting also in that Mr. Harris has chosen to write in the style of the Commedia dell'arte, an Italian Rennaisance form of theatre filled with stock characters and fantastic bits of physical activity. The famous character Harlequin (*Arlechino* in Italian) comes from this period, as does Pantalone, the miser, the Bragging Captain, and, of course, the pair of *Inamorata,* or Lovers. All of these characters appear in this version of the fable. The director, the actors, and the designer, have all studied this theatrical style in order to faithfully interpret Mr. Harris' intentions in the production of his script. The choreographer has also chosen music and dance steps of this period to make the dances fit in with the overall style.

Plot Summary   A group of Commedia actors build their platform stage and enact a play. In the play, Pantalone, a miser, is determined to prevent his niece Isabella from marrying Lelio, because he is unwilling to give up her dowry, which he holds for her. The slave Androcles is enlisted to help the lovers elope. Pantalone hires a fierce Captain to guard his niece. Androcles tricks the Captain, however, and Isabella escapes. Unfortunately, she forgets to take the dowry with her. Androcles runs after her to give her the money. Because he ran away, Androcles is declared a fugitive, and chased into the woods. There he meets a Lion. Just as the Lion is about to spring at Androcles, it steps on a thorn and howls in pain. Androcles bravely pulls the thorn out, and befriends the Lion. Later, Androcles is captured by Pantalone and the Captain and thrown into the pit to be eaten by a wild animal. As it happens, the very same Lion is released to devour Androcles. Of course, he refuses to eat his friend, and turns instead on the two villains. The lovers end up happily reunited, Androcles and the Lion are freed, and the miser and the braggart get their deserved punishments.

The Cast   The program credits for this production are as follows:

Androcles (Harlequin)	Jack Smith
Isabella	Ethel Jones
Lelio	Fred Jones
Pantalone	Jim White
The Captain	Joseph Blake
The Lion and The Prologue	Rita Ryan

Directed by Bill Doe

Designed by Myrtle Doe
Choreographed by Jane Doe

Classroom Activities   The teaching ideas which follow are more of a grab bag than a sequential guide. It is hoped that by using one or more of these suggestions, the teacher can maximize the experience of the play.

Before the Play

1. Knowledge of what makes up a play: review the background information with the class, discussing the different jobs which go into the making of a play. Have the students read the original fable and try to decide what the characters should wear. It might be fun to draw these before seeing what the actual costumes look like. Try to draw pictures of the locales—a Roman street, the forest, the arena. Read a short scene from the play (script attached to the study guide) and try to imagine different ways in which it might be acted. Discuss the differences between seeing a story on television, in the movies, or on a stage.

2. Knowledge of the story: read and discuss the synopsis above. Discuss questions like: do you know of other stories where man has made friends with animals? how was it accomplished? what does the story say about slavery and freedom?

3. Art projects: make a collage from magazine clippings or your own drawings that represent the relationships between man and animals or different kinds of slavery.

4. Creative dramatics or improvisation: create lions through the techniques of creative dramatics. Encourage the students to think about the way a lion moves, eats, sleeps, or laughs. Improvise scenes from the story, or any other story, guiding the children to create their own locale, characters, and dialogue through your open-ended questioning. (Refer to bibliography for books on creative dramatics.)

After the Play

1. Discussion of the children's favorite parts, and the play's theme, style, etc.

2. Create the class's own play using creative dramatics.

3. Choose another fable from Aesop, or elsewhere, and write a play based on it as a class.

4. Use the suggestions above to make a collage, or have the children make a visual representation of their favorite moment in the play, or favorite character.

Bibliography

1. Fables: Aesop, *Aesop's Fables,* many editions and illustrators and Arbuthnot; May Hill, *Time for Fairy Tales,* Scott, Foresman, 1952.

2. Books on theatre.

3. Books on creative dramatics.

Feedback   In addition to the students creative work, all comments by students, teachers, sponsors, and parents are welcomed by the theatre as we attempt to improve our program through your suggestions. Comments on the helpfulness of this study guide are also welcomed. Send all reactions to:

Bill Doe, Director
Hereandnow Children's Theatre

SELECTED BIBLIOGRAPHY

books

ALLEN, JOHN, *Going to the Theatre*. London: Phoenix House, 1949.

BAUMOL, W. and W. BOWEN, *The Performing Arts: The Economic Dilemma*. New York: The Twentieth Century Fund, 1966.

BIRNER, WILLIAM, *Twenty Plays for Young People*. Anchorage, Kentucky: Anchorage Press, 1967.

CHERNIAVSKY, L. N., ed., *The Moscow Theatre for Children*. Moscow: Cooperative Publishing Society, 1934.

CHORPENNING, CHARLOTTE, *Twenty-One Years with Children's Theatre*. Anchorage, Kentucky: Anchorage Press, 1955.

COREY, IRENE, *The Mask of Reality*. Anchorage, Kentucky: Anchorage Press 1968.

COURTNEY, RICHARD, *Play, Drama, and Thought*. London: Cassell, 1968.

DAVIS, JED, ed., *A Directory of Children's Theatres in the United States*. Washington: American Educational Theatre Association, 1968.

———— and M. J. L. WATKINS, *Children's Theatre: Play Production for the Child Audience*. New York: Harper & Row, 1960.

DORIAN, FREDERICK, *Commitment to Culture*. Pittsburgh: University of Pittsburgh Press, 1964.

FISHER, CAROLINE and HAZEL ROBERTSON, *Children and the Theatre*. Palo Alto: Stanford University Press, 1950.

217

FORKERT, O. M., *Children's Theatre That Captures Its Audience.* Chicago: Coach House Press, 1962.

HERTS, ALICE MINNIE, *The Children's Educational Theatre.* New York: Harper & Bros., 1911.

JOHNSON, RICHARD, *Producing Plays for Children.* New York: Rosen Press, 1971.

KASE, ROBERT, *Children's Theatre Comes of Age.* New York: Samuel French, 1956.

KERLINGER, FRED, *Foundations of Behavioral Research.* New York: Holt, Rhinehart, 1964.

KERMAN, GERTRUDE, *Plays and Creative Ways with Children.* New York: Harvey House, 1961.

McCASLIN, NELLIE, *Theatre for Children in the United States: A History.* Norman: University of Oklahoma Press, 1971.

MACKAY, CONSTANCE D'ARCY, *Children's Theatre and Plays.* New York: Appleton, 1927.

————, *How to Produce Children's Plays.* New York: Holt, 1915.

MAUER, MURIEL for Seattle Junior Programs Inc., *Children's Theatre Manual.* Anchorage, Kentucky: Anchorage Press, 1951.

MIKHAILOVA, A. Y., *The Theatre in the Aesthetic Education of School Children.* Moscow: Aesthetic Education Institute, 1966.

MORTON, MIRIAM, *The Arts and the Soviet Child.* Riverside, New Jersey: The Free Press, 1972.

MOSES, MONTROSE, *Another Treasury of Plays for Children.* Boston: Little, Brown, 1926.

————, *A Treasury of Plays for Children.* Boston: Little, Brown, 1921.

————, *Concerning Children's Plays.* New York: Samuel French, 1931.

The Performing Arts: Problems and Prospects, Rockefeller Panel Report. New York: McGraw, Hill, 1965.

POGGI, JACK, *Theatre in America: The Impact of Economic Forces, 1870–1967.* Ithaca: Cornell University Press, 1968.

SIKS, GERALDINE, *Creative Dramatics: An Art for Children.* New York: Harper & Row, 1958.

———— and H. DUNNINGTON, *Children's Theatre and Creative Dramatics: Principles and Practices.* Seattle: University of Washington Press, 1961.

SLADE, PETER, *Introduction to Child Drama.* London: University of London Press, 1958.

SPOLIN, VIOLA, *Improvisation for the Theatre.* Evanston: Northwestern University Press, 1963.

SWORTZELL, LOWELL, *All the World's a Stage.* New York: Delacorte, 1972.

WALKER, STUART, *Portmanteau Plays.* Cincinnati: Stewart & Kidd, 1919.

WARD, WINIFRED, *Playmaking with Children.* New York: Appleton, 1947.

————, *Theatre for Children,* 3rd ed. rev. Anchorage, Kentucky: Anchorage Press, 1958.

WAY, BRIAN, *Development Through Drama.* London: Longmans, 1967.

WHITTON, PAT, ed., *Participation Theatre for Young Audiences: A Handbook for Directors.* New York: New Plays for Children, 1972.

ph.d. dissertations

GOLDBERG, MOSES, "A Survey and Evaluation of Contemporary Principles and Practices at Selected European Children's Theatres." University of Minnesota, 1969.

GRAHAM, KENNETH, "An Introductory Study of the Evaluation of Plays for Children's Theatre in the United States." University of Utah, 1947.

KINGSLEY, WILLIAM H., "Happy Endings, Poetic Justice, and the Depth and Strength of Characterization in American Children's Drama: A Critical Analysis." University of Pittsburgh, 1964.

LEECH, ROBERT MILTON, "Education through Theatre for Children." University of Texas, 1962.

McCASLIN, NELLIE, "A History of Children's Theatre in the United States." New York University, 1957.

SOSIN, GENE, "Children's Theatre and Drama in the Soviet Union, 1917–1953." Columbia University, 1958.

VAN TASSEL, WESLEY, "Theory and Practice in Theatre for Children: An Annotated Bibliography of Comment in English Circulated in the United States from 1900 through 1968." University of Denver, 1969.

periodicals

These periodicals publish articles on children's theatre on a regular basis:

Children's Theatre Review (official CTA journal).
Drama.
Educational Theatre Journal.
Information Bulletin—ASSITEJ (published quarterly by the Czechoslovakian Center of ASSITEJ).
International Bibliography of Children's Theatre Plays in Translation (published bi-annually by Michael Pugh, 10 Adamson Rd., London).
Players Magazine.
The Playground.
Recreation.
Theatre and School (published bi-annually in Moscow).
Theatre: Childhood and Youth (official ASSITEJ journal).

INDEX

* Boldface numbers indicate photographs.

Donahue, John Clark, 47, 48
Don Quixote of La Mancha, 141, 143
The Dragon, 145
Drama, as process (*see* Creative dramatics)
Drama League, 28:
  periodical, 33
Dramatic play, 102–4
Dramaturge, 190

Eastern Michigan University, **43**
East Germany, children's theatre in, 74–75
Economic Opportunity Act, 31
Educational dramatics, 5
Educational Theatre Journal, 34
Ego conflicts, 99
Emergencies, 198
Emerson College, 29
Emil and the Detectives, 65, **66**, 163
Emotional truth, 138–40
Empathy (*see* Identification)
The Emperor's New Clothes, 37
England, children's theatre in, 59–62
English, John, 60
Entertainment, 129–31:
  importance of, 184–85
Equity, 32
Erevan Theatre of Young Spectators, **172**
Evanston, Illinois, 14
Evanston Children's Theatre, 29, **40**
Everyman Players, 33, 37
Expectations (*see* Audience, child, visual expectations)
Expressionism, **173**, **174**

Facilities, 190–92
Family theatre, 109–10
Faulkes, Margaret, 60
Fauquez, Arthur, 134
Faustus, 140
Federal Theatre, 30
Feedback, from schools, 90
Fifreli de Lutin, 63
The Firebird, 35
The Firebird and the Red Fox, **69**
Flanagan, Hallie, 30
The Flight to Grenada, **173**
Florida State University, 30, **176**, **177**:
  goals, 45
  operation, 45–46
Formal *vs* informal theatre, 90–91
Formal setting, **175**
Foundations, 31 (*see also* Patronage)
France, children's theatre in, 62–63
Frank, Yasha, 15
Friendship Theatre, **66**, 75:
  theorists at, 94, 95

Funding:
  benefit of research, 117
  governmental, 31:
    in Eastern Europe, 57, 73
  of Minneapolis Children's Theatre Company, 47
  need for public relations, 194
  in Palo Alto, 35
  use of Board, 186
  (*see also* Patronage)

Genres, East and West, 58
Gibberish, 142, 164
Glyndebourne Children's Theatre, 60
Goals, stating, 183
Golding, William, 128
Good and evil, 95–96:
  affected by casting, 146–48
  at ages seven-nine, 82
  balance of, 96, 125
  levels of, 95
  for teenager, 84
Good Luck, **67**
Goodman Children's Theatre, 29
Good Morning, Mr. Tilly, 48
Governments:
  as children's theatre sponsors, 30–31
  funding in Minneapolis, 47
  municipal, 31, 35–36
  (*see also* Funding, Patronage)
Graham, Kenneth L., 14
Greet, Ben, 60
Guitry, Lucien, 142

Hang on to Your Head, **44**, 48
Hansel and Gretel, 48, 149:
  actor control of participation, 161
  reveals cruel parent, 99
Happy endings, 96–97
Harris, Aurand, 134, 212, 213
Head Start, 31
Henry Street Settlement, 27
Hero (*see* Identification)
Herts, Alice Minnie, 27
The Hide and Seek Odyssey of Madeline Gimple, 143
High School children's theatre, 37
The Hobbit, 35
Hoffman, Christel, 94
Hogle, Imogene, 29
Holiday Theatre, 36
Holland, children's theatre in, 76
Hopkins Eisenhower High School, 37, **39**
House management, 196–98
Hull House, 27
The Hunchbacked Pony, 65

Idealism, 96–97